Men's Cinema

Men's Cinema
Masculinity and *Mise en Scène* in Hollywood

Stella Bruzzi

EDINBURGH
University Press

Edinburgh University Press Ltd
22 George Square, Edinburgh EH8 9LF
www.euppublishing.com

Typeset in 11/13 Ehrhardt by
Servis Filmsetting Ltd, Stockport, Cheshire,
and printed and bound in Great Britain by
CPI Group (UK) Ltd, Croydon CR0 4YY

A CIP record for this book is available from the British Library

ISBN 978 0 7486 7615 6 (hardback)
ISBN 978 0 7486 7616 3 (paperback)
ISBN 978 0 7486 7617 0 (webready PDF)
ISBN 978 0 7486 7619 4 (epub)

Contents

Figures

Acknowledgements

Thanks are due mainly to friends and family members who helped me as I wrote this book: to my children, Frank and Phyllis, with whom I've watched and re-watched many of the films and, of course, to my husband Mick. I owe a very special debt of gratitude to Daniela Berghahn whose generosity in agreeing to read my typescript with such care and interest was simply incredible. I should also like to thank my editor at Edinburgh, Gillian Leslie, for taking on this project, and my colleagues at Warwick, especially Charlotte Brunsdon whose encouragement kept me going.

Men's Cinema has evolved from several years of teaching and is dedicated to my 'Class of '97', two of whom I've cited in the book.

Introduction: towards a masculine aesthetic

The image on the cover of this book is from *Mission: Impossible – Ghost Protocol* (Brad Bird, 2011), the fourth in the series. This sequence, in particular, is a good place to start my analysis of men's cinema as it exemplifies many of the styles and traits I shall later go on to discuss. Roughly halfway through the film, the action relocates to Dubai as the Impossible Mission Force seeks to intercept stolen nuclear missile triggering codes. Agent Ethan Hunt (Tom Cruise) arrives at a hotel suite alongside fellow agents Benji Dunn (Simon Pegg), Jane Carter and William Brandt; some setting-up business ensues as Benji, who is action hero Hunt's geeky sidekick in charge of assuming control of the computer systems, warns: 'slight wrinkle, but nothing to worry about. We're just going to have to go in to the server room from the *outside*.' Behind Benji is a vast window, in effect a glass wall, giving out on to the sandy landscape of Dubai, but Benji reassures everyone: 'I'm telling you, we can get to it from the outside,' to which Hunt, responds monosyllabically: 'We?'. As Benji is 'on the computer' and Brandt is just the team's 'helper', it falls to Hunt to don the hi-tech lycra climbing gear, goggles and a pair of computer-controlled sucker gloves with which he is supposed to scale eleven storeys up and seven units along in 26 minutes to override the computer settings. After helping to remove one of the glass windows (wincing 'Oh, that's high' as he carries it off), Benji explains the gloves' simple colour-coded light system: 'blue is glue', 'And red?' Ethan asks – 'is dead', Benji replies as nonchalantly as he can. The next edit heralds excitement, anticipation and dread: framed from behind, Cruise steps gingerly on to the discarded window's ledge; the smooth camera follows, goes up and over his shoulder and continues on until it is looking vertically down over his head. Vertiginous images of the heroes' seemingly impossible feats or escapes from tall buildings are commonplace in the modern action film, couched within technically audacious, visually complex sequences, made up of a rich array of images, angles,

Figure I.1 *Mission: Impossible – Ghost Protocol* (Brad Bird, 2010). Agent Ethan Hunt scaling a Dubai skyscraper.

Figure I.2 *Mission: Impossible – Ghost Protocol* (Brad Bird, 2010). Hunt putting his sucker gloves to work.

shot lengths that doubtless many spectators watch only with their eyes half shut.

In *Ghost Protocol*'s rendition of this obligatory sequence, Cruise steps out into the whistling wilderness; the camera rolls behind him to get a better look, giving the impression that we – as we will feel at various junctures in the sequence – are stranded in mid-air with nothing to support us. Cruise attaches a sucker mitten purposefully to the glass windows that reflect back the surrounding scenery, thereby minimising still further any distinctions between building and atmosphere. After cutting to a reverse shot from inside the IMF team's makeshift headquarters, Cruise's feet disappear from frame and there follows a high, slightly angled view of Ethan at the corner of the glass tower, hero and simulacra conjoined in a disorienting kaleidoscope of refracted, incomplete reflections.

The spongy thud of Hunt's gloves making contact with the glass is a comic touch (in both senses: Bird, the film's director had previously directed *The*

Incredibles and *Ratatouille*) and, for a few seconds more, the faint electronic wheeze, as they continue to attach and detach themselves, provides fleeting respite from the escalating tension. All is absurdly calm until Brandt exclaims 'What the hell is that?' at which point we cut to Ethan Hunt in close-up and see reflected in the glass an approaching sandstorm. Cruise turns around to take a proper look, the camera shadowing him. Upon being assured by Benji that it is a long way away and 'shouldn't be a problem', Hunt continues to climb the building, square jawed and grimly determined until his right glove starts to crackle and flicker, at which stage a tighter image of Cruise shows him looking over at his hand. This happens twice until the mitten's light turns red and Cruise discards it, forcing him now to ascend by wedging his hands and feet against the protruding uprights between windows. The camera chooses this moment (when Hunt needs us most, so to speak) to pull out and, with an elegant swoop away from the glass tower, abandon our hero until he is just a small black spider against an expanse of mirrors. The active camera's circular airborne motion is again generically familiar, which is comforting, but its retreat from Hunt also raises interesting questions about identification and proximity. Brandt radioes that it is now '23 minutes to door knock' (that is, to when the terrorists after the nuclear codes are due to arrive) reminding us that this frenetic sequence is ironically unfolding in near-enough real time. Cruise, in close-up from behind, continues skywards as the wayward glove comes into view, attached to the glass next to him, before it emits one final fizzle and flutters away.

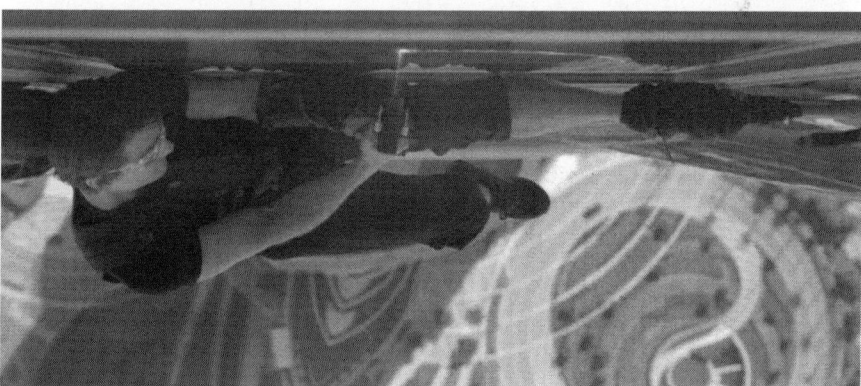

Figure I.3 *Mission: Impossible – Ghost Protocol* (Brad Bird, 2010). Hunt cutting the glass to the computer floor.

Seen from behind the glass, Hunt's imminent arrival at the corridor which houses the computers is announced, his one good glove raised upwards and the other (again with a view to practicalities) shielding his eyes so he can see in. In a movement that recalls the weightless waltzes around the space station in *2001: A Space Odyssey* (Stanley Kubrick, 1968) Hunt rotates until he is parallel with the top and bottom of frame. With an edit to a distorting, low-angle, exterior close-up of him extracting a glasscutter from his back pocket, he begins cutting the glass. Thus far, these close images, while remaining totally implausible, have helped to make the sequence psychologically manageable – that is, until now, when sparks splutter, Ethan loses contact with the building and plummets earthwards, the tranquilising close-up having been replaced by the indispensible, vertical, high-angle shot that switches to a mid-shot only as the one functioning glove miraculously succeeds in attaching itself once more to the building. Brandt radioes that it is now '22 minutes to door knock', at which point Hunt snarls that the countdown is 'not helping'. He gets back to server level but, after failing to punch in the glass, realises that the only way to get inside is to swing his legs out and then back again, an action he performs three times before crashing into the computer corridor.

Figure I.4 *Mission: Impossible – Ghost Protocol* (Brad Bird, 2010). Hunt trying to get back to base in time.

Ethan sorts out the computers with pragmatic efficiency but then realises the only means of getting back to his colleagues is the way he came. Making effective use of an anchored roll of cord (again, the precariously secured rope or cord has become a regular men's cinema motif), he hurls himself through the window with the cord tied around his waist. The introductory chords of the *Mission: Impossible* theme tune start up as, like some anarchic virtual reality fairground ride, the camera throws itself smoothly out after Hunt, hurtling towards the ground. Ethan's idea is to run down the sheer side of this glass tower and, as the image cuts to a relatively normalising angle looking straight at him, the thud of his feet making contact with the building are in synchrony with the first proper beat of the classic soundtrack. Synchronicity between music and editing is another effective and familiar trope in men's cinema's repertoire. The camera pans down, following Ethan's scamper to the IMF suite until there is a cut to a low-angle shot from the point of view of Brandt who is standing at the glassless window looking up. The cord runs out and Ethan is stopped in his tracks, leaving Brandt to shout up helpfully (from yet another angle – this time from over Hunt's shoulder looking down): 'your line's not long enough'. Ethan replies, 'no shit', looks (framed tightly now) over his shoulder and, as a robust, assertive, brass-led arrangement of the *Mission: Impossible* music blasts away, charges back the way he came, perpendicular to the skyscraper. As he gets to the building's corner, Ethan, on the beat, releases himself into the sky in a perfect arc. The macho leitmotif is suppressed and gives way to altogether wispier and more tentative violins as, spanning a patchwork of short and diverse individual shots, Agent Hunt builds up sufficient momentum to launch himself at the window where Brandt and Carter are standing. A quick-fire montage is strung together to relay the moment when Hunt misses his target, rebounds back off the building, is caught by Brandt (who, in turn, is being held on to by Carter) and is finally, after one last hairy, suicidal look straight down past his dangling figure, winched in. A common way to conclude such hyper-adrenalin-inducing sequences is via a shift in tone, and undercutting macho heroics has been, certainly since *Die Hard* (John McTiernan, 1988), another staple feature of Hollywood action films. In this case, Benji walks in, having spent the time Ethan Hunt has spent executing his death-defying stunts switching the numbers on hotel doors as part of the ruse to get the nuclear codes, a little out of breath and exclaiming with relief: 'Whoah . . . that was not easy . . . but I did it . . . What did I miss?'

The spectator is here placed, as in many other examples of 'men's cinema', in a position of quasi-identification, not so much with the hero as with the film's visual style. The excitement and camaraderie, which *Ghost Protocol* strives to make us feel while watching its action sequences, emanate from, but are not necessarily tied to, its representation of men and masculinity. These adrenalin-driven emotions are not simply the result of more conventionalised identification with the muscular male hero, the figure of idealised masculinity on the screen; they are also responses – less intellectual, more instinctive, physical, visceral – shaped by a noticeable conjunction of stylistic elements. Frequently (but by no means exclusively) spectacular, 'men's cinema' uses style and *mise en scène* to convey masculinity, not merely to represent it. Such evocation of masculinity or transmutation of its sensibility on to a film's aesthetic are the reasons for it having become increasingly imperative to go beyond pervasive critical preoccupations with issues of representation and the body and, consequently, for feeling the necessity to posit a fluid, non-genderised model of audience response that supplants older models of identification. This introduction is more cobweb-like in form than linear and, in it, I shall interweave selected moments from film theory, gender studies, queer theory, psychoanalysis and sociology in order to establish the critical framework for one way of looking at 'men's cinema' and understanding how, within Hollywood, masculinity is interpreted, understood and conveyed via aesthetics.

FILM STUDIES, MASCULINITY AND ISSUES OF REPRESENTATION

The title of this introduction, 'Towards a masculine aesthetic', is adapted from Silvia Bovenschen's 1976 essay 'Is there a feminine aesthetic?' which attempted a definition of the style, not merely the ideology, of 'women's cinema'. Three decades have elapsed since Bovenschen's essay, and much criticism has appeared, but, for all the writing about masculinity and cinema, a comparable, extended study of 'men's cinema', as grounded in the relationship between masculinity – its ideology as well as representation – and aesthetics, has not been attempted. Instead, with a few notable exceptions, masculinity in cinema is still being framed in ways almost exclusively indebted to Laura Mulvey's foundational essay from 1975, 'Visual Pleasure and Narrative Cinema', with its emphasis on sexual difference, representation and narrative. One of the enduring legacies of Mulvey's essay (and later work that takes 'Visual Pleasure' as the starting point for analyses of cinema and gender) is the centrality of the body to discussions of masculinity in cinema. This continues through subsequent film criticism: 'The Body' is the first subheading of Kirkham and Thumim's introduction to their anthology *You Tarzan: Masculinity, Movies and Men* (1993); Steve Cohan's *Masked Men: Masculinity and the Movies in the Fifties* (1997) contains two chapters explicitly focused on the body ('The Body in the Blockbuster', 'The Age of the Chest') as well as several further allusions to its predominance; Yvonne Tasker's *Spectacular Bodies: Gender, Genre and the Action Cinema* (1993), as its title suggests, equates strong masculinity with muscularity; Peter Lehman's edited collection of essays, *Masculinity*, is subtitled *Bodies, Movies, Culture*. It is also conspicuous that all these titles place a bare-chested image of a man, usually an actor, on the front cover: Johnny Weissmuller, Kirk Douglas, William Holden, Jean-Claude van Damme, and so on. Whether the masculine body is 'triumphant' or 'in crisis', it is invariably through images of muscularity that masculinity is defined (Tasker, 1993: 109). The more recent anthology of essays *The Trouble with Men: Masculinities in European and Hollywood Cinema* (Powrie, Davies and Babington, 2004) sets out once more the genealogy I have outlined above as if it were the only way to look at men's cinema. Its introduction, after stating 'The study of men in film has assumed increasing importance since the 1990s', declares:

> The study of *the representation of men in films* has been widespread in Film Studies; after all, it is hardly possible to write about a number of film genres – the western, the war film, the gangster film, romantic comedy, the biblical epic, film noir all spring immediately to mind – without touching on masculinities. *However, what concerns us in this volume* – the systematic exploration of masculinities anchored in

the gender paradigm, and which we shall call 'Masculinity in Film Studies' for short – *developed as an afterthought of the feminist-inspired spectatorship paradigm of the period 1975–1985*. (Powrie, Davies and Babington, 2004: 1, my italics)

What I would like to draw attention to here is the automatic conclusion that the sum total of 'masculinity in film studies' is 'the representation of men in films'. Powrie et al. make the additional assumption that such critical reductivism is due to the over-reliance of 'masculinity in film studies' on 'the feminist-inspired spectatorship paradigm of the period 1975–1985'. It is true that this has become the received view of the way in which masculinity has been approached by film studies but it is not the only way as I hope this study will demonstrate.

Though rightly viewed as a seminal text, it remains intellectually troubling the extent to which Mulvey's radical but incomplete template has become reduced to its (in)famous, axiomatic sound bites ('Woman as object/man as bearer of the look'; 'the male gaze', etc.) and also how her polemic (this was, after all, a feminist rallying cry) has been taken as fact rather than as argument. Mulvey's first essay bestrides the history of film and gender studies like a colossus. For many, the first encounter with 'Visual Pleasure' will have unlocked the pleasures, if not of Hollywood, then of studying film. But, for all its brilliance, 'Visual Pleasure' has not only opened doors but closed them, too. On the one hand, the scope of the essay itself has, over time, been reduced, for example through the relative marginalisation of its status as feminist polemic and manifesto,[1] as feminism became secondary to the interpretation of narrative cinema through psychoanalysis and, in particular, a series of gendered binary oppositions (male/female; active/passive; subject/object and so on). On the other, the overwhelming attraction of Mulvey's schema has, in turn, closed down alternative ways of interpreting gender operations in mainstream, principally Hollywood, films, so that subsequent writing on gender and film has nearly always taken as its starting point 'Visual Pleasure and Narrative Cinema', and has almost just as frequently taken its terms as read.

Exemplary of Mulvey's pervasive influence is E. Ann Kaplan's *Women and Film: Both Sides of the Camera* (1983) which establishes, right at the start of its introduction, that Mulvey's idea of the 'male gaze' (that power and subjectivity reside with the male presence on-screen and the masculine position off it) must be the foundational basis for 1980s feminist film criticism (Kaplan, 1983: 1–2). In her subsequent chapter (under the interrogative title: 'Is the gaze male?'), however, Kaplan does suggest that the gaze 'is not necessarily male (literally), but to own and activate the gaze, given our language and the structure of the unconscious, is to be in the "masculine" position' (Kaplan, 1983: 30). Kaplan raises the issue of the potentially ungendered, even performative, spectator, without resorting to the tortuous formulations of oscillating and transvestite patterns of identification Mulvey proposes in 'Afterthoughts on "Visual Pleasure and Narrative Cinema"'.

Kaplan and others soon detected (as did Mulvey herself), some of the limitations of 'Visual Pleasure' and its inflexible advocacy of gender fixity and sexual difference as the best tools to define the pleasures of Hollywood spectatorship; as Steve Cohan and Ina Rae Hark wrote as relatively late as 1993, however, film criticism 'in the wake of Mulvey's article has pretty much expanded upon her thesis about visual pleasure' (Cohan and Hark, 1993: 2). As a result, they suggest,

> not much attention has been paid to the problems arising – in texts and for audiences – from the secure and comfortable 'norm' of masculinity which, according to the theoretical model that continues to circulate in film theory, drives the representational system and its institutional apparatus only by being *disabled*. (2)

The conflations occurring here are interesting, if somewhat extreme: for example, that 'the scant attention paid to the spectacle of men ends up reinforcing the apparent effacement of the masculine as a social construction in American culture' (2–3). Is the suggestion here that men, by virtue of not having been analysed in terms of spectacle, have been effaced in culture? Again, this supports the assumed parallelisms that underpin Mulvey and so much gender film criticism since, namely that gender and sexual difference on screen are understood via the analysis of representation and image, and that there remains a necessary conflation between patriarchy/men/images of men. Before exploring some alternative perspectives [such as Eve Kosofsky Sedgwick's comment in *Epistemology of the Closet* that 'a damaging bias toward heterosocial or heterosexist assumptions inheres unavoidably to the very concept of gender' (Sedgwick, 1994: 31)], I shall look at Steve Neale's 1983 essay, 'Masculinity as Spectacle: Reflections on Men and Mainstream Cinema', with which Cohan and Hark open their edited collection, *Screening the Male*.

Neale, having identified the need to analyse heterosexual masculinity in similar ways to femininity (not yet identified more particularly as *heterosexual* femininity), explicitly takes 'Visual Pleasure' as its 'central, structuring reference point' and as a framework within which to 'open up a space . . . for a consideration of the representation of masculinity' (Neale, 1993: 10). In so doing, Neale singles out Mulvey's priorities – identification, looking and spectacle – and discusses them in turn in order to 'pose some questions as to how her remarks apply directly or indirectly to *images of men*, on the one hand, and to *the male spectator* on the other' (10). I have added the italics to draw attention to how, for Neale, the male spectator and the subjective position he occupies are simply assumed objectively to exist, and how he is likewise presumed to have a binding and natural bond of identification with images of men. That Neale automatically set out to discuss masculinity in terms of representation and gendered identification is made explicit a little later when Neale concludes: 'Every film thus tends to specify identification in accordance with the socially defined and constructed categories of male and female' (11).

Though in his discussion (indebted to Paul Willemen) of Sergio Leone's westerns in which, as he observes, 'male struggle' frequently becomes 'pure spectacle' (17), Neale does posit the beginnings of an alternative mode of looking at gender on screen, and he swiftly represses the more radical implications of his idea of spectacle as taking over from or freezing narrative when he writes how, in Leone's shoot-outs:

> We are offered the spectacle of male bodies, but bodies unmarked as objects of erotic display. There is no trace of an acknowledgement or recognition of those bodies as displayed solely for the gaze of the spectator. (Neale, 1993: 18)

Ultimately, masculinity is stopped from descending into 'pure spectacle' by the acceptance of Mulvey's psychodynamic paradigm, a paradigm that is here reiterated at the expense of any further discussion of style and aesthetics as generators of meaning. Neale reinforces the division – predicated on Mulvey's active/passive binary model – between male bodies on display in 'masculine' genres, such as westerns and action films, and the more feminised representations of men to be found in more conventionally 'feminine' genres such as melodrama. Whereas in the more 'feminine' films, the male body can explicitly become 'the object of the erotic look' through being feminised (18), in the more 'masculine' films, involvement in action determines the way in which we look at male bodies, so 'We see male bodies stylized and fragmented by close-ups, but our look is not direct, it is heavily mediated by the looks of the characters involved' (18). 'Feminised' and 'feminisation' as terms are put in inverted commas or italicised by Neale as if we are meant simply to accept this actually quite problematic conflation of gender identities. Ultimately, Neale endorses the basic premises of 'Visual Pleasure' and falls back on traditionally heterosexist formulations of sexual difference. He concludes that 'the spectatorial look in mainstream cinema is implicitly male' and that if, as Mulvey argues, the male spectator 'is reluctant to gaze at his exhibitionist like' (Mulvey, 1985: 310), male bodies in mainstream cinema are either 'masculine', active and not circumscribed by their 'to-be-looked-at-ness' (309) or passive, 'feminised' and accepting of the spectator's gaze, as he finds Rock Hudson in Sirk's melodramas to be.

There were, though, other ways of looking at men and masculinity in film. At the outset of 'Male Sexuality and the Media' (written two years after 'Masculinity as Spectacle') Richard Dyer outlines the possible reason for the absence hitherto of critical writing on masculinity as a concept and a style when he remarks:

> One would think that writing about images of male sexuality would be as easy as anything. We live in a world saturated with images, drenched in sexuality. But this is one of the reasons why it is in fact difficult to write about. Male sexuality is a bit like air – you breathe it in all the time, but you aren't aware of it much. Until quite recently, what was talked about was the mysterious topic of female sexuality, or else, the subject of deviant male practices. Ordinary male sexuality was simple sexuality, and everyone knew what it was. (Dyer, 1985: 28)

In terms of how to theorise masculinity on screen, Dyer starts where Neale left off. Rather than take as axiomatic the division between masculinity as the 'ideal' which is 'implicitly known' and femininity as 'by contrast, a mystery' (Neale, 1993: 19), he treats ironically the assumption that male sexuality is so straightforward. The 'masculine' has been the universal, the known, not the 'other' that merits and necessitates critical definition and scrutiny. Even when it *has* merited scrutiny, the male on-screen has been found to be especially interesting when he takes on, or can be seen to possess, attributes usually attributed to the female form: vulnerability, masochism, etc. Following the 'crisis' of 1970s' sexist exclusion of women, 'crisis' became a term, particularly in the 1980s, virtually synonymous with masculinity: men are the new women.

Once more moving the arguments on (but again taking as her starting point 'Masculinity as Spectacle'), Tasker in *Spectacular Bodies,* written a decade later, attends to the problem inherent in Neale's conclusions about Rock Hudson when she reveals how the 'circular logic' of Neale's Mulvian argument is in danger of describing Hudson as feminised '*because* he is eroticised in these films' (Tasker, 1993: 115; italics in original). Such equations, Tasker suggests, 'are premised on a stable gender binary, which is underpinned by a heterosexual understanding of desire and difference' (115). Like so many analyses of masculinity and film since, however, Tasker's study of action cinema is ultimately all about bodies and so remains wedded to the notion that gender must necessarily and reductively be discussed through and as *representation.* This neat, attractive syllogism needs to be critiqued and I would initially like to do this by recalling some other, neglected aspects of early film studies criticism, discussions of gender and cinema – and more specifically masculinity and cinema – that could have developed along different lines had pieces of early film criticism, other than 'Visual Pleasure' and 'Masculinity as Spectacle', become the automatic reference points for later criticism.

After having discussed the (1970s) work of Claire Johnston, for instance, Alison Butler suggests the potential usefulness and value of an approach to women's cinema 'which prioritises discursive structures over looking relations' (Butler, A., 2002: 13), positing, in a way that overlaps with Thomas Elsaesser four decades earlier, that meaning is generated not merely through form and narrative but less systematically via 'a variety of articulations, which may be aesthetic, semantic, ideological and social' (Butler, A., 2002: 13). The definition of 'women's cinema' was always a different project from any potentially comparable definition of 'men's cinema', as the former necessarily had an urgent political and ideological root, and aesthetics were inevitably allied to this political struggle. The manner in which Johnston and others sought to define women's cinema in the 1970s and 1980s as a political act, however, or how Bovenschen pondered what might constitute 'a feminine aesthetic', went beyond the more narrowly focused debates that came to constitute the main body of feminist film criticism. As Bovenschen notes:

> The exclusion of women from vast areas of production and the public sphere has directed women's imagination along other lines . . . Is there a feminine aesthetic? Certainly there is, if one is talking about *aesthetic awareness* and *modes of sensory perception*. Certainly not, if one is talking about an unusual variant of artistic production or about a painstakingly constructed theory of art. (Bovenschen, 1976: 49)

Several notable early feminists argued that women have been compelled to communicate using 'man-made language'[2] and that part of the feminist struggle (and Hollywood was self-evidently a crucially contested site) was to find alternative means and modes of articulating female subjectivity and of describing feminine experience. In the words of British feminist Sheila Rowbotham (writing in the 1970s): 'As soon as we learn words we find ourselves outside them . . . Language is part of the political and ideological power of the rulers' (1973: 32–3). From a very different perspective, the writings of French literary theorist Hélène Cixous to an extent have formulated and advocated alternative and 'feminine' modes of expression, clustered around the idea of '*l'écriture féminine*'.[3] Although Cixous is specifically not suggesting that '*l'écriture féminine*' (loosely translatable as 'feminine writing') is tied to biological difference, she is referring to the idea that opposition to patriarchy can be the foundation for an alternative form of expression which she allies to the feminine. Within film studies, the articulation of a similar opposition has taken various forms and, like Cixous, a writer such as Claire Johnston, in 'Women's Cinema as Counter Cinema' (1974), advocated the importance to women of working within the mainstream, within the realm of entertainment as well as finding alternative forms through which to conceptualise their political struggle.

If, as I have suggested, the genderisation of aesthetics and, more specifically, the interpretation of masculinity via aesthetics were not prioritised by much early film and gender theory, where might one look for pertinent antecedents? At the risk of sounding facetious, a good place to start is by looking at the substantial body [sic] of early film criticism that did not overly concern itself with sexual difference or the politics of gender. If we take as representative of that early scholarly output a standard anthology many of us older scholars grew up with – namely Bill Nichols's *Movies and Methods* (1976) – then we swiftly see that around seventy pages are taken up with what the editor terms '*Mise-en-scene* Criticism' (including Henderson's 'The Long Take' and Place and Peterson's 'Some Visual Motifs of *Film Noir*') and that later, in 'Part 3: Theory', several essays are included that explicitly foreground issues of aesthetics and style (such as Pasolini's 'The Cinema of Poetry' and Metz's 'On the Notion of Cinematic Language'). 'Film theory' was to be a broad church; for valid political reasons, feminist film theory was not and, in overdetermining ways, set itself up in direct opposition to its less politicised forefathers. As Robin Wood asserts in the 'Prologue' to the revised edition of *From Vietnam to Reagan . . . And Beyond,* 'it should be impossible to separate the aesthetics from the politics (in which I include sexual politics), the analyses from the radical attitude that animates and pervades them' (Wood, 2003: xvi), and when I come on to discussing the ways in which Hollywood films wield aesthetics as essential tools for interpreting and conveying masculinity, I hope to reinforce this point.

Even within this 'broad church', some Hollywood genres were inevitably deemed to be more noteworthy than others in terms of how they deployed aesthetics and style, and melodrama was quickly held up as uniquely interested in encouraging, as Elsaesser identified in 1972, 'a conscious use of style-as-meaning' (1985: 175). As studies of the Hollywood melodrama (or 'the woman's film') came to be dominated, entirely legitimately, by feminist film criticism, other debates and issues predominated but, in Elsaesser's 'Tales of Sound and Fury: Observations of the Family Melodrama', as well as in his 1973 essay 'Narrative Cinema and Audience Aesthetics: The *Mise-en-Scène* of the Spectator' or Geoffrey Nowell-Smith's 'Minnelli and Melodrama' (from 1977), one can find the foundations for an alternative way of bringing out issues of gender via aesthetics and film style. Elsaesser focuses on melodrama because, as a genre, he found it to be representative of Hollywood's intentions through style:

> Everyone who has at all thought about the Hollywood aesthetic wants
> to formulate one of its peculiar qualities: that of direct emotional
> involvement . . . Since the American cinema, determined as it is by an

ideology of the spectacle and the spectacular, is essentially dramatic
. . . and not conceptual . . . the creation or re-enactment of situations
which the spectator can identify with and recognise (whether this
recognition is on the conscious or the unconscious level is another
matter) depends to a large extent on the aptness of the iconography (the
'visualisation') and on the quality (complexity, subtlety, ambiguity) of
the orchestration for what are trans-individual, popular mythological
(and therefore generally considered culturally 'lowbrow') experiences
and plot structures. In other words, this type of cinema depends on the
ways 'melos' is given to 'drama' by means of lighting, montage, visual
rhythm, décor, style of acting, music – that is, on the ways mise-en-
scène translates character into action . . . and action into gesture and
dynamic space. (Elsaesser, 1985: 176)

I have excised some of the parenthetical comments from Elsaesser's second,
especially Miltonic, sentence but his underpinning observation that the
Hollywood aesthetic, as exemplified by melodrama, is defined by how the stylistic elements of *mise en scène* are mobilised in the construction of meaning, is
nevertheless intact. Elsaesser and other early critics (such as Geoffrey Nowell-
Smith in 'Minnelli and Melodrama') detect and exploit the dynamic interlo-
cution between narrative, aesthetics and *mise en scène* that exists in Hollywood
melodramas. Though the taxonomy of women's films or the genealogy of
feminist film criticism might have been different if these discussions had been
extended, it is important and revealing that even Elsaesser is, in small part,
guilty of sending things in a different direction.

Immediately after the energising paragraph quoted above, Elsaesser turns
to other more 'masculine' genres, such as the western and crime-centred films,
observing that 'although the techniques of audience orientation and the possibility of psychic projection on the part of the spectator are as much in evidence
in a melodrama . . . as they are in a Western or adventure picture, the difference of setting and milieu affects the dynamic of the action' (Elsaesser, 1985:
176). The assumption is that *mise en scène* 'translates character into action' so
successfully in melodramas because of the films' interiority – 'The world is
closed, and the characters acted upon' (177); conversely, if the milieu is the
masculinised '"open" spaces' (176) of the western, it is as if the powerful signifiers within the *mise en scène* automatically become less important. And so an
especially interesting slippage occurs across these two pages: the 'conscious
use of style-as-meaning' (175) is 'sharply defined' in 'the domestic melodrama' because the range of '"strong" actions is limited' (177). A year later,
in 'Narrative Cinema and Audience Aesthetics', Elsaesser relaxes the genre
specificity he asserted in 'Sound and Fury' when he writes about what characterises the output of 'the directors we now think of as "classical"' (his examples

are, in this instance, varied: Ford, Lang, Minnelli, Preminger, Welles, Ray and Sirk). In their films, Elsaesser argues, we see the 'transformation of action into subjective vision accomplished by the *mise-en-scène*' so that 'the image not only codifies a certain spatial configuration, but serves as the metaphoric expression of a (state of) consciousness and its comment on the action and setting' (Elsaesser, 2012: 102). It remains the case, though, that any discussion of the detailed use of 'lighting, montage, visual rhythm, décor, style of acting, music' (Elsaesser, 1985: 176) is reserved for the 'woman's film'. Though I shall also consider masculinity in the classical Hollywood melodrama, part of what I hope to achieve later when I come to discussing in detail some examples of 'men's cinema', is the recuperation of interiority and an expressive aesthetic in more overtly masculine genres as well.

Though masculinity and cinema have, as already signalled, become a persistent and common subject of film criticism, there is still relatively little criticism that engages with what men's cinema looks and feels like in the way Elsaesser treated melodramas. Borrowing from Elsaesser's approach, this book seeks to go beyond intellectual responses to mainstream *representation* of men and masculinity to encompass and explore some of the ways in which Hollywood's treatment of masculinity also *looks* and *feels*. Much more recently, Elsaesser and Malte Hagener, with *Film Theory: An Introduction Through the Senses*, expand on Elsaesser's early work on film aesthetics when they set out to produce a book whose central focus is 'the relationship between the cinema, perception and the human body'. They go on:

> Each type of cinema (as well as every film theory) imagines an ideal
> spectator, which means it postulates a certain relation between the
> (body of the) spectator and the (properties of the) image on the screen
> . . . What is called classical narrative cinema, for instance, can be
> defined by the way a given film engages, addresses and *envelops the
> spectatorial body*. Films furthermore presuppose a *cinematic space that
> is both physical and discursive*, one where film and spectator, cinema and
> body encounter one another. (Elsaesser and Hagener, 2010: 4)

The italics above are mine, used to highlight how Elsaesser and Hagener have developed the much earlier writing on style to include not only the relationship between spectator and film but also the effect certain types of movies have on the spectator. (Here classical narrative cinema is singled out. Does this mean that other forms of cinema are, by default, *non*-affective, cerebral, intellectual?) My parenthetical concerns apart and, though Elsaesser and Hagener subsequently apply these ideas more to spatio-temporal relationships on the screen than the effect of the image on the body of the spectator, this physical and dynamic view of cinema's affective-ness is nevertheless crucial for me in that it draws attention to some of the ways in which style and aesthetics function physically and viscerally within men's cinema in prompting responses in spectators that are not only emotional and instinctive but also non- or pre-conscious, asubjective or pre-subjective.[4]

Whereas for Elsaesser and Hagener the effect of classical narrative cinema on the spectator is viewed as overwhelming, an affective response with the potential to negate the cerebral response, for Vivian Sobchack 'carnal thoughts' bring the two aspects together. After identifying the theme of *Carnal Thoughts* to be 'the embodied and radically material nature of human existence and thus the lived body's essential implication in making "meaning" out of "bodily sense"' (Sobchack, 2004: 1), Sobchack writes that the book's intention is to offer 'an appreciation of how our own lived bodies provide the material premises that enable us, from the first, to sense and respond to the world and others' and also to charge 'our conscious awareness with the energies and obligations that animate our "sensibility" and "responsibility"' (3). Sobchack's notion of the physicalities of cinematic spectatorship, that we make 'conscious sense from our carnal sense' while 'watching a film, moving about in our daily lives and complex worlds' (1), lay the foundations for 'a *materialist* – rather than *idealist* – understanding of *aesthetics* and *ethics*' (italics in original, 3) in a way that I want to pursue and expand upon in this book when discussing the complicated, often contradictory or equivocal, relationships between image and the 'spectatorial body' in 'men's cinema'. As I will argue, in 'men's cinema' the spectator is often 'enveloped' by a film's aesthetics but this does not preclude them from also finding themselves distanced from a film, made aware of its constructedness. Starting out by identifying some of the key elements of Hollywood's masculine aesthetic, I want to go beyond merely describing masculinity through visual style as well as through dialogue and action, and to proffer a more positive, affirmative notion that 'men's cinema' exists as a cinematic category, based on the stylistic consistency, or even homogeneity, found in a whole host of 'men's' films. A crucial and potentially liberating result of this formulation of 'a masculine aesthetic' is that it proposes ways in which men's cinema is not limited by genre and does exist beyond, for example, the cinema of action and spectacle. The multifarious affects of the films, I will argue, are in part brought together by the envelopment Elsaesser and Hagener identify as a trait of classical narrative cinema's effect on 'the spectatorial body' as there is an often intense and overwhelming feeling of camaraderie engendered by a sequence, such as the skyscraper-scaling sequence in *Mission: Impossible – Ghost Protocol* (discussed earlier), that both draws the individual spectator towards the image and creates a sense of a communal viewing experience.

The tradition of focusing on the more phenomenological aspects of the spectatorial response, into which *Carnal Thoughts* falls, echoes Steven

Shaviro's *The Cinematic Body*, at the outset of which its author identifies how the book is 'personal' in both its idiosyncratic choice of films and 'in the sense that it foregrounds visceral, affective responses to film, in sharp contrast to most critics' exclusive concern with issues of film, meaning and ideology' (Shaviro, 1993: viii). In bringing together gender (in the form of masculinity) and aesthetics, *Men's Cinema* enters into a comparable negotiation, as remarked on earlier, with a predominantly meaning- and ideology-driven critical lineage. The approach and the tone Shaviro adopts in his analysis of Kathryn Bigelow's *Blue Steel* (1989) are extremely relevant here, not merely because he feels that it is 'not doing justice to *Blue Steel* when I discuss it only in terms of scripts and performance, of character plot and genre', but also because of the way he articulates this need: that, for example, 'Bigelow pushes the action film's tired formulas to a point of delirious frenzy through specifically cinematographic means' and creates 'a perverse and powerfully stylized exercise in visual excess' (Shaviro, 1993: 1).

Shaviro's excitement at recalling the pleasurable viewing of *Blue Steel* is richly evoked, and is comparable to my pleasurable excitement at revisiting some of Elsaesser's early work in which *he* expressed the palpable, physical exhilarations offered by film viewing, and similar to the visceral responses that I identified at the very start of this introduction in response to *Ghost Protocol*. 'Men's cinema', as I shall go on to define it, is emotionally and instinctively engaging, thrilling, anxiety inducing or exhausting to watch, and comprises 'the excitement and passivity of spectatorship' (Shaviro, 1993: 9). It does, to my mind, display identifiable and unique ways in which it interacts with, and plays upon, its audiences' sensibilities, or adopts strategies, effects and affects that are inextricably linked to the body *of the spectator* more than they arguably are to the centrality of the cinematic male body. It is limiting, therefore, to view the physicality of 'men's cinema' as pertaining exclusively, or even chiefly, to the physical presence and physique of male characters on-screen. Much of the theoretical writing on masculinity and cinema has offered the more detached, scientific approach Shaviro detects, more pervasively, in film theory which, he argues, 'tries to assume as great a distance as possible from its object' (Shaviro 1993: 10). Too little writing, he maintains, has given a sense of the 'seduction, delirium, fascination, and utter absorption in the image' (10).

I would like now to make some links between these ideas about cinema and responsive spectatorship to arguments about masculinity and the potential for non-fixed gender definitions. In her critique of Paul Smith's introduction to his edited anthology, *Boys: Masculinity in Contemporary Culture*, in which she accuses Smith, among other things, of electing to 'focus on dominant white masculinity to the exclusion of the other masculinities he has listed' (Halberstam, 1998: 16), Judith Halberstam mounts an argument against Smith's contention that although it may well be the case, as some influential voices often tell us, that masculinity or masculinities are in some real sense not the exclusive 'property' of biologically male subjects . . . in terms of cultural and political *power*, it still makes a difference when masculinity coincides with biological maleness. (Smith, 1996: 4)

I shall return in more detail to Halberstam's term 'female masculinity' in a moment but first I want, via Smith's logical but not unproblematic assumption that masculinity and biological maleness are equivalents, to explore arguments for fluid, ungendered modes of cinematic identification. Smith's presumed alliance between image and gender instantly raises questions about more phenomenological and liberated conceptualisations of the spectator evoked (both explicitly and implicitly) by Elsaesser, Shaviro and others, also raising critical issues for 'Men's Cinema' in which the physical presence of men is an important and inherent component. My focus on style and *mise en scène*, as the primary routes to understanding and enjoying men's cinema as opposed to representation, is rooted in the belief that spectatorship and patterns of iden-tification are fluid, instinctual and not necessarily gendered in a limiting way. So what if these are also films that are, if not always *by* or *for* men, then *about* men and masculinity? Taking note of Halberstam's criticism of Smith, what men's cinema offers is what Marjorie Garber might call a 'third term', that cat-egory that 'does not belong' within existing binary oppositions (other 'thirds' that Garber highlights are: the Third World, Sophocles' third speaker and Lacan's Symbolic [Garber, 1992: 11]) but rather 'questions binary thinking and introduces crisis' (11). Like Garber's 'third' (the cross-dressed figure), the act of identification, when it comes to men's cinema, is with a sort of Symbolic masculinity (to continue with the Lacanian thread a little longer) as opposed to a literal representation of a man. This symbolic abstraction of 'masculinity' on to style and *mise en scène* problematises and destabilises that representational image's fixity and, following Garber's template, forces gendered binaries into crisis. Within this triangular structure, the two binaries would be the men on the screen and the multi-identitied audiences who enjoy and respond to men's cinema, while the third dimension is the style and the surface of the film, invested with both the symbolic meaning of masculinity and the specta-tors' unfixed desires and instinctual responses to these nebulous and ambigu-ous characteristics. Our supposed identification with Ethan Hunt in *Mission: Impossible* is effectively channelled through the films' energetic style, and is thereby linked more to the excitement of experiencing the abstract enactment of what it might feel like to be Ethan Hunt than to the character per se.

For all its desire to question and then destabilise existing beliefs in sexual difference, gender inequalities and identities, a significant portion of film and gender criticism ultimately fails satisfactorily to dislodge many assumed correspondences between gender fixity, mainstream cinema and patriarchy. Masculinity, as a concept and a style within film studies, was taken for a long time to be the universal, the known, not the 'other' which more urgently merited critical scrutiny and redefinition. Just as whiteness has also done, it 'secures its dominance by seeming not to be anything in particular' and yet, under scrutiny, 'is often revealed as emptiness, absence, denial, or even a kind of death' (Dyer, 1993b: 141). Similarly, in subjecting to scrutiny 'masculinity' in Hollywood movies, and *not* taking either masculinity's or Hollywood's invisible hegemony as givens, is symbolically to bring 'a kind of death' to both. Extending Dyer's ideas, Nicola Rehling, in *Extra-Ordinary Men: White Heterosexual Masculinity in Contemporary Popular Cinema*, identifies her reasons for examining Hollywood films:

> Popular films are often far more complex than they tend to be given credit for (rather like straight men) and frequently contain ruptures, gaps, tensions, and incoherencies that indicate collective anxieties and desires, as well as ideological conflict (as do straight men). (Rehling, 2009: 9)

My study takes as its starting point the need to examine what 'everyone knows', namely the most mainstream, omnipresent and 'ordinary' forms of cinema, and identifies within this universal what can positively be defined as 'men's cinema' as opposed to what is merely taken for granted.

Raewyn/R. W. Connell's[5] definition of 'hegemonic masculinity' is pertinent here as Connell, after Gramsci, proposes that 'Hegemonic masculinity can be defined as the configuration of gender practice which embodies the currently accepted answer to the problem of the legitimacy of patriarchy' although (and this becomes especially relevant to issues of masculinity, representation and identification) 'This is not to say that the most visible bearers of hegemonic masculinity are always the most powerful people. They may be exemplars, such as film actors, or even fantasy figures, such as film characters' (Connell, 2003: 77). Connell rounds off this passage by concluding: 'Nevertheless, hegemony is likely to be established only if there is some correspondence between cultural ideal and institutional power, collective if not individual' (77).

Connell connects this issue of hegemony with the notion of 'the patriarchal dividend', namely the idea that men as a group – and women who might benefit – all have a vested interest in 'maintaining an unequal gender order' (Connell, 2009: 142). Important to Connell's notion of the 'patriarchal dividend' is the awareness that it is also upheld by men (and women) who 'do not embody hegemonic masculinity' but who, nevertheless, have 'some connection with the hegemonic project' (Connell, 2003: 79). What Connell is identifying is a 'system of symbolic relationships, not fixed facts about persons' which, in turn, 'makes acceptance of the phallic position a highly political act. It is always possible to refuse it – though the consequences of refusal are drastic' (Connell, 2003: 20).

In *Female Masculinity* (that this term is not pluralised is potentially problematic) Halberstam opens by looking at masculinity from the other end of the telescope as it were. After asking: 'What is "masculinity"? . . . If masculinity is not the social and cultural and indeed political expression of maleness, then what is it?' (Halberstam, 1998: 1), she swiftly responds: 'Masculinity, this book will claim, becomes legible as masculinity where and when it leaves the white male middle-class body' (2). Halberstam seeks to explode conventional definitions of masculinity to recognise that 'in the 1990s has finally been recognised as, at least in part, a construction by female- as well as male-born people' (13) and that 'the topic of female masculinity' becomes the means by which 'a queer subject position that can successfully challenge hegemonic models of gender conformity' can be explored (Halberstam, 1998: 9). Despite acknowledging that 'because the definitional boundaries of male and female are so elastic, there are very few people in any given public space who are completely unreadable in terms of gender' (Halberstam, 1998: 20), there is a persistent assumption that the only truly radical and radicalising 'female masculinity' is butch lesbianism: that while Halberstam has 'no doubt that heterosexual female masculinity menaces gender conformity in its own way' it 'all too often represents an acceptable degree of female masculinity as compared to the excessive masculinity of the dyke' (28).

However challenging to received definitions of hegemonic (white, heterosexual) masculinity Halberstam's counternotion of female masculinity is, as a category it nevertheless does not altogether challenge fixed ideas of gender and sexuality. Conversely, Eve Kosofsky Sedgwick's determining premise in *Between Men* and in *Epistemology of the Closet* was the desire to un-fix categories and gender and sexuality and to suggest slippages between them. To return specifically to the issue of identification, Sedgwick returns in *Epistemology*, for example, to *Between Men* and one of the fundamental problems with gendered identification when commenting how the earlier book

> tried to demonstrate that modern, homophobic constructions of
> male heterosexuality have a conceptual dependence on a distinction
> between men's *identification* (with men) and their *desire* (for women), a
> distinction whose factitiousness is latent where not patent. (Sedgwick,
> 1994: 62)

For Sedgwick, individualism and an uneasy relationship to group identification are pervasive concerns; so that, about her own work she concludes:

'Realistically, what brings me to this work can hardly be that I am *a* woman, or *a* feminist, but that I am this particular one' (Sedgwick, 1994: 59). She then goes on to argue, when writing specifically about 'strong group-identification across politically charged boundaries, whether of gender, of class, of race, of sexuality, of nation', that it is never going to be the case that '"everyone *should* be able to make this identification". Perhaps everyone should, but everyone does not, and almost no one makes more than a small number of very narrowly channelled ones' (59–60). Perhaps most importantly for my introductory arguments here, Sedgwick offers a model for a radical, non-gendered, non-sexed spectatorship – and so an implicit model for a potentially radical, non-gendered, non-sexed aesthetic conceptualisation of masculinity – when she observes that 'Many people have their richest mental/emotional involvement with sexual acts that they don't do, or even *want* to do' (25), to which we might add that neither do people necessarily have their richest mental/emotional responses to cinematic images that they can most readily and superficially identify with. The spectator of *Mission: Impossible – Ghost Protocol* might not be a hegemonic male or subscribe to the 'patriarchal dividend', but this does not prevent him or her from investing in and developing a strong emotional involvement with the exploits of Tom Cruise.

Extending these questions of ambiguity and identity to cinema and questions of identification, it becomes possible to argue that the almost universal presence of often narrowly defined images of masculinity at the centre of men's cinema does not necessarily mean that patterns of identification cannot be far more complex and varied than the superficial stability of masculinity as image might suggest. The presence of by-and-large white, heterosexual men on the screen does not automatically leave these images untroubled or their ostensible hegemonic status unquestioned, as a notable pleasure granted by cinema is that of reading images against the grain, of formulating a critique of, or mounting an opposition to, an image at the same time as feeling an affinity for it or being overwhelmed by it.

In a different and cinema-specific way Robin Wood considers gender difference and, by implication, issues of identification in his prologue to the revised 2003 edition of *Hollywood from Vietnam to Reagan . . . and Beyond*. Wood first identifies potentially retrogressive gender binary oppositions (that men are 'responsible for at least 90 per cent of the evils and suffering in the world that are not caused by natural disasters'; 'Did women invent and develop the atomic bomb?' etc [xviii]) but then problematises these via the breaking down of the category of 'masculinity'. Though it appears that Wood initially equates 'masculinity' (and gender hegemony) with 'heterosexual masculinity', he soon distinguished between 'masculinity' and 'masculinism', or 'the cult of masculinity', which claims that 'men have a natural right to power and domination' (xviii) and then complicates 'masculinity' still further when commenting that:

> There is no reason to believe that what have traditionally been regarded
> as the 'masculine' virtues (strength, courage, energy, . . .) are the
> exclusive property of men, or that what have been regarded (especially,
> and conveniently, by men) as the 'feminine' virtues (gentleness,
> tenderness, nurturing qualities, supportiveness, passivity, . . .) are
> exclusive to women. The ideal human being would combine the two
> sets of virtues in balance. My own perfect embodiment of this is the
> music of Mozart . . . (Wood, 2003: xviii–xix)

Wood here evokes antimasculinist perfection as the *music* of Mozart – in terms
of my argument, this separation between composer and music is vital. Just as
Wood identifies the *music* of Mozart to be his 'own perfect embodiment' of 'the
ideal human being', so for the films I am discussing here as representative of
'men's cinema', the fact that they largely centre on men and masculinity, does
not necessarily mark them out as NOT FOR WOMEN (in the way, perhaps,
that some feminist films produced in the highly charged political environment
of the 1970s and 1980s were made 'for and by women' with the intention, quite
possibly, of BEING NOT FOR MEN). Later in *Hollywood: from Vietnam
to Reagan*, Wood, in a preamble to his discussion of Scorsese, revisits the
question of his dissatisfaction with 'current theoretical accounts of the construction of the viewer's position by classical cinema, especially with regard
to the dichotomy of male/female spectatorship' (Wood, 2003: 220). Apropos
of Hitchcock's films, which, he believes, 'frequently encourage identification
with the female position for viewers of either sex', Wood raises the 'phenomenon of transsexual identification' which, in certain instances, undermines
'beyond all possibility of recuperation' the 'male identification position'.

In the provocatively titled chapter 'The End of Sexual Difference?' Judith
Butler, in *Undoing Gender*, ruminates on some of the problems of the term
'sexual difference'. Butler first contends, after French feminist Luce Irigaray,
that 'sexual difference is not a fact, not a bedrock of sorts . . . On the contrary,
it is a question, a question for our times' (Butler, J., 2004: 177), going on to
challenge the appropriation within queer studies of 'sexuality and sex' as the
'"proper" object' of gay and lesbian sexualities, separate, for example, from
feminism which 'is said to have *gender* as its object of inquiry' (181). 'Such
understandings', Butler continues, 'evacuate gender as well, but only because
gender stands for feminism and its *presumptive heterosexuality*' (Butler, J.,
2004: 184; my italics). Butler's notion of 'presumptive heterosexuality' as
dominant within even recent discussions of sexuality offers a significant way
forward for discussing a potentially flexible and inclusive notion of cinematic
masculinity, as does her suggestion that 'heterosexuality doesn't belong exclusively to heterosexuals' for the reason that 'heterosexual practices are not the
same as heterosexual norms . . . No doubt, practicing heterosexuals have all

kinds of critical and comedic perspectives on heterosexual normativity' (199). Just as 'sexual difference' needs to be understood as 'a border concept' or 'the site where a question concerning the relation of the biological to the cultural is posed and reposed' (186), so Butler suggests that the concept of 'universal entitlement' deserves scrutiny. After explaining that 'the universal' as a term is 'culturally variable' and that 'specific cultural articulations' of it 'work against its claim to a transcultural status' (190), Butler examines the twinned issues of 'the universal' and exclusion:

> To be excluded from the universal, and yet to make a claim within its terms, is to utter a performative contradiction of a certain kind . . . The universal begins to become articulated precisely through challenges to its *existing* formulation, and this challenge emerges from those who are not covered by it, . . . but who, nevertheless, demand that the universal as such ought to be inclusive of them. (Butler, J., 2004: 191)

One of the 'problems' of masculinity has been, as already discussed, that it is collapsed too easily and with insufficiently nuanced critical scrutiny into 'the universal': that 'as an ideal, at least' it is 'implicitly known' whereas femininity remains 'a mystery' (Neale, 1993: 19). As Connell later argued, Simone de Beauvoir's treatment of genders in *The Second Sex* as, in Connell's words, 'different ways of life rather than fixed character types' had not, in 2003, been 'explicitly applied to the First Sex, as a theory of masculinity' (Connell, 2003: 19). Connell thus sought to problematise, scrutinise masculinity, much as Butler later does the 'universal'. Both Connell's inner recognition that there is no explicit theory of masculinity and Butler's performative model of gender and sexuality offer models for my approach to 'men's cinema'. The performative ambiguities and fluidities that characterise 'men's cinema' make it possible for it to be *inclusive* rather than exclusive of the genders and sexualities that the superficially more straightforward images of hegemonic masculinity in the films appear to perform or represent. In identifying more complex and flexible notions of identification and gender I also want to propose a fundamental reassessment of the role aesthetics, style and *mise en scène* play in our understanding of identity and our subsequent enjoyment of 'men's cinema'.

It might seem contrary, having reached the relatively radical and fluid definitions of gender and sexuality offered by queer theory, to revert at this juncture to the first of Sigmund Freud's 'Three Essays on the Theory of Sexuality' (1905), but this is what I propose to do, for, as with so much of Freud's writing on gender and sexuality, the essay on the sexual aberrations is not only pertinent but it has too often been simplified and misrepresented. R. W. Connell opens the revised 2003 edition of *Masculinities* by recalling how in depth psychology's 'scientific account of masculinity' there was 'radical potential . . . from the start' (Connell, 2003: 8). Though believing that 'Freud opened more doors than he walked through' (9), what, in Connell's estimation makes his work the 'starting point of modern thought on masculinity' despite most later researchers having 'known little and cared less about the detail of his ideas' (8), is that he 'disrupted the apparent natural object "masculinity"' (8) and furthermore argued for each personality as 'a shade-filled, complex structure, not a transparent unit' (Connell, 2003: 10). It was as a result not of Sigmund Freud's work but of psychoanalysis's move to the right between 1930 and 1960, Connell maintains, that

> adult heterosexuality, which Freud had seen as a complex and fragile construction, was increasingly presented as an unproblematic, natural path of development. Anything else was viewed as a sign of pathology – especially homosexuality. (Connell, 2003: 11)

In the first of his *Three Essays on Sexuality* Freud outlines what constitutes 'normal' sexuality and, by extension (and for the purposes of my argument), 'normal' masculinity. I want to discuss this essay not because I want then to impose a Freudian 'reading' on the films to be examined later but because Freud's articulation of what constitutes the 'normal' sexual aim and, by contrast, a 'perversion' offers an invaluable insight into why definitions of masculinity have proved so problematic. Firstly, I feel it is necessary to stress that 'The Sexual Aberrations' can be most productively read as a polemic in which Freud himself can be seen to be grappling with, and deliberately exaggerating, the fundamental issues and problems of human sexuality, as opposed to an agenda-less account of sexuality.

So what, to Freud, in this seminal 1905 essay is 'normal' sex? At the outset, he establishes the *'sexual object'* as 'the person from whom sexual attraction proceeds' (Freud, 1991: 45–6)[6] and the *'sexual aim'* as 'the act towards which the instincts tend' (1905: 46). He also sets out the complex and inherently contradictory binary opposition between 'normal' and 'perverse' sexual practice, identifying the 'normal' sexual aim as being 'the union of the genitals in the act known as copulation' (1905: 61) and the 'perversions' as

> sexual activities which either (a) *extend*, in an anatomical sense, beyond the regions of the body that are designed for sexual union, or (b) *linger* over the intermediate relations to the sexual object which should normally be traversed rapidly on the path towards the final sexual aim. (Freud 1991: 62)

From the start of 'The Sexual Aberrations', there is a discernible tussle in Freud's thinking between an overt mission to prove that there is such a thing as normative sexual practice and the repeated tacit acknowledgment that such a position is untenable because the human libido is necessarily the result of a dynamic (unstable, impulsive) relationship between the 'normal' and the 'perverse'.[7] Having offered an excessively narrow, almost parodic definition of the 'normal sexual aim', Freud immediately identifies his definitions' flaws, as if even he is straining to believe his own argument. Subsequently, the bulk of 'The Sexual Aberrations' comprises a series of carefully nuanced definitions of the 'perversions' and their relationship to the supposedly 'normal' sexual aim.

Freud opens by discussing the most significant (though not necessarily the most prevalent) 'perversion', namely 'inversion', before progressing to 'bisexuality', 'fetishism', 'touching and looking' and 'sadism and masochism'. In each case he argues that these become 'perversions' if they take the place of and supplant the act of (heterosexual) copulation, that is, if they pervert the course of 'normal' sex. Simply counting the number of times Freud uses the word 'normal' in these brief descriptions of the 'perversions' gives some indication to the reader that he doth protest too much. The image of a road always springs to mind when I read 'The Sexual Aberrations' – a crumbly, distressed road similar to the fateful one taken by Oedipus in Pasolini's *Edipo Re* – liberally strewn with stones, debris and other obstacles; at the end of the road resides, oracle-like, the 'normal' sexual aim while the 'perversions' are the impediments that potentially trip us up, deflect us from our course or, in the most unfortunate cases, prevent us from attaining our putative goal altogether. Is the road linear or circular, however? Freud seems anxious to establish the libido's *linearity* while finding it to be resigned to *circularity*, forever side-tracked or blown off course, as are his descriptions of it. Freud metaphorically throws up his arms in resignation when he elaborates under 'The Perversions in General' that:

> No healthy person, it appears, can fail to make some addition that might be called perverse to the normal sexual aim; and the universality of this finding is in itself enough to show how inappropriate it is to use the word perversion as a term of reproach. (1991: 74)

Freud's argument is, I am convinced, intentionally not just circular but contradictory, in that he itemises in such detail each 'perversion' and identifies why and how it might be pathological, only to conclude that 'perversions' are essential to the 'normal sexual aim' and so not aberrations, as he has initially defined them, at all. All the itemising and dissecting of the perversions, all these meandering and contradictory internalised debates Freud enters into with himself as much as with us, have the perverse effect of rendering the perversions less perverse. That Freud can discuss them with such granulated clarity results paradoxically in the aberrations' 'normalisation'; the 'putting into discourse of sex' (Foucault, 1976: 12) which, as Michel Foucault argued, is simultaneously an act of transgression and an act of sanitisation. If one is then to treat 'The Sexual Aberrations' as a polemical and inherently contradictory piece, then the 'normal sexual aim' becomes the ultimate perversion by virtue of being nearly impossible to attain or embody in its 'pure' state. Indeed, in one of Freud's many unexpected volte-faces, he surmises that *neuroses are, so to say, the negative of perversions* (Freud, 1991: 80; italics in original), that their symptoms originate not 'at the cost of the so-called *normal* sexual instinct' but 'at the cost of *abnormal* sexuality' (80). This rich final discussion of neuroses succinctly makes the case for the normalisation of perversion as well as for the pathologisation of normality.

Opened up to revisionist scrutiny, 'The Sexual Aberrations' offers a fascinating template for understanding heterosexual masculinity, so often assumed to occupy the position of the given, the un-Other, the 'normal'. Not only, like the 'normal' libidinal pursuits, is (heterosexual) 'masculinity' repeatedly defined by and against what it is not but it comes into being as a category through the attempted, but unsuccessful, repression of various perversions, homosexuality in particular. Just as the 'normal sexual aim' cannot come into being without permitting and assimilating a degree of perversity, so masculinity cannot function without having assimilated some aspects of the subject positions it strains so hard to repress: femininity, homosexuality, bisexuality and so on. Just as the 'normal sexual aim', in its purest manifestation of heterosexual penetrative sex, is neurotic so heterosexual masculinity, in its most pared down form (Sylvester Stallone's monosyllabic Rambo, for example), is hysterically two-dimensional, stripped of normality and ultimately perverse. Men might aspire to an ideal of masculinity but, unless they are odd and dysfunctional, they cannot embody it, for to do so successfully would be perverse. Masculinity, like 'normal' sexuality, is the sum of its perversions.

Hollywood seems like a promising place to start an examination of 'men's cinema' for in its films it has repeatedly enacted this precarious balance between normality and perversity in its many conceptualisations of masculinity. Perversity, for certain, is more often than not embedded and repressed but it frequently surfaces through style and *mise en scène* as a means of defining and refining the more overt manifestations of 'normal' masculinity. So many examples exist in which the struggle between 'normal' and 'perverse' forces is discernibly enacted on the level of blocking, acting, framing, camera movement, editing (let alone narrative), that masculinity, like the sexual 'normality' it purportedly embodies, does not simply exist in opposition to, or separate from, the repressed aspects of male sexuality, but because of them. If we liken the surface of the film to the body, then the latent, anterior 'symptoms' of the repressed perversities that ultimately *denote* masculinity come to be expressed through and on the surface of a film. It is for this reason that discussing masculinity mainly (or only) in terms of representation – its primary overt manifestation – is not enough as its physical presence might not end up being where masculinity resonates or where it is understood on an emotional, figurative or psychic level. And where it is understood on these multiple levels is in and through its freely identifying, multigendered, spectatorship. There is an argument to be made, pursuing Freud's polemic in 'The Sexual Aberrations', for masculinity as cinema's ultimate perversion because, in its most narrowly defined terms, it hardly exists at all and, outside this, is perpetually construed in relation to the perversions around which it is constructed but which the ultimate representative of that masculinity (the 'man') so strenuously represses. Many Hollywood films which enact the 'strain' of heterosexual masculinity on the level of surface convey (in terms of how the spectator watches and receives them) the 'strain' on a physical, almost visceral, level via its formal and stylistic strategies. Far from being its determining force, heterosexual masculinity is so frequently a film's unrealisable ideal, an uncertain, troubled and phantasmagorical textual presence.

Point Break (Kathryn Bigelow, 1991), for instance, is a satisfyingly complex example of men's cinema which sets out its stall from the off. It opens with a title sequence that, to the dreamy wisps of Mark Isham's score and the soporific sounds of waves folding into sand, juxtaposes two alternative images of masculinity: the more socially acceptable, professional one represented by rookie FBI agent, Johnny Utah (Keanu Reeves) on a firing range; and a more extreme, marginalised surfer subculture one, exemplified by Bodhi (Patrick Swayze). The two are not made to look completely dissimilar: both introductory strands feature water, for example, as Utah is drenched by virtue of having to undertake this training exercise in torrential rain but, whereas Utah's thread is shot mainly at full speed, the images of the surfers are exclusively slow motion and, whereas Bodhi's story is an elliptical, beautiful and abstract montage of surfers catching waves, Utah's timed shooting exercise has an identifiably linear narrative structure. Only one of these stories immediately makes us want to be there, as boards scythe through the sea, surfers' silhouettes swoop towards us against a golden sky and droplets of water glisten. Starting with these evocative but gendered titles, surfing, throughout *Point Break*, functions as a loosely defined metaphor for masculinity but one that has defiantly rejected its roots in, and severed its ties with, its patriarchal, hierarchical and hegemonic 'other', exemplified by the FBI. It encapsulates a state of being that affects us, that washes over and sensuously engulfs us. *Point Break* develops both aspects of masculinity established in its title sequence: it follows a taut plot in which Utah infiltrates the surfer community to track down the Ex-Presidents, a group of masked bank robbers, and it interrupts this with several ecstatic interludes of uncontaminated spectacle, as characters lose themselves to extreme physical activity, be it

Figure I.5 *Point Break* (Kathryn Bigelow, 1991). Surfing masculinity.

surfing or skydiving, which exists both within and beyond the confines of narrative.

The first time we see Bodhi surfing is after Johnny Utah has had his first successful surfing lesson with Tyler (Lori Petty). He turns around and, as he becomes transfixed by Bodhi riding a wave, a jaunty pop song ('I Will Not Fall') fades out to be replaced by spacey Mark Isham music accompanying slow-motion images of the surfer partnering the unruly foam in an athletic ballet or arching back inside the breaking wave's tunnel. Tyler turns to Johnny and tells him 'That's Bodhi . . . he's a real searcher', searching for 'the ultimate ride'. In *Cinema and Sensation* Martine Beugnet argues for the possibility of cinema being able to overturn the 'conventional conception of the observer/observed relation' in which the observer's self 'theoretically stands as a separate entity' and 'the effect of looking and listening takes on a mimetic quality' that 'pre-empts or supersedes' a 'state of detached self-awareness' in which the 'border between subject and object collapses' (Beugnet, 2007: 5). In *Point Break*, just such a convergence occurs during these rarefied spectacular interludes. After stepping in to prevent Johnny Utah from being beaten up, Bodhi tells him that surfing is 'a state of mind; it's that place where you lose yourself and you find yourself'. Johnny finally experiences this after a party that night, when the surfers head out for a night-time surf, after which he confesses to Tyler, 'I can't describe what I'm feeling', to which her response, against the romantic gleam of the water, is 'you don't have to'. Like the 'demon in the sky' in *The Right Stuff* (Philip Kaufman, 1983) or the raging fire in *Backdraft* (Ron Howard, 1991), surfing, especially going for the big wave ride (which Tyler dismisses as being 'a macho asshole with a death wish') is ambiguously and not unproblematically coded as masculine. This exchange between Johnny and Tyler, however, comes a few seconds before they succumb to the eroticism of the moment and spend the night together on the beach. Surfing, like Lacan's phallus, is both linked to masculinity and an abstract notion, an undescribable and unattainable thrill whose identity is fluid and which transcends sex and gender boundaries (for it is over surfing that Utah bonds with Bodhi and falls for Tyler) and is there to be understood by everyone.

Point Break inverts the conventional relationship between 'normal' and 'perverse' masculinities, as the ordinary, professional masculinity represented by the FBI via the film's action plot becomes secondary to the orgiastic, unconstrained experiences of surfing or skydiving. I would therefore question Barry Keith Grant's treatment of *Point Break* in which he frames it in terms of how it exhibits 'a masculine homosocial hysteria mapped onto the excessive display of the male body' and argues that the mid-air hand-clasping between Johnny and Bodhi is simply 'a hysterical visualization of the repressed homoerotic subtext of the buddy movie' (Grant, 2011: 187). *Point Break* remains one of the strongest cinematic evocations of masculinity precisely because it neither limits nor defines it; it does not just transport us, in the extreme action sequences, into a 'delirious frenzy' but it transports us beyond sexual difference and homosocialism. Certainly there are gender divides in *Point Break* – it is a surfing movie not a utopian vision – but it seems crucially important (though it is also she who, minutes before, had declared 'there's too much testosterone here') that it is Tyler and not Bodhi who understands Utah's inability to describe what he is feeling after the night-time surf. Just as, when the film elicits a visceral, emotive response from its viewers as well as an intellectual one, this is in response to its liberating, intense visual style just as much as to any nebulously defined notion of the phallus.

Point Break concludes, just as it opens (amid slicing rain), with Utah in Torquay, Australia, having finally tracked down Bodhi, waiting to ride the 'biggest wave the planet has ever seen'. Bodhi is looking out to sea, not the enticing green of before but rather a grey and menacing cavalry, thundering towards the shore. Utah catches up with him, tells him 'you've gotta go down' and they fight. The two men brawl but not only that – Bigelow films their fight in extreme close-ups using a hand-held camera that jerks and rolls with the punches, as it might do in a conventional cop movie: Bodhi, this suggests, is almost ensnared by the more predictable masculinity he has so far avoided, especially as the fight ends with Utah cuffing him. Utah ultimately releases him, however, so he can catch 'one wave before you take me' because 'my whole life has been about this moment'. Intercut with the exasperated federal officers (who have arrived just in time to be too late to cart him off) peering through their binoculars, Bodhi is on top of a massive, unforgiving wave. He falls, crashes and is engulfed: the last ocean image being a close, dislocated shot of the raging foam after which there is a cut to Utah walking along the shore and throwing his FBI badge into the water. Masculinity is 'a state of mind' –

in metaphorical terms, the waves that take over the screen – but it is also the not-so-ethereal federal officers.

NOTES

1. See Mandy Merck's analysis of 'Visual Pleasure and Narrative Cinema' as a manifesto in 'Mulvey's Manifesto', *Camera Obscura* Volume 22, No. 3 66, pp. 1–23, 2007.
2. This is the title of Dale Spender's 1982 book about patriarchy and language.
3. Cf. Cixous's notion of '*l'écriture féminine*'.
4. Cf. Introduction to Steven Shaviro *Post-Cinematic Affect*, Ropley: O-Books/ John Hunt Publishing Ltd (2010).
5. Raewyn Connell is a transgendered woman who, earlier in her career, pubished as Robert, Bob and R. W. Connell. Of the two works cited by me, the author of *Masculinities* (first edition published 1995, second edition 2003) was R. W. Connell, while the author of *Gender* (second edition, 2009) is Raewyn Connell.
6. This is an intriguing use of the term 'sexual object' as Freud here is referring to what most readers would take to be the sexual subject.
7. As Freud suggests even early on in 'The Sexual Aberrations': 'But even in the most normal sexual process we may detect rudiments which, if they had developed, would have led to the deviations described as "perversions". For there are certain intermediate relations to the sexual object, such as touching and looking at it, which lie on the road towards copulation and are recognised as being prelim sexual aims' (Freud, 1905: 61–2).

CHAPTER ONE

How *mise en scène* tells the man's story

The title for this chapter makes reference to Jane Gaines's brilliant and oft-quoted 1990 essay 'Costume and narrative: how dress tells the woman's story', in which, having identified the normative model adopted by most Hollywood costume designers of the classical era, she explores certain instances, such as in the melodrama *Dark Victory*, when female costumes function differently and more obtrusively. Using Elsaesser's 'Sound and Fury' as one of her formative touchstones, Gaines argues that 'a woman's dress and demeanour, much more than a man's, indexes psychology; if costume represents interiority, it is she who is turned inside out on the screen' (Gaines, 1990: 181). Though elsewhere I have critiqued and extended Gaines's statement with specific reference to the costuming of masculinity (for instance, in the Hollywood gangster film), my starting points here are different. The first is to use the idea of *mise en scène* to tell the man's story to challenge the critical tendency, when it comes to classical Hollywood, in particular, to believe that masculinity and male identity are not so fragile, not so 'turned inside out on the screen' because somehow normative men and masculinity assume ownership of the screen and the *mise en scène*. The second is to extend Gaines's notion of telling a gendered story via the too frequently neglected element of costume by proposing that, in many instances, men can likewise be seen to be 'turned inside out' on the level of *mise en scène*, that their interiority can, like women's, be indexed in ways that problematise the relationship between the integrity and cohesion of Hollywood narrative cinema and the hegemony of masculinity. In such instances, doubts concerning masculine authority often come to be expressed as a loss of control over the *mise en scène*.

While the second half of this book will focus predominantly on the specific development of a masculine aesthetic in more recent and contemporary Hollywood cinema, this chapter will begin to map out the terrain for that discussion by centring on the notion of film style and *mise en scène* being deployed to tell the man's story. My discussion here will be divided into three sections and will look mainly at examples from the classical era, starting with how 'classical' Hollywood cinema made use of non-narrative ways of framing and expressing hegemonic masculinity. This normative mode, though more prevalent in the pre-1970s era, was never, even then, left entirely unchallenged, so I will then look at two ways in which the challenge to hegemonic, stable masculinity was mounted, using as my two exemplars masculinity and anxiety and masculinity and perversity, examining how these are examined and articulated through style and *mise en scène*.

MASCULINITY AND THE NORMATIVE MODEL

As has been cited many times in discussions of Hollywood cinema (see, for example, Bordwell et al. 1988; Langford 2010), the derivation of the term 'classical', when applied to Hollywood's style, probably dates to André Bazin who, in 'The Evolution of the language of cinema', declared that Hollywood had reached 'a level of classical perfection', brought to the cinematic art 'its perfect balance, its ideal form of expressions . . . a complete harmony of image and sound'. 'In short', as Bazin concludes, 'here are all the characteristics of a classical art' (Bazin, 1967: 29–30). David Bordwell, in 'An Excessively Obvious Style', the opening chapter of *Classical Hollywood Cinema*, sees parallels between Bazin's idea of classicism and art historian E. H. Gombrich's enquiries into classicism and art, surmising that, although 'Film historians have not generally acknowledged the place of the *typical* work . . . in other arts the ordinary work is granted considerable importance'. Bordwell then sets out to define the system that created 'not the aberrant film that breaks or tests the rules' but the 'quietly conformist film that tries simply to follow them' (Bordwell et al., 1988: 10). Bordwell, Staiger and Thompson were, above all, interested in defining a system not hitherto deemed necessary of definition because 'We all have a notion of the typical Hollywood film', a film that 'strives to conceal its artifice through techniques of continuity and "invisible" storytelling' in order to appear 'comprehensible and unambiguous' (Bordwell et al., 1988: 3), and which possesses and displays 'aesthetic norms' (4).

The Classical Hollywood Cinema first appeared in 1985, the same year as Richard Dyer's essay on 'Male sexuality in the media' in which Dyer similarly sought to define some of the aspects of another system, namely hegemonic masculinity which, at the time, was considered to be just as 'excessively obvious', its mechanisms for dominance just as 'invisible'. *Men's Cinema* does not set out to offer an exhaustive Bordwellian description of the 'aesthetic norms' of Hollywood masculinity but, just as there are intellectual links between the endeavours of Bordwell, Staiger and Thompson and Dyer, so *Men's Cinema* does set out at least to contextualise subsequent discussions against an understanding of the parallels between the invisible styling of masculinity and male subjectivity in Hollywood. As Bordwell identifies, it is frequently the case that the most interesting and provocative examples within a genre or group are those that rupture 'classical' norms, or the under-stylisation of the 'styleless style' as Elizabeth Cowie (again, after Bordwell) terms the classical Hollywood aesthetic (Cowie, 1998: 187). Just such a fissure occurs in Frank Capra's use of freeze-frame in *It's a Wonderful Life* (1946) at the moment when George Bailey is essentially choosing between a life of travel and exploration or domesticity – incompatible alternatives for the 1940s' American male and a moment when 'the normally invisible ideological mechanism became apparent, and a viewer could become aware of the cinematic apparatus' (Ray, 1985: 204).

So many great films of such fundamental importance to the twin development of Hollywood and of Hollywood's perception and definition of masculinity do not fit the norms (most of Hitchcock; the melodramas of Sirk, Minnelli and Ray – which is no doubt why so many analyses of Hollywood style and *mise en scène* start with them; the *noirs* of the late 1940s) that it is tempting to disregard the 'excessively obvious' altogether and simply cut to the chase. But, just as Cowie set out to 'find a way to challenge the hegemony of this [*Classical Hollywood Cinema*'s] account of classical narrative' (Cowie, 1998: 188), so I will seek in this opening chapter to achieve two things: firstly, to identify some of the notable ways in which the classical system upholds the hegemony of white, middle-class, heterosexual masculinity and, secondly, to progress towards a discussion of how, via formal and stylistic devices and *mise en scène*, the hegemonic model is challenged from within its own system, thereby questioning the definition of masculinity as straightforwardly 'typical' or 'ordinary'.

My doctoral thesis was on the political use of trials in film, theatre and television, and, while writing it, I soon discovered that classical Hollywood tended to revolve its courtroom dramas around white, heterosexual, middle-class and, more often than not, middle-aged, male lawyers. The films also ostensibly offered several examples of Hollywood's transparent, invisible style, as what was being said on the screen generally took precedence over how it looked. For some directors, filming in either an actual or purpose-built courtroom became a sort of straightjacket. An exasperated Stanley Kramer, for example, discovered, when on location shooting for *Judgment at Nuremberg* (1961), that courtrooms were, by virtue of being confined and cumbersomely furnished spaces, extremely difficult to film in. The courtroom's multiple diegetic and non-diegetic audiences (jury, lawyers, public galleries, spectators) add to this sense of claustrophobia and reinforce the centrality of the hegemonic male lawyer at the centre of the case. Hollywood's conscience-driven trial film is arguably another of Bill Nichols's 'discourses of sobriety' (Nichols, 1994: 67), the category he created to characterise how many people view documentary film. In an attempt to appear objective and impartial, its visual style is often excessively straight and unobtrusive. Bordwell emphasises the importance, within classical Hollywood cinema, of the Aristotelian unities of time and space when he contends that:

> The consensus among contemporary theorists is that the classical sequence possesses the Aristotelian unities of duration, locale and 'action', and that it is marked at each end by some standardized punctuation (dissolve, fade, wipe). (Bordwell et al., 1988: 63)

Conventional trials have inbuilt narrative linearity and logic and therefore abide naturally by such unities.

An effective example of the good liberal male lawyer is Atticus Finch in Harper Lee's *To Kill a Mockingbird* who, in 2003, came top of the American Film Institute's list of top fifty cinema heroes. Finch is asked by the Maycomb county sheriff to defend an African American, Tom Robinson, who has been accused of raping a white teenager, Mayella Ewell, 'Maycomb', being a fictional town standing in for Monroeville, Alabama, Harper Lee's childhood home, whose courthouse is replicated on the sound stages at Universal Studio. Tom Robinson's trial is the centrepiece of both book and film; in the adaptation especially, however, its lugubrious and stodgy liberal intentions almost kill off what, until that point, has been a subtle and nuanced film about childhood. In a thoughtful discussion of 'woman and the authorial voice' in *Mockingbird*, Amy Lawrence argues that 'During the trial scene, Scout and the voice of the narrator are shunted aside' (Lawrence, 1991: 174) in favour of Atticus's identification with his son Jem (sitting, within a segregated courtroom, in the upper African American public gallery alongside his sister Scout). Exemplary of how this happens and how *Mockingbird* is hijacked effectively by the forces of male subjectivity and Atticus in particular is Atticus's moving but wooden summation to the jury, shot apparently in a single nine-minute take with, in the final version, the insertion of selected cutaways.

The summation opens with a wide, high-angle shot from the perspective of the upper gallery with Atticus, his back to camera, facing the jury. For the most part, however, Atticus's rousing speech to the (all-white, all-male) jurors is framed using a low-ish, frontal mid-shot from the point of view of the jury benches. Camera movement is restrained and, throughout the trial generally, there is very little stylistic expressivity, with the exception of the dramatic zoom into Mayella Ewell's face during Atticus's heavy cross-examination of her. Atticus is literally nearly always central to each frame (bar the few reverse shots or cutaways to the public galleries), and Peck generally delivers the summation to just left of the tripod-mounted camera as if to reinforce this and the predominance, during the trial, of the spoken word. If Atticus does walk away from the jury, the camera pans to follow him but invariably stops short of zooming in to capture more straightforwardly emotive close-ups. The result is an intense and oppressive unity between character, movement and place in which we – the just off-screen alternative jurors (more diverse, hopefully more broad-minded) – become another of Atticus's attentive audience.

Parallels between cinema spectators and on-screen jurors are emphasised especially clearly during Atticus's statement about justice, a portion of the summation aimed at an early 1960s American public as much as it is at 1930s Alabama. After a pause, Atticus turns to the jury and says: 'Now, gentlemen, our courts are the great levellers. In our country all men are created equal,' at which point, Peck scans the jury from left to right before a rare edit to the African American upper gallery, listening intently. He then continues, as the stiff tripod mid-shot resumes: 'that is no ideal for me, that is a living, working reality'. For the summation's conclusion ('In the name of God, do your duty . . .'), the framing becomes a little tighter but, at the repetition of 'In the name of God', there is a cut – not to a close-up of Jem looking down at his father (which, in terms of the scene's heavily Oedipal connotations, would have made sense) but, much more contrarily, to a wide, high-angle shot of Atticus, his back to camera, pleading with the jurors. Reverting to the framing of the establishing shot, while making more straightforwardly emotive character identification difficult, reinforces the heavily laden notion of the cinema audience's alliance with the anti-racist forces of Finch, the good liberal lawyer, and the wronged African American communities of Alabama and 1960s US society. As he continues ('In the name of God, believe in Tom Robinson . . .') formal stability is restored as the image reverts to the frontal mid-shot of Atticus, here leaning on the jury bench, before panning (not zooming) synchronously with him walking away from the jury to sit down at his table alongside Tom.

Tom Robinson's trial offers an instructive lesson in invisible but persuasive liberal film-making – in what US documentary director Emile de Antonio termed 'democratic didacticism'. Atticus presents the arguments for Tom's innocence objectively – the point, I would suggest, of the distant, theatrical blocking of his lengthy summation with minimal emotional interference to detract from its dry ideological message. There is, therefore, only ever one interpretation effectively open to us, and that this does not tally with the 'guilty' verdict meted out by the all-white jury, is, in narrative terms, immaterial. The shot that Gregory Peck reputedly believed won him the Oscar in 1963 was the high-angle image of a defeated, yet morally triumphant, Atticus leaving the courtroom at the end of the trial. Atticus slowly organises his papers as his remaining diegetic audience (the African Americans in the upper gallery – their victorious white counterparts have all left) look on in silent respect and then stand in unison as he exits the courtroom, his head bowed. This wrapping-up shot cements the symbolic bond between hegemonic masculinity, ideology and audience, a unification achieved through the synchronisation of Atticus's subjective authority and the sequence's archetypal 'self-effacing craftsmanship and cool control of the viewer's response' (Langford, 2010: xiii).

In *To Kill a Mockingbird* (Robert Mulligan, 1962), the narrative significance of the 'Maycomb' county courthouse is determined by its over-identification with Atticus, the archetypal lawyer–father. The courthouse is very differently introduced, for example, in the pre-title sequence of *Twelve Angry Men* (1957) as Sidney Lumet immediately reverses the controlling relationship between trial, ideology and liberal protagonist simply by adopting a much more mobile and, by implication, responsive and unfixed camera style. In *To Kill a Mockingbird*, the result of the trial scene's virtually imperceptible stylisation and unremarkable *mise en scène* is 'democratic didacticism'. Though the inherent structure of a trial is to put forward alternate and oppositional points of view, not only is the male subjective position in these films confirmed as the strongest but also the arguments and ideology they speak for are, in tandem, the more persuasive. In *Mockingbird*, Atticus's centrality in the trial scene marginalises the hitherto much more important point of view of his children, especially Scout.

Though the unities present in *To Kill a Mockingbird*, however, appear to be present at the outset, they are ultimately challenged and overturned in another justice-centred Hollywood film, Fritz Lang's last Hollywood film, *Beyond a Reasonable Doubt* (1956). Following on from earlier films, such as *M*, *Fury*, *You Only Live Once*, *Scarlet Street*, *Secret Beyond the Door* and *The Big Heat*, the visual style of Lang's final examination of personal justice and the fallibility of the law is uncharacteristically oppressive and matter-of-fact, a curiously unmoving film that, as one of its fans, Jacques Rivette, put it, feels like 'a description of an *experiment*' (Rivette, 1977: 67). Its extreme visual flatness (within the potentially emotive narrative context of a critique of capital punishment) borders on the perversely unsatisfying but Lang's tonal detachment is, at least partially, explained by the end of the film. A vital component of this perversity, and the one that the majority of its many critics focus on, is *Beyond a Reasonable Doubt*'s overly schematic plot in which writer Tom Garrett (Dana Andrews) sets out, with his future father-in-law and newspaper editor, Austin Spencer, to expose the fallibility of capital punishment laws by framing himself for a murder he did not commit, thereby 'proving' that it would be possible for an innocent person to receive the death penalty. In his evocative 1957 review for *Cahiers du cinéma*, Rivette argues that, whereas in earlier films, such as *Fury* or *You Only Live Once*, innocence possessed 'all the appearance of guilt', in *Beyond a Reasonable Doubt* the relationship is reversed, as guilt assumes 'all the appearances of innocence'. So, Rivette asks: 'Beyond appearances, what are guilt and innocence?' (Rivette, 1977: 68). *Beyond a Reasonable Doubt*, therefore, is motivated by a paradox: it affects an invisible, transparent style while, at the same time, being all about surface and performance. Lang deploys an ostentatiously unintrusive 'classical' style which, alongside his excessively functional characterisation of Tom, in particular, he purposefully reduces down to its minimalist bare necessities. Just as Tom, in a totally unanticipated final twist, is revealed as a fraud and to have murdered a wife nobody knew he had and to have used Austin's anti-capital punishment ruse as cover, so Lang's hysterically unforgiving visual style is likewise exposed as a con and a smokescreen, and thus raises doubts about Hollywood's classical style, in the same way as its plot raises doubts about the judicial system's ability to uncover a murderer. Ultimately, we find it impossible to believe 'beyond a reasonable doubt' in the credibility of classical masculinity either. Rather like Hitchcock's *Suspicion* (1941), another film in which Joan Fontaine plays the gulled partner, *Beyond a Reasonable Doubt* does not add up any more convincingly once we know how it ends. Innocence and guilt remain indistinguishable.

What I shall do here is look briefly at the two key early scenes in which Austin outlines his idea for proving how innocence can masquerade as guilt and Tom's dominant and fraudulently sincere role in them. The first scene takes place in Austin's sitting room, just after Tom, in a coldly perfunctory scene, has asked Susan Spencer to marry him. The two men are seated opposite each other, a little distance apart, like stilted actors in a poor social-problem play. They are also clearly set apart from the camera, a framing that remains largely consistent throughout this monotone exchange about the wrongs of capital punishment. The expressionless camera is rooted to the spot, hardly moves, as Austin furnishes some further details of his plan. Even though Austin is the ostensible focus of the scene, it responds to Tom only, for example, by undertaking a small tilt up and forward as he gets up from his chair and goes to stand at the mantelpiece. This exchange ends with Tom dismissing Austin's idea with a wave of the hand and: 'a case like that doesn't come up once in ten years'. Over a dissolve to a close-up of an opened newspaper carrying straplines of a report on the murder of nightclub dancer, Patti Gray – 'Dancer Strangled', 'Scene of Murder' and 'Police Baffled' – Austin repeats these exact words, as a prelude to the pair's next discussion of his plan. Hindsight tells us that this is probably the moment – during the handy temporal elision marked by the dissolve – when Tom hatched his murderous plans but, apart from an almost indiscernible wobble of the camera, there is nothing that gives this away.

The edit from the close-up on the newspaper report to a wider shot of Tom and Austin effectively resumes where the last scene left off, that is, with a stiff and detached camera, clunky theatrical blocking and Tom maintaining his central, ballast-providing position. Again, there is little about this innocuous scene and its functional style that implicates Tom or intimates that we should not trust him or his innocence, or what the film is telling us, even though, in retrospect, we come to realise that he had killed his wife even before Austin had alighted on the case and chosen Tom as the 'guinea pig' whom he will help frame for her murder. But even knowing this, there is no suggestion that our previous trust in Tom – always dull, always central to action and frame – was misplaced. As, at the end of the scene, Austin returns to his desk, and both men assume virtually identical positions to the ones they were in at the start of it, Tom remarks: 'you make this all sound very simple'. Stylistically, *Beyond a Reasonable Doubt* is very simple but its strangulated straightforwardness – like Tom's – is its ultimate deceit.

Tom's over-determined narrative role finds parallels in his physical positioning within the *mise en scène* and in the symbiotic ties between his movements and those of the camera. He is literally, for instance, central to the sequences in which he features, which is nearly all of them. The effect of Tom's excessive, dogged centrality is that it makes *Beyond a Reasonable Doubt* an unengagingly claustrophobic viewing experience, even at the climax of the film as Tom, so relieved that he is about to be pardoned, makes the fatal slip of revealing to Susan that he was the killer after all. To return to Rivette's critical observation that, in Lang, innocence and guilt look the same: *Beyond a Reasonable Doubt* hardly skips a beat, hardly changes tonal or aesthetic register, even after Tom has blurted out to Susan what he did. Yes, the bland but insistent score in which the film has been swaddled from the outset stops in its tracks at the moment of her realisation but, visually, the film is never liberated: it opened with a man being led from 'death row' to execution and ends with another one awaiting the same fate. As Rivette observes, in such an over-determined, disaffected world, 'all men are guilty *a priori*, and the one who has just been mistakenly reprieved, cannot prevent himself from immediately incriminating himself' (Rivette, 1977: 68).

Lang's clinically intellectual style in *Beyond a Reasonable Doubt* reveals 'experimentation' beyond testing the judicial system, namely that fixation on appearance also becomes a metaphor for Hollywood's 'invisible' style. Its 'openness' promises to keep us, the audience, in the loop but, as Doug Pye points out, the 'suppressive narrative' at work in *Beyond a Reasonable Doubt* does not function as it might in more conventional mystery or suspense contexts (Pye, 1992: 98), that is, keeping us guessing but also suggesting that we are being fed clues with which we will ultimately be able to solve the final mystery. Instead, style and narrative play tricks on us as well as on the other characters. The seamlessness of Lang's visual style papers over the cracks of the film's successfully suppressive and elliptical storytelling; it seems honourable enough but is, in fact, an obstruction not an aid, and knowingly sends us off the scent. Though the smooth look of the film glides over the fissures, Lang withholds a wealth of information from his audience including, as Pye identifies, the beginnings and ends of scenes. But what of the links between style and masculinity? In fooling his audience into believing the expressionless, ostensibly objective look of his film, Lang casts doubt on the classical Hollywood style as a transparent representational system. The tight links between *mise en scène* and Tom's determining subjective position further suggest that the colourless, straight hegemonic masculinity he purports to represent is, likewise, so nearly plausible but, in the end, turns out to be just as fraudulent and untrustworthy, Tom's self-incrimination ultimately exposing the superficialities and performative frailties of the archetypal Hollywood hero. Lang pushes his distrust of justice and invisible narration to the limit and, in the process, intimates that, alongside distrusting the straight, 'ordinary' style, we should also come to the realisation that straight, 'ordinary' masculinity, which seems so at ease and in control of the 'ordinary' style, is not so dependable either.

MASCULINE ANXIETY AND VISUAL STYLE

Masculine anxiety or anxiety about masculinity as issues, when they exist, are commonly expressed via non-narrative means. Examples are readily, but certainly not exclusively, found in genres such as melodrama and film noir, genres that both deal in suppressive narratives and are readily associated with the deployment of *mise en scène* features (costume, lighting, editing, camera) to tell the woman's story. As illustrations of comparable factors being mobilised to tell the man's story, this chapter will examine the discursive, aesthetic strategies used in certain melodramas and noirs to signal masculine anxiety, indicative of suppressed emotional responses that would otherwise remain half hidden or unacknowledged. I argued at the end of the previous section that normative masculinity is, even in the most ostensibly straightforward Hollywood films, an unrealisable ideal, and it follows that the anxieties and contradictions that surface as a result of this conclusion having been reached will frequently be resolved at a non-narrative level. The films I shall be discussing here are troubled and anxious in themselves, enacting on the surface of the films the anxiety and strain of not being able to live up to the fantasy of masculinity.

The strains, the repressive instincts, the disavowals and all the other attendant strategies deployed to hold up the 'normality' and hegemony of white, middle-class, heterosexual masculinity emerge furtively but frequently within classical Hollywood cinema, at a time when the explicit questioning of masculinity's status would have been more problematic. Though the cinematic expression of male anxiety is evidently not confined to melodramas and film noir, the evocation of the 'strain' of masculinity is particularly interesting when functioning within a markedly feminised space. Added to which, both melodrama and noir adopted a particularly expressive visual style. As Elsaesser remarked about Hollywood's 1940s and '50s 'domestic melodrama in colour and widescreen', it is 'perhaps the most elaborate, complex mode of cinematic signification that the American cinema has produced' (1987: 52); and, as Paul Schrader commented, it is, as a category, defined not so much 'by conventions of setting and conflict, but rather by the more *subtle qualities of tone and mood*' (1972: 81; my italics). Exemplary of the complexity of *mise en scène* as a signifying discourse in these genres are the 1950s melodramas of Vincente Minnelli in which masculine anxiety is variously signalled via an obviously anxious or anxiety-inducing setting or style. In *The Cobweb*, for instance, the sanatorium's director, Stewart McIver (Richard Widmark), probably seems like the least troubled character in the film, and yet Minnelli's trademark use of jarringly obtrusive decor and costume to signal repressed desire or unacknowledged personal doubt or fear is most clearly manifested in relation to him. McIver is *The Cobweb*'s least imaginative character, and his inability first to comprehend and then to control the tensions threatening to engulf the diegetic world he supposedly directs is expressed via his inability to understand the symbolic importance of the new curtains his clinic needs. That the curtains are externalised manifestations of McIver's lack of introspection is most clearly suggested by the eccentric design of the curtains, featuring prominent screen prints of a patient's drawing of McIver's face, that are eventually chosen for the clinic's drawing room windows. McIver is not anxious until (briefly) at the end, and yet spectators experience anxiety on his behalf.[1]

Here, fears, desires and anxieties become 'almost conscious' through existing in the *mise en scène* as they do in both *East of Eden* and *Inherit the Wind*, for instance, as Kazan and Kramer respectively use tilt shots at particularly tense and dramatic moments, such as the two crucial Oedipal father/son exchanges in *Eden*. In these cases, non-verbalised male anxieties are transferred on to the body of the film via an obtrusive use of the camera, and the 'almost-conscious' is a state many of the anxious males in this chapter inhabit, as psychological anxieties surface in the form of non-narrative elements, such as performance, blocking, editing and use of camera. The films' stylistic excesses not only explain but *transmit* the emotional intensity to the spectator, prompting an excited, agitated, distinctly uncerebral form of viewing culminating in the 'utter absorption in the image' Shaviro experienced in response to *Blue Steel* (Shaviro, 1993: 8). Defined through a series of binary oppositions, at the heart of masculinity there lies a symbolic dividing line between 'desirable' masculine instincts and 'undesirable' ones that need to be repressed (the most prominent of which is homosexuality). This and other symbolic divides are sources of tension and self-doubt, and it is not surprising that barriers – literal as well as figurative – feature prominently in several films focused on masculinity and anxiety, from the many literal barriers in the domestic settings (stairs, window frames, curtains), to the quasi-physical use of the non-diegetic film frame in the first sequence of *Rebel Without a Cause*, or the hero's loss of spatial, emotional and intellectual control in *Out of the Past* and *The Lady From Shanghai*. A prominent element of the melodramas, especially, is not merely that the elaborate visual style and the use of barriers *compensate for* the male characters' repressive instincts and lack of introspection or self-knowledge, but that the male characters – whose bodily gestures often act in tandem with the films' visual excesses – *are also conscious of, but are disavowing*, the tensions and anxieties voiced within the *mise en scène*. The 'strain' and anxieties in these examples are, almost, palpable.

There's Always Tomorrow is one of the most melancholy of Douglas Sirk's melodramas and. in terms of its portrayal of male unhappiness and desperation, one of the most depressing. Alongside *The Wrong Man, Bigger than Life* and *The Man in the Gray Flannel Suit, There's Always Tomorrow* is one of a cluster of Hollywood films from 1955 to 1956 in which the breadwinner patriarch, the supposedly hegemonic male of 1950s America, is shown not to be as content and secure as might be expected but, conversely, to be miserable, desperate and insecure.[2] The pervasive and enduring malaise of these films is far from alleviated by their tacked-on and deeply implausible 'happy endings'; the hopelessness by this point is woven into the films' fabric and has been signalled from the outset on the level of *mise en scène*.

The second sequence of *There's Always Tomorrow* illustrates this, resonating as it does with Cliff's unhappiness and sense of redundancy, and setting the tone for the rest of the film. The 'barrier' in this scene is the family home's stairs which dominate the physical environment. Cliff (Fred MacMurray) arrives back from the office, having bought flowers and two tickets for the theatre in anticipation of being able to celebrate his wife Marion's (Joan Bennett) birthday with her *à deux*. As he opens the front door, he enters a deep-focus shot dominated by Vinnie, his teenage son, who is on the telephone. Arriving home is an alienating, not a welcoming, event. As Cliff, still in the background, calls up the stairs to Marion, Vinnie commands his father to 'ssshhh' and Cliff meekly obliges. Andrew Klevan comments that 'This begins a pattern in the sequence of Clifford left behind, left stranded in his house' (Klevan, 2005: 54), and the ensuing action revolves around Cliff but does not include him. Frankie, the youngest of two daughters, then rushes past her father on the stairs, barely acknowledging him, as Cliff continues up to the landing where he presents Marion with the birthday bouquet. As he does, he leans forward to kiss her, an advance from which she visibly recoils, thankful it seems that one of her children has called out to her so she can go and tend to them instead. This brief exchange is shot from a low angle further down the staircase and through the spindles, heightening the sense of Cliff's entrapment by, and alienation from, the home, and his marginalisation and entrapment within it.

Figure 1.1 *There's Always Tomorrow* (Douglas Sirk, 1955). Cliff tries to give Marion a birthday kiss.

Cliff attempts to salvage the situation by telling Marion how special she is and how her birthday is the one day of the year which should be dedicated to her but Marion tells Cliff regretfully that she cannot go to the theatre as she had promised to attend Frankie's first ballet performance that evening. Cliff and Marion are now centre frame but Cliff's speech is interrupted both by Frankie, fussing over getting ready, and then by their other daughter, Ellen, on her way out to discuss 'emotional problems' with a friend. Cliff (whose actions so far have all been reactive) once more follows the action, this time back downstairs, now pleading with Marion 'Let's go away some place . . . alone'. She is only half listening and the inelegantly high camera angle reflects Cliff's growing redundancy as he hovers on the outskirts of the frame as if about to fall out of it completely. No one, not even the family cook, wants the two tickets, and everybody bar Cliff tumbles out of the door and he is left to have dinner alone.

This sequence so far has been marked by frenetic choreography – children and wife running up and down the stairs, going in and out of different rooms and most importantly rushing past Cliff – as blocking, framing and the stairs are synchronised to construct a domestic world that barely remembers he is there. If ever there was an example of a man rendered insignificant by the female domain of the home it was this – but then the doorbell rings and at the door is Norma Vale (Barbara Stanwyck), an old flame from years earlier, and finally, as he goes to the door, Cliff becomes both central to the narrative and the frame. His status is not entirely uncompromised, however, as Cliff has gone to the door wearing an apron and carrying a coffee pot that has just bubbled over. While the erupting coffee functions as a metaphor for Cliff's dormant desire for Norma, the apron works as a bathetic reminder of his precarious hegemonic status [as Russel Lynes, one of many 1950s champions of the strong male, noted: 'the man in the apron has no one to blame but himself' (Lynes, 1953: 54)]. Boundaries continue to be important: as the coffee breaks free from its pot, so Norma has intruded upon and disrupted the sterile stability of Cliff's family home. Later Clifford reaches the point of being able to articulate his feelings of redundancy to Marion when he rails, 'I'm tired of the children taking over, I'm tired of being pushed in the corner, I'm tired of being taken for granted'; but it is Norma's much earlier transgression of the boundary between home and outside that marks the moment at which his despair bubbles over into consciousness.

As in *There's Always Tomorrow*, stairs frequently function as a visible line of demarcation between the traditional home's public and private domains; for the breadwinner father like Cliff, they often become the location for a fraught negotiation and oscillation between conflicting aspects of the man's identity, and they feature prominently as devices to link psychology to narrative in several 1950s male-centred melodramas, including *Bigger than Life, Rebel Without a Cause, Written on the Wind, Tea and Sympathy* and *The Man in the Gray Flannel Suit*. These domestic staircases serve a specific metaphoric function as sites of friction, decision-making and trauma. In *Rebel Without a Cause* (Nicholas Ray, 1955), for instance, two confrontations between Jim Stark (James Dean) and his father occur on the family stairs, once when Jim has returned home following the fight outside the planetarium and once after the fatal 'chicken run'. The first time Jim finds himself confronted with the Oedipal trauma of his (again) apron-clad father carrying a tray (the son is literally lost for words at this uncomfortable image of masculinity, only able to stutter 'Dad . . . stand . . . don't . . . I mean don't . . . what are you?') while the second staircase confrontation is filmed from another distortive low angle and culminates in Jim (having not received the support he had wanted from his parents following Buzz's death) pushing his father to the floor and running out of the house, in the process kicking in 'a portrait of his mother as a younger and lovelier woman' (Slocum, 2005: 128).[3] In both instances, as in the two big stair scenes in the earlier *Bigger than Life* (Ed's collapse and his near-fatal fight with Wally in the penultimate scene), Nicholas Ray stages divisive and definitive family fights on staircases using a heady mix of hyperbolic camera moves and angles: for example, magnifying Jim's Oedipal anxieties over his weak father by filming the crouching figure of Frank Stark (Jim Backus) from a low viewpoint through the spindles, thus accentuating his entrapment and infantilism. These sequences share a complexity that invites layered and nuanced levels of engagement, involvement and identification; they straightforwardly anticipate responses to staircases as signifiers for domestic unhappiness and the sites of confrontation but they also, via the deployment of self-conscious and intrusive framing, camera angles and movement, prompt more complex and abstract forms of identification with not merely the intensities of the narrative situations but also the scenes' stylistic excess.

Another of Sirk's melodramas, *Written on the Wind,* features a scene in which Lucy (Lauren Bacall) tells her husband Kyle (Robert Stack) that she is pregnant, the bedroom window here becoming an idiosyncratic metonym for masculine anxiety. This sequence (if we follow Nowell-Smith's argument that 1950s melodramas, in 'siphoning off' meaning on to music and *mise en scène*) works as an example of conversion hysteria, an affecting and effective illustration of the painfulness of watching a man enact *on the surface of the film* a barely repressed internal trauma. *Written on the Wind* more generally also contains two of the best examples of the transference of internal anxiety into bodily symptom in the performances of Stack and Dorothy Malone as the two wayward Hadley children. Crippled by the mystique of masculinity, the weight of patriarchal expectation comes crashing down on Stack in the bedroom window scene, in whose case the conversion of internalised anxiety into bodily symptom is manifested firstly in the excruciating affectedness of his speech, as if the process of uttering words summons into consciousness his repressed pain (as Elsaesser remarks, Stack's voice sounds 'as if every word had to be painfully pumped up from the bottom of one of his oil-wells' (Elsaesser, 1985: 173)). And secondly, as in this sequence, in the similarly tortuous and tortured physicality of Stack's bodily performance: his cricked neck and infantile, feral gestures.

Kyle has again returned home drunk, and Lucy escorts him upstairs to their bedroom. Both, in terms of decor, immediately stand out from their surroundings, as their clothes' sober strains of dark grey and black contrast with the crimson chairs, the deep-red carpet, the boldly patterned oriental screen and the wafting white chiffon curtains. The vibrancy of the colours perversely augments Kyle's misery. His doctor has told him that Lucy is having difficulty getting pregnant owing to a 'weakness' in him, which Kyle misconstrues as total infertility so, when Lucy here tells him that she is pregnant, Kyle's neurotic assumption is that he has been cuckolded by his best friend Mitch. As Kyle's conversation with Lucy progresses, Stack's delivery becomes increasingly strangulated and mannered as his body folds in on itself. Then, in a movement reminiscent of the physicalised histrionics of German expressionist cinema, he goes over to the opened window and half leans out, literally acting out his fear that he is precariously poised on the edge of neurotic collapse. The window and frame function as divides between life and fantasy, their permeability accentuated by the fluttering curtains, half outside and half inside the room. As the couple continue to talk, Kyle turns back into the room, only to recoil back into the window frame around the moment when he verbalises his fantasy that Lucy is pregnant by Mitch ('You shouldn't have done this to me'). He is therefore doubly framed, by the window and by the film, just as he

Figure 1.2 *Written on the Wind* (Douglas Sirk, 1956). Kyle Hadley framed by the window.

is trapped by, and shrinking from, both his wife and his own wild imaginings. Stack's position within the window functions more literally than a metaphor, externalising, but also helping to shape, his deep-rooted anxieties. Adding to the painfulness of this sequence is the physicality of Kyle's traumatised state, that he is so labouredly, consciously enacting his torment that we cannot but assume that he is also incapable of repressing it any longer from himself.

The 'frame' in *Written on the Wind*, though resonant with symbolism, is ultimately still a diegetic frame – one of Sirk's many over-determined signifiers. In a last example from 1950s melodrama of how unconscious masculine anxiety is conveyed through the *mise en scène*, I shall discuss the opening scene of *Rebel Without a Cause* in which there is a transferal on to the film frame (the parameters of the CinemaScope image itself) of Jim Stark's semi-acknowledged familial anxieties. Jim (James Dean), Judy (Natalie Wood) and Plato (Sal Mineo) are three adolescents recently brought into the local police station. Jim has been detained, as the title sequence shows, for underage drinking, and the heightened visual style used for the histrionic exchange with his family establishes the tense mood of the rest of the film. From off-screen comes the sound of Jim's mother calling his name as Jim waits to be interviewed by the station social worker, seated in a leather shoeshine chair set on a raised platform. As he hears his parents' and grandmother's arrival, Jim slowly stands up, an action marked, as is so much of the film, by an affected, intrusive *mise en scène*. Jim, who at this point, is positioned to the extreme left of the widescreen image, assumes only a semi-upright position, prevented, or so it seems, by the frame of the image from standing up straight, as if he finds himself physically wedged up against the ceiling of an *Alice in Wonderland*-esque undersized house. The extreme low angle at which the camera is set destabilises this already unstable

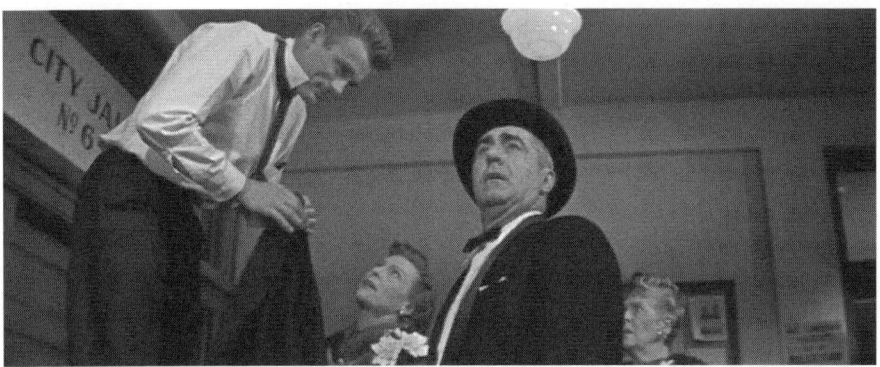

Figure 1.3 *Rebel Without a Cause* (Nicholas Ray, 1955). Jim Stark trapped by CinemaScope.

image, an insecurity further accentuated by the height at which James Dean is standing: the bottom of the frame roughly level with his knees. This heavily obtrusive framing remains constant as the heads and shoulders of Jim's parents and grandmother come into shot, with Jim left hanging over them like a semi-collapsed marionette. The veritable cacophony of stylised techniques spreads anxiety and has the cumulative effect of bringing to the surface, of enacting performatively, Jim's still unarticulated insecurities as well as the specific generational gulf between him and his parents.

Jim then falls back into the chair, at which point he comes down to his family's level. Once the image has stabilised, he does (and can) stand up straight. After the social worker has finished talking to Plato, he invites Jim and his family into his office. The contrast between the two diegetic spaces (Fremick's office and the waiting area outside) is as marked as the juxtaposition between its cramped-ness and the width of the CinemaScope image. It is, however, this more visually unexceptional sequence that explains, or rather gives a context to, the excesses of its predecessor, as Jim and his parents immediately start to squabble. A localised argument about Jim's drunkenness swiftly escalates into a wider metaphorical one about parent–son relations, as Jim's father, Frank, asks of his son (apropos of nothing much) why he keeps 'slamming the door in my face', before progressing to: 'We give you love and affection, don't we? Then what is it?' It is after this mushrooming of the petty argument that Jim emits his talismanic teenage cry: 'You're tearing me apart!', a grossly exaggerated response to the petty and bad-tempered familial exchange but one that, nevertheless, is in keeping with the film's highly wrought visual style. Ray's pointed use of CinemaScope, the depth of field and the breadth of the image (anomalously majestic for such a prosaic setting) function broadly in two ways: to lose Dean within the frame by prioritising, or drawing attention to, subsidiary actions; and to show him trapped by it. The opening scene thus establishes the relationship between melodramatic character dynamics and mannerist use of the camera that characterises *Rebel Without a Cause* throughout. The frequently tight framing used for James Dean is crucial to the sequence's overall effect. Charles Barr counters the suggestion that the format was incapable of using the close-up when he observes that:

> In CinemaScope the close-up, so far from being impossible, is for the first time fully acceptable: it *cannot* be a mechanical, all-purpose CU . . . and it cannot be detached, it must include a genuine and not just a token background. (Barr, 1963: 19)

The unmechanical and self-conscious use of the juxtapositions between close-up, width and depth is evident in 'Rebel' and goes against Bordwell's belief that 'In mainstream usage . . . widescreen filmmaking was but another instance of trended change, a new set of stylistic devices brought into line with the classical schemata' (Bordwell et al., 1988: 361). Ray's style is extreme and insistent. Coupled with CinemaScope's potential in the 1950s for, as Barr notes, adding authenticity, one of the effects of the police station is that the audience is more able to feel an affinity with Jim as the film's visual expressiveness provides a means of exploring and conveying his internalised conflicts on a primal, physical level. It is not only that Jim's repressed anxiety finds its most fulsome expression in the film's non-narrative elements, nor that the generic extravagances of the melodrama's *mise en scène* relate above all to the characters [Elsaesser's comment, for instance, that the men in these films are trying to live up to an exalted vision of man (Elsaesser, 1985)], but that our empathetic anxiety is awakened by the parallels between what is going on at the literal level of plot and what is being implied by the visual style.

The emotive deployment of aesthetics in film noir, though used to similar ends, looks and feels quite different. In 'How Hollywood Deals with the Deviant Male', Deborah Thomas examines how the strains of masculinity are played out in noir through the films' *mise en scène*, noting noir's 'essential male-centredness' and its 'pervasive mood of anxiety' which she argues:

> . . . pervades the entire fabric of such films, and does not merely accrue to its duplicitous women, appearing to linger on despite the resolutions of the narrative and the frequent restoration of its hero to his 'rightful' place. (Thomas, 1992: 59)

Thomas couches the masculine anxieties in noir principally in terms of motifs and plot and uses slightly different psychoanalytic terms from the ones I have outlined above, remarking, for example, that 'much of Hollywood cinema has grappled more or less explicitly with a kind of male schizophrenia which both puts an enormous pressure on men to be "normal" and yet represents such normality in contradictory terms' (1992: 59). Nevertheless, the acting out in noir of male anxiety on the level of *mise en scène* is a fundamental idea that I would like to explore further.

Anxiety is commonly attributed to noir's expressionist *mise en scène* and extensively permeates much of the attendant criticism – that, for example, there remains so little consensus about how noir can be defined and whether or not it is, in fact, a genre.[4] Whatever its generic or non-generic classification, the contours of noir's style are well known and need minimal rehearsal here (the indebtedness to German expressionism of the films' chiaroscuro lighting, disorienting camera angles, wide-angle lenses, disconcerting close-ups, and so on), so what I want to do instead is to examine two sequences in detail that, coming when they do in their respective films, serve to indicate how the underpinning anxiety of noir's *mise en scène* operates succinctly in relation to masculinity. Often it seems as if noir's extreme visual style works on the spectator in conjunction with – or, more accurately, at odds with – the hero's perspective and relative ignorance of the situation unfolding around him. We therefore come to feel an anxiety to which the hero is oblivious until, in terms of narrative resolution, it is too late. Though the conventional noir *mise en scène* is richly stylised, it is also elliptical and elusive when it comes to proffering meaning, in uneasy collision with the films' usually complicated plots which are seldom neatly resolved.

Dictating the tone of the group of films traditionally grouped as Hollywood film noir is the (vain) attempt to control chaos. Richard Dyer has identified the basic structure of noir as 'a labyrinth with the hero as the thread running through it' (Dyer, 1993a: 53), and there are various ways of profitably extending this. There are in most noir films three interlinked levels to the male protagonist's embroilment in the labyrinthine plot. Firstly, what occurs in several noir films of the 1940s and '50s (*Double Indemnity, The Postman Always Rings Twice, Out of the Past*) is that, as the hero gets sucked into it, the labyrinthine plot becomes less comprehensible or solvable, thereby functioning in contradistinction, as Dyer notes, to the classic thriller conventions of Agatha Christie or Sir Arthur Conan Doyle, in which each twist and turn takes the hero and reader closer to, not further away from, solving the mystery. Secondly, it seems that, in many cases, the more complex the labyrinthine plot becomes, the less possible it is for the hero to exert any control over it, though this is not evident to the hero himself at the time. Finally and paradoxically, the more control over, and independence from, the plot the hero thinks he has, the less independent or in control he, in fact, is and the more embroiled in the plot he is becoming. This last stage of the hero's imprisonment is, for those watching, particularly satisfying and compelling because it is often enacted on the level of *mise en scène*, and so is not tied exclusively to character but open to more instinctual and emotive patterns of response.

Out of the Past (Jacques Tourneur, 1947) illustrates the duality at the heart of the male experience in noir, and the paradox is contained within its structure. Tourneur imposes a superficially coherent narrative structure (its cyclic quality) on to events that are not satisfactorily resolved (the film ends on a lie). Symptomatic of Jeff's status within this paradoxical structure is how he is situated within its *mise en scène*. At the heart of the film is an extended sequence in San Francisco when Jeff (Robert Mitchum) goes in search of Kathie and Leonard Eels. It is in this section that, despite early on remarking to his cab driver that he realises he is being framed 'but all I can see is the frame', Jeff feels he is closest to unravelling the deceits of Whit and Kathie. How Tourneur uses this motif of 'framing' is crucial to the sequence's tone and to how it conveys that Jeff is more trapped than ever in a tortuous plot he does not understand. Between his first conversation with the cabbie and finding the dead body of Leonard Eels, Jeff enters and exits numerous dimly lit buildings and doors – going through, as it were, frame upon frame, a suggestion of entrapment and ignorance emphasised by the bareness of many of the doorways and buildings he traverses, which at times resemble stark German expressionist sets. There is an ostensible purposefulness to Jeff's chasing but, ultimately, he gets nowhere, a futility that is underlined by the number of doors, apartment buildings, clubs he goes in and out of. After finding Eels's body, Jeff encounters Kathie (who tells him she was forced to have Eels killed) and he senses he is getting closer to the truth but, again, the image contradicts this as the lovers are here so deeply in shadow as to be almost unreadable.

A variant on this relationship between the noir protagonist's voice-over and *mise en scène* comes at the end of Orson Welles's contemporaneous *The Lady from Shanghai* (1947). As Michael O'Hara (Welles) recovers consciousness in the Crazy House fairground, his voice-over starts with conviction and certainty: 'I was right, she was the killer, she killed Grisby and now she was going to kill me'. But his rational and confident-sounding words are emitted against the expressionist backdrops of wild, intersecting lines, tilted and distorted images and *The Cabinet of Dr Caligari*-esque stage sets. It is, ironically, at precisely the point at which O'Hara deduces that he has been the fall guy that the film's already mannerist visual style becomes especially unstable and fragmented, with Michael careering down a slide, being propelled across spinning stages and ending up in the hall of distorting mirrors. As Frank Krutnik comments of the parallels between expressionism and noir: 'the distorted *mise-en-scène* serves as a correlative of the hero's psychological destabilisation' (1991: 5). As Elsa (the 'she' of the scene's opening voice-over, played by Rita Hayworth) enters the hall of mirrors, her image is refracted and multiplied as the screen comes to resemble an unruly zoetrope, compounded by the entry of Elsa's husband, Bannister, who, on his crutches, moves across the various mirrors like a dispirited clockwork toy. It is tautological to suggest that the

Figure 1.4 *Out of the Past* (Jacques Tourneur, 1947). Jeff lost in the city.

fragmented images reflect the chaotic situation or the chaos in O'Hara's head but the repetitiveness of the mirrored images are, I think, meant to be just that: tautological illustrations of what we, by this point, already know, namely that O'Hara has realised too late that he 'has nothing' (Kaplan, 1983: 69) and that the multiple Elsas are but a painful reminder of that. The final shoot-out between Elsa and Bannister is almost comic in its violent pandemonium, as glass shatters with each random bullet fired, each felling randomly the images of the other, no longer capable of differentiating between the real figures and their reflections. The hall of mirrors thus becomes the exemplary metaphor for noir, with its omnipresent lack of clarity, stable identities and sound knowledge. Only as Michael walks out into the palpable sanity of the blank, bright outside world does the craziness end but, even here, there is ambiguity as his last voice-over starts: 'Well, everybody is somebody's fool'.

In film noir there is always information that cannot be conveyed through the discourses of action and character, and so, as in Freudian conversion hysteria, a 'conversion takes place onto the body of the text' (Nowell-Smith, 1987: 73) and it is through visual style, rather than the more direct means of plot or dialogue, that these films convey what the male protagonists refuse to acknowledge, namely that they are done for. Even Michael O'Hara in *The Lady from Shanghai*, who walks away from the final shoot-out relatively unscathed, indicates through his morose voice-over that the effect of Elsa will never leave him and that he will remain a fool in perpetuity.

The determining male 'anxiety' is not that masculinity is foolish or easily mocked, but that, having thought it was the identity position against which its 'Others' were defined, it discovers, in fact, that it is the most precarious and unsustainable of identity positions. The disquieting relationship between anxiety and masculinity finds expression in the elaborate and extreme visual style of a film, such as *The Lady from Shanghai*, as the men in the melodramas and noirs are perpetually thwarted in their quest to escape the 'dull' ordinariness they outwardly represent. In Nicholas Ray's *Bigger than Life*, there is the coupling of Ed Avery's illness and collapse, his cortisone-induced delusions of grandeur and Ray's use of tilts, extreme camera angles and expressionist colour schemes. In *Bigger than Life*, the *mise en scène* tells us, the enemy to 'normal' masculinity is internalised; conversely, in J. Lee Thompson's *Cape Fear* (1962), there exists a dangerous *externalised* symbiosis between 'good' masculinity (Sam Bowden) and 'bad' (Max Cady), again played out on the level of style as well as narrative. As does *Bigger than Life*, *Cape Fear* concludes with the 'good' male protagonist's restitution to hegemonic centrality; but, also as in *Bigger than Life*, this recuperation of the secure masculine position has been effected too easily to be plausible. *Cape Fear* ends with a physical fight between the lawyer Bowden (Gregory Peck) and convicted rapist Cady (Robert Mitchum) on the lake 'Cape Fear', against a noir-ish backdrop of dark tangled trees and gleaming, moonlit water. It looks as if Cady is going to triumph, as Bowden is left for dead under the water. Like the classic horror monster from the deep (in a poignant reversal of morality and roles), however, Bowden resurfaces to club Cady on the head, incapacitate him and hold him at gunpoint until he can be arrested. The water's limpid, threatening surface is crucially symbolic, as the distinctions between what is above the line and what below it (in terms of morality, knowledge, masculinity) become blurred and, ultimately, irrelevant. *Cape Fear*'s concluding shot is of the Bowden family leaving the lake on a motorboat, a family superficially safe, but now profoundly undermined, a fracturedness conveyed, as it has been previously, by the three of them sitting together but looking in different directions.

MASCULINITY AND PERVERSITY

With the transition from 'anxiety' to 'perversity', the level of internalised torment and stylistic intrusiveness is significantly increased. In terms of the films to be discussed in a moment, whereas, in *The Deer Hunter* and *Strangers on a Train,* the divisions between ordinary and perverse masculinity are just about upheld, in a film such as *Dead Ringers* the symbiosis between perversity and straight(forward) masculinity has become irreversible as the 'perverting' of masculinity invades the film's textual fabric. Though Michel Foucault in *The History of Sexuality*, Volume 1: *An Introduction* considers fetishism to be 'the model perversion' which 'served as a guiding thread for analysing all other deviations' (Foucault, 1976: 154), in terms of masculinity, homosexuality is the more significant perversion, as it is so often the repression of homosexuality on which a successful performance of normative, heterosexual masculinity depends. This is only a starting point, though, because masculinity is destabilised by many other perversities, as well as finding itself defined by its proximity to, as well as distance from, the sexualities it purports to reject. I will have argued by the end of this chapter that heterosexual masculinity, as I intimated in the introduction, becomes the ultimate or 'model' perversion as a result of three things: by virtue of being defined by its relationship to the 'perversions' as more conventionally conceived; by proving incapable of existing autonomously from them; and for being, in a form unadulterated by perversity (as conventionally conceived), conspicuously rare.

To be 'a man's man' (John Wayne, Charlton Heston, Peckinpah's 'wild bunch', Jean-Claude Van Damme, Bruce Willis, Wesley Snipes, Will Smith) is not to be a man's man at all when it comes to sexuality. It is only on a superficial level that heterosexual masculinity operates in binary opposition to homosexuality, as this segregation is virtually impossible to enforce, an awkwardness that resonates through much Hollywood 'men's cinema', in which normative masculinity is so frequently enriched by a complex dependency on its unspeakable, unconscious, repressed Other. It is this symbiotic, as opposed to dualistic, relationship that underpins my argument for (heterosexual) masculinity as the ultimate perversion for, without its Other, it is nothing. Similarly, as many films suggest, the heterosexual male's desired sublimation of homosexuality is doomed to failure and so, in so many ways and in so many films, hegemonic masculinity is understood *through*, and not in *contradistinction to*, homosexuality, a realisation that endlessly enriches studies of men's cinema.

The interactive, not to say mutually sustaining, relationship between heterosexuality and homosexuality is not a unique insight (see Freud's 'Three Essays on the Theory of Sexuality', for example, discussed in the introduction) though it is a realisation that is sometimes too readily (hysterically?) repressed. In the chapter 'Homosexual Outlet' in *Sexual Behavior in the Human Male*, post-war sexologist Alfred Kinsey and his research associates Wardell Pomeroy and Clyde Martin discuss at length the 'heterosexual–homosexual balance' (Kinsey, 1948: 636) and use their scientific, interview-based approach [in the introduction Kinsey had set out that one of the aims of the book was to represent 'an attempt to accumulate an objectively determined body of fact about sex which strictly avoids social or moral interpretations of the fact' (5)] to test preconceived ideas and stereotypes of homosexuality and to challenge the belief that heterosexual masculinity depended on the suppression or absence of homosexuality. Kinsey lays out in illuminating detail what he and his researchers take to be the 'commonly believed' characteristics of 'homosexual males', namely that they are: 'rarely robust physically', have 'fine skins, high-pitched voices . . . a feminine carriage of the hips . . . a considerable crop of hair . . . more often interested in music and the arts, more often engaged in such occupations as bookkeeping, dress design, window display, hair-dressing, acting' (Kinsey, 1948: 637). When reading this chapter in Kinsey's most infamous book, I invariably find myself thinking of Vincente Minnelli (who worked as a window dresser before getting into movies) and his exquisite melodrama about the sexuality that has no name, *Tea and Sympathy* (1956), in which John Kerr as Tom 'sister-boy' Lee has a best friend Al who tries to help him to learn to walk in a more manly way and whose house master Bill Reynolds's neurotic public displays of masculinity and love of outdoor pursuits mark him out as just as tormented as Tom.

Before challenging post-war certainty and homophobia, Kinsey initially surmises that 'The characterizations are so distinct that they seem to leave little room for doubt that homosexual and heterosexual represent two very distinct types of males' (Kinsey, 1948: 637). He then drew a table for the 'Heterosexual–homosexual rating scale', which went from 0 to 6, 0 being the male who was 'Exclusively heterosexual with no homosexual' and 6 being the male who was 'Exclusively homosexual' (639). In contradistinction to public opinion, the bulk of this table is taken up with the variegated categories of men who have had both heterosexual and homosexual sexual experiences. Kinsey now suggests that 'the heterosexuality or homosexuality of many individuals is not an all-or-none proposition' (638), and, the crudity of the table notwithstanding, he and his researchers reach the refreshingly radical conclusion (certainly for its time) that

> Males do not represent two discrete populations, heterosexual and
> homosexual. The world is not to be divided into sheep and goats . . .
> Only the human mind invents categories and tries to force facts into
> separated pigeon-holes. The living world is a continuum in each and
> every one of its aspects. The sooner we learn this concerning human
> sexual behavior the sooner we shall reach a sound understanding of the
> realities of sex. (639)

Kinsey, like Freud, was considered both profoundly influential and dubious in his methods but his 1948 view of male sexuality often seems more enlightened than, for example, much of the defensive, hysterical writing that emerged during the backlash, 'masculinity in crisis' men's movement of the 1980s and early 1990s when masculinity studies started in earnest, too much of which sought positively to reaffirm the firmly heterosexual stability and supremacy of hegemonic masculinity.

The fear of homosexuality drives many cultural representations of masculinity; positive masculine identification is so hysterically tied up with an obsession with *not being homosexual* that – rather like the ultimate conundrum offered by 'The Sexual Aberrations' being that perversity is the ultimate normality – homosexuality, through needing to be systematically repressed, becomes the *sine qua non* of masculinity. In so many narratives the man's fear is the fear of an externalised 'Other' that is actually, as it turns out, the embodiment of his own perceived internal inadequacies, most significantly homosexuality. The intended but frequently unsuccessful repression of homosexuality is a pervasive characteristic of many Hollywood films that, ostensibly at least, promote hegemonic masculinity. They display several strategies for coping with or containing the perceived threat of homosexuality, such as the convenient killing off of gay characters towards the end of the movie (for example, Plato in *Rebel Without a Cause*), the omission of any reference to a character's homosexuality (*Cat on a Hot Tin Roof*), the weaving in of opaque but, to the attuned spectator, detectable gay subtexts and innuendo (*Red River, Ben Hur*) or the creation of diversions and/or idiosyncratic euphemisms for homosexuality (Tom Lee's love for an older woman in *Tea and Sympathy* and his father's embarrassment that his son's ambition is to become a folk singer). There is as much disavowal in these strategies as there is rejection and, at times, the syphoning off of potential homoerotic desire comes perilously close to affirming and embracing it, as occurs in *Some Like It Hot* as Jerry (Jack Lemmon) appears rather too attached to his drag persona Daphne and Osgood, Daphne's fiancé, in turn intimates at the end not merely that he does not mind when Daphne reveals herself to be a man but that he has realised this – and been attracted to it – all along.

The convenient distillation of potential homoerotic desire occurs also around the construction of narrative scenarios, as in buddy movies, in which men bond with each other more readily than they bond with women (*Butch Cassidy and the Sundance Kid, Lethal Weapon, Die Hard*). In a film such as *Die Hard*, there is the added 'threat' of the sexually ambiguous Hans Gruber (Alan Rickman) who, in his narcissism, his love of clothes, his flowing hair and his wit, suggests an altogether more polymorphously perverse masculinity, to which I will return after having examined in greater detail the repressed presence of homosexuality as a destabilising force within the overtly masculinised setting of Michael Cimino's *The Deer Hunter* (1978).

Cimino's Vietnam movie is part war film, part melodrama, and, like other melodramas discussed in this book, its emotive and expressive visual style conveys much about 'being', or more accurately perhaps, 'becoming' a man. In this it borrows from earlier films such as *Rebel Without a Cause, There's Always*

Tomorrow and *Written on the Wind*, in which the troubled heroes' anxieties were acted out in part via the films' highly wrought visual style. In *The Deer Hunter*, what is being disavowed or hidden from view is specifically homosexuality, and this specific 'perversion' finds its expression, equally specifically, in the film's use of editing. *The Deer Hunter* is a film ostensibly 'about' the Vietnam War, featuring a trio of friends who go together to Vietnam. Unlike the almost acknowledged, on-the-surface-of-the-films repressions that drove the male characters of the noirs and melodramas previously discussed, the attraction between Michael (Robert de Niro) and Nick (Christopher Walken) in *The Deer Hunter* remains submerged.

Veiled homoeroticism in *The Deer Hunter* has been commented on before, for example by Christine Gledhill who remarks on Walken's feminisation and 'androgynous performance' that, in the bar scene in which Nick dances and sings along to 'I Can't Take My Eyes Off You' while playing pool on the eve of Steve's wedding, 'momentarily escapes the constricting male stereotypes of leader or lead' (Gledhill, 1995: 80). Walken trained as a dancer (he later shimmied his way effortlessly through Spike Jonze's video for Fat Boy Slim's 'Weapon of Choice' and danced memorably with his wife in Spielberg's *Catch Me if You Can*) and in this scene offers an elegant disruption of the film's overt heterosexuality. As Gledhill again observes, the 'undercurrents of unexpressed male desire between Mike and Nick' (1995: 80) first surface in this scene, as Nick explicitly becomes the focus of Mike's as well as the camera's gaze (1995: 80).

Robin Wood, in *Hollywood from Vietnam to Reagan*, discusses Walken's persona as mediating 'the cultural definitions of masculinity and femininity' (Wood, 2003: 260) and offers an earlier and fuller reading of *The Deer Hunter*'s homosexual subtext:

> The narrative of *The Deer Hunter* is posited on, largely motivated by, the love of two men for each other, but this, far from being a problem, is assumed to be unequivocally positive and beautiful; therefore, the film is compelled to permit the spectator to pretend that its sexual implications do not exist. At the same time, it leaves remarkably clear, if not always coherent and consistent, traces, so that those who wish to see may do so. (Wood, 2003: 260)

I concur entirely with the crux of Wood's interpretation, and it is the eroticised permeability of the heterosexual war film text by the homosexual melodrama that interests me here, as it invites the spectator not merely to read the film against the grain by unearthing a concealed subversive subtext but also to see that subversive subtext come out at a textual level. Wood identifies key points on a narrative level when this occurs; what I would like to do is to discuss in detail a couple of scenes in which the tense interrelationship with homosexuality is drawn out specifically through editing.

The first key example is the exchange of looks between Mike and Nick during the dancing at Steve and Angela's wedding. This shotgun wedding in Clairton, Pennsylvania (which dominates the first half of a long film) is not unequivocally joyous, coloured as it is by its 'ominous proximity to Vietnam' (Wood, 2003: 252), as Mike, Nick and Steve are leaving for the war the next day, an eventuality signalled by a banner wishing them well and huge black-and-white high school photos of the three of them hung on the walls. At this Russian Orthodox wedding, Nick and his girlfriend Linda (Meryl Streep) form part of a dancing group alongside Steve and others. Mike (having already been identified, for instance in the first deer-hunting sequence, as a loner) is drinking alone at the bar. His first look over towards the dance floor is ostensibly aimed at Linda, as in the reverse shot she is central. Shortly after, however, there is another shot of the dancing group, and this time Nick is clearly centre frame, after which, following a brief shot of an older couple eating, there is a cut back to Mike, walking away from the men at the bar and towards a doorway from which he can gain a clearer view of the revellers. On this occasion the reverse shot indicates that Mike's gaze definitely alights on Nick. When we return to Mike, he is still looking in the direction of the dancing but now in a different direction – as it turns out, towards the large photo of a younger Nick hanging on the wall. When Mike then reverts to looking at the dancers again, there is an exchange of looks between Nick and Mike, though it is Linda who becomes self-conscious as she mistakenly senses she is the one being looked at, an attraction tentatively confirmed a little later as Mike makes a drunken pass at her at the bar.

This rapid sequence of shot/reverse shots can really imply only one thing: that, as Wood suggests, *The Deer Hunter* revolves around an unutterable love story between two men, Mike and Nick, lent legitimacy through the implication of Linda as the third corner of their erotic triangle – the woman through whom the men indirectly express and eventually consummate their illicit love for each other. The most erotic and poignant look is Mike's towards the photo of Nick on the wall, an enigmatic and dreamy image of Walken in a home-knit sweater gazing out into the middle distance, a sort of matinee idol shot weighed down by innocence and nostalgia: the innocence of youth [prior to the 'experience' of an adulthood represented first by (Steve's) marriage and then by Vietnam] and the nostalgia for a pre-adult stage when loving your friend as Mike does Nick was not so problematic. It is important, at this point, that there is never a comparable exchange of glances between Mike and Nick to the one between Mike and Linda; homosexual possibilities are here buried deep within the sensuous dreaminess of unconsummated homosocialism.

This incomplete love affair between Mike and Nick, and the resultant

Figure 1.5 *The Deer Hunter* (Michael Cimino, 1978). Steve's wedding: Michael looking at the dancers.

Figure 1.6 *The Deer Hunter* (Michael Cimino, 1978). Steve's wedding: Linda, Nick and Steve dancing.

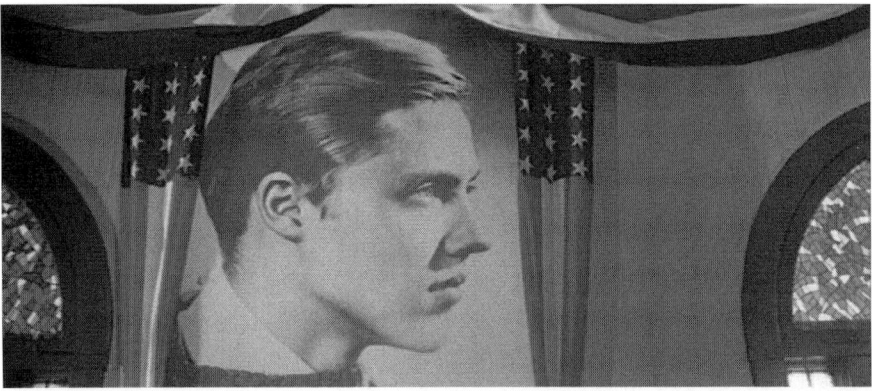

Figure 1.7 *The Deer Hunter* (Michael Cimino, 1978). Steve's wedding: Nick's photograph.

Figure 1.8 *The Deer Hunter* (Michael Cimino, 1978). Steve's wedding: Linda thinks Michael
is looking at her.

erotic triangle involving Linda, are revisited later, again around a photograph.
Suffering from shock after traumatic active duty and almost unable to recall
his parents' names, Nick is in hospital. Seated on a veranda wall, he opens his
wallet and with his thumb slides out from one of its compartments a passport
image of Linda, an action he repeats when, having been discharged, he tries
unsuccessfully to telephone her. Upon returning to Pennsylvania a decorated
war hero, Mike repeats precisely this action of looking at the same picture of
Linda. Arriving at his hotel room, in a pose that mimics Nick's on the hospital
veranda, Mike squats against the wall and takes out Nick's wallet, repeating
the gesture of slipping out Linda's photograph with his thumb, an action that
is then followed by a mid-shot of Mike and then a cut back to the photo, mirroring the sequence of shots in the hospital. Mike's solitary contemplation of
his best friend's snapshot of his fiancée is one of the film's many emotionally
and erotically charged uncanny moments and, to make sense of it, one needs,
in turn, to make sense of the intervening sequence in Saigon.

Upon being discharged from hospital, Nick ventures into the threatening
buzz of Saigon. Walking the streets in a traumatised fug, he mistakes another
man for Mike, a misrecognition that triggers a frantic and self-destructive
series of events which culminates in him going underground and becoming
a professional Russian roulette player. After an aborted visit to a prostitute
(whom he wants to call 'Linda'), Nick meets a sleazy, enigmatic Frenchman,
Julien, who, in a dim back alley, offers him a glass of champagne. A gunshot
from a game of Russian roulette rings out and the Frenchman tries to interest
Nick in going to see it, but Nick at this stage replies: 'You've got the wrong
guy'. He changes his mind, however, and finds himself, in an indirect echo
of the wedding dance sequence, the focus of two gazes: the Frenchman's and
Mike's who, with preposterous melodramatic coincidence, just happens to be

there. The erotic triangle is at this stage composed of three men. Nick, whose actions are no longer rational, grabs the roulette revolver, holds it to his head and fires, but the cartridge is blank. He runs out, with Mike in pursuit. Rather than be reunited with Mike who had been the object of his quest only moments earlier, however, Nick drives off with Julien. From Julien's car he glances back, seemingly in Mike's direction, with, on his gaunt face, a discernible look of annoyance. In a decisive move that sees him unshackle himself from his past, Nick then throws a wad of money up into the air, an action that both symbolises liberation and represents his severance from Mike who, finding himself on the other side of a curtain of fluttering notes that have inevitably attracted a swarm of opportunistic locals, is unable to pursue Nick further. This is a moment of transition. Nick turns his back on his past, on Mike's nostalgic attachment to unspoken, unconsummated love and seems to embrace a life of danger, self-destruction – and homosexuality, for what is Julien doing when he plies Nick with champagne and whisks him off in his fancy car if it's not wooing him or treating him like a gigolo? Despite its lengthy wedding sequence, heterosexuality in *The Deer Hunter* is precarious. When we see that Mike has Nick's wallet, we assume that he salvaged the wallet – the lover's token – as the Saigonese pounced on the money. In repeating Nick's gesture of taking out Linda's image, Mike revisits the moment when his lover was lost and, once back in Clairton, both he and Linda try to re-find Nick by starting a lugubrious sexual relationship with each other.

As Victor Perkins invaluably pointed out to me, the similarities between Mike's return to Saigon at the end of *The Deer Hunter* to bring Nick home (and earlier when he had pursued Julien's car) and the myth of Orpheus's descent into the underworld to save Euridice are unmistakeable, a parallel that helps explain not only the intensity of the final, fatal roulette contest which culminates in Nick's death but also why, after so much time of having been lucky, his luck turns at precisely the moment when his lover comes back for him. Exchanges of looks are again vital. Just as Orpheus cannot help himself and turns around to check that Euridice is following him (despite knowing that if he does so he will lose her forever), so Nick's foggy recognition of Mike (and the association of the Russian roulette's 'one shot' with his deer-hunting past) precipitates the luck running out: after so many indirect, refracted looks, Nick looks directly into Mike's eyes, repeats 'one shot' and blows his brains out. Their love is an 'affair' but one compelled to remain unconsummated and repressed.

The formative role played by the repression of homosexuality in the formation of masculinity is outlined particularly clearly by Eve Kosofsky Sedgwick as she puts forward her definition of 'homosocialism' in the opening chapter of *Between Men: English Literature and Male Homosocial Desire* (1985). Sedgwick posits that heterosexual masculinity can be satisfactorily constructed only if its opposite, homosexuality, is denied and actively repressed – as in *The Deer Hunter* with the juxtaposition of various heterosexual institutions (the wedding, the war, the steel factory, deer hunting) and unacknowledged homoerotic desire. Sedgwick argues that men who have successfully repressed homosexuality, will nevertheless need to find a means of interacting erotically with other men via what she terms 'male homosocial desire', which she defines thus:

> 'Male homosocial desire': the phrase in the title of this study is intended to mark both discriminations and paradoxes. 'Homosocial desire', to begin with, is a kind of oxymoron. 'Homosocial' is a word occasionally used in history and the social sciences, where it describes social bonds between persons of the same sex; it is a neologism, obviously formed by analogy with 'homosexual', and just as obviously meant to be distinguished from 'homosexual'. In fact, it applies to such activities as 'male bonding', which may, as in our society, be characterised by intense homophobia, fear and hatred of homosexuality. (Sedgwick, 1985: 1)

Having identified her terrain as that which centres on desire, Kosofsky Sedgwick develops her idea of the 'continuum' that links the polarities of both male and female sexual, erotic experience, when she argues that, while in men the opposition between the 'homosocial' and the 'homosexual' is dichotomous and discontinuous, for women there is a fluid continuum from one potential polarity to another, that 'however conflicting the feelings . . . women in our society who love women, women who teach, study, nurture, suckle, write about, march for, vote for, give jobs to, or otherwise promote the interests of other women, are pursuing congruent and closely related activities' (1985: 2–3).

There is a simplicity and relaxedness about the various sexual and non-sexual women's relations and how they inform and interact with each other that is lacking in the comparable relations between men but Kosofsky Sedgwick's argument about men is more convincing on this point of the continuum, and it becomes increasingly clear that it is men and the complexities of desire that surround and define them, that really intrigue her. The proposal that all female experience is part of a solid continuum is utopian and, as a theoretical idea, relatively unformed. Conversely, writing in the mid-1980s (Susan Jeffords's 'hard' bodied Reagan era), Kosofsky Sedgwick argues more convincingly that 'it has apparently been impossible to imagine a form of patriarchy that was not homophobic', that 'homophobia directed against males and against females is not arbitrary or gratuitous, but tightly knit into the texture of family, gender, age, class and race relations. Our society could not cease to be homophobic and have its economic and political structures remain unchanged' (1985: 3–4). To believe in itself, she suggests, heterosexual masculinity must repress and vilify homosexuality; desire between men is diverted on to intense 'bonding' activity whose direct link to sexual desire has been broken but which nevertheless still possesses a suppressed erotic component.

In the next chapter of *Between Men*, Sedgwick then outlines and applies an idea of René Girard's that an 'erotic triangle' exists between a woman and two men in which 'the bond that links the two rivals is as intense and potent as the bond that links either of the rivals to the beloved; that the bonds of "rivalry" and "love", differently as they are experienced, are equally powerful and in many senses equivalent' (Sedgwick, 1985: 21). A woman desired by two men thereby becomes the figure through whom two men – unable to express their desire for each other openly – can find an outlet for this desire for each other. This could have been written with the triangular relationship between Mike, Nick and Linda in mind. What is strikingly relevant about Kosofsky Sedgwick's notion of homosocialism to men's cinema is that it enforces both the repression of homosexuality by masculinity while still permitting homosexuality to retain a pivotal role in defining masculinity. There are few texts that illustrate this quite as clearly as *The Deer Hunter*, a film emblazoned with its disavowal, proclaiming itself to be a film *about* Vietnam, while really being about a set of personal relationships wrecked by Vietnam, most notably the shattered friendship between Mike and Nick.

In 'The Sexual Aberrations' Freud's term for homosexuality is 'inversion' and, in *Between Men* or a film such as *The Deer Hunter*, it does function symbolically as the inverse of its heterosexual counterpart. As intimated earlier, though, this is far from the only perversion to define as well as destabilise conventionalised forms of masculinity and, for the remainder of this chapter – and recalling the discussion in my introduction of Kosofsky Sedgwick's *Epistemology of the Closet*, I want to focus on some aspects of more abstract, polymorphous perversities and their relationship to masculinity.

In his introduction to *Flaming Classics: Queering the Canon*, Alexander Doty identifies some of the ways in which the terms 'queer' and 'queerness' have been used, starting with the idea that they are synonyms 'for either gay, lesbian, or bisexual' (Doty, 2000: 6) but swiftly extending his list to include 'any non-normative expression of gender, including those connected with straightness', 'non-straight things that are not clearly marked as gay, lesbian, bisexual, transsexual, or transgendered, but that seem to suggest or allude to one or more of these categories, often in a vague, confusing, or incoherent manner' and 'those aspects of spectatorship, cultural readership, production, and textual coding that seem to establish spaces not described by, or contained within, straight, gay, lesbian, bisexual, transsexual or transgendered understandings and categorizations of gender and sexuality' (7). Doty then cites Mark Simpson when he refers to 'the queer world' as 'not a world of homosexuality . . . but rather a world put out of order, out of sorts, out of joint; a world of queasy dislocation and general indeterminacy' (quoted in Doty, 2000: 8). It is to these fluid, indeterminate perversities that I will now turn, with specific reference to sequences from films by Alfred Hitchcock and David Cronenberg, two directors with an enduring fascination with polymorphous 'queerness'.

Hitchcock's films are always erotic, though frequently uncomfortably so, and unspecified perversity looms over most (even the straightest) of them like Norman Bates's stuffed birds do over his parlour. As Doty explains, the scene in which the examples of taxidermy appear – the light supper scene after Marion Crane has arrived at the Bates motel – 'is perhaps the sequence that causes most first-time viewers to consciously think there might be something "wrong" with Norman' (Doty, 2000: 159). The issue is, however, that the 'something "wrong"' with Norman Bates is never, even by the end of *Psycho*, precisely defined: one could label him 'transvestite', 'homosexual', 'bisexual', even 'asexual', but, as Doty has earlier suggested, Norman is more 'queer' than anything else, and enacts a particularly complex interrelationship between 'nonheteronormative gender and sexuality' (156–7). Norman's 'queerness' is consolidated and confirmed by Hitchcock's mannered and disorienting directorial style: his contravention of 'audience expectations in and the sedate conventions of Hollywood montage', for example, his 'notorious manipulations and infringements of narrative decency' (Langford, 2010: 91) or the aestheticised brutality of the shower scene (see Perkins, 1972: 108).

A film that signposts its queerness from the outset is *Strangers on a Train* (1951). In this example, 'queer', as Doty proposes, can be 'understood as a suggestive rather than a prescriptive concept' which destabilises 'existing categories' (6–7), as the film's edgy, hysterical stylisation dictates tone and intrudes upon any easy development of, or identification with, elements such as plot and character. The film's tone is set by the opening scene between Bruno and Guy, the eponymous 'strangers on a train'. After the establishing shots of the title sequence, there is an edit to a low, flat close-up of the bottom half of a cab door being opened by a flunky who lifts out a suitcase. The music changes to a jauntier brass score as an ensemble of ostentatious black-and-white brogues, grey wool socks and busily lined turn-ups (which we soon learn are Bruno's) follow the suitcase out of the car, turn towards the cab (presumably to pay) and swivel round again, progressing towards the station. Cut to a second cab door out of which emerges a far more conformist and less agitated dark-grey outfit of shoes and trousers (which we learn are Guy's). Shots of the two sets of lower legs are intercut as if about to converge, Bruno from right of frame, Guy from left. A reverse-angle shot shows a crowd, including the two so far anonymised men, going through the bottleneck of a ticket barrier as a train is called. The image then cuts to a shot from the perspective of the driver's compartment of railway tracks coming towards a set of points: one track heading straight, the other sidling off to the right. Predictably, the train takes the curved route, at which stage there is a dissolve to Bruno's obtrusive footwear walking through a carriage, stopping as he sits down and crosses his legs. Then Guy's feet enter, this time from left of frame and stop as he sits opposite Bruno.

The opening liminal frames of *Strangers on a Train* are destabilising. Perhaps the instabilities that ensue could be argued to be expressive evocations of Bruno's manipulative fantasies but such a reductive interpretation would undersell the sequence's unappropriated, yet insistent, queerness that persists beyond the first line of dialogue which is Guy's 'Excuse me' as he inadvertently nudges Bruno's foot when crossing his legs. Continuing on from the close-ups of the shoes, there are, just after Bruno has sauntered chummily over to Guy's side of the carriage and struck up a conversation, other close-ups, this time of their faces in the extreme foreground. At the moment at which Guy offers Bruno his lighter (which will later be such a crucial bit of evidence after the murder has taken place) Bruno is in distorting close-up to the extreme right of frame. Then, as for the reverse shot, Guy is in a parallel position to the extreme left. This intrusive framing underlines the topic of conversation which is Guy's unhappy marriage, his desire for a divorce and his current romance, the fragmentariness of the image (the different planes created by the shallow depth of field, for instance) augmenting the fractured excitement of his personal life. Then it is Bruno's turn. As the two men dine in his compartment, Bruno is lying to the right of the picture with his feet up on the seat looking over at Guy. In the extreme foreground this time are the soles of his shoes, silhouetted like ominous shadows against the light of the window, the dandy's demonic underside. None of this opening sequence is *about* homosexuality as such, though such a reading is readily supported; instead, it is indicative of the delight Hitchcock takes, as does Patricia Highsmith who wrote the novel of *Strangers on a Train,* in choreographing and staging a more slippery perversity. It would be easier to think of Bruno – a stammerer like Norman Bates or Brandon in *Rope* (see Rothman, 1982: 271) – as gay but this brand of 'motiveless malignity',[5] is suggestive of an altogether more disturbing and threatening masculine sexuality.

Though Hitchcock's suspenseful films are overtly preoccupied with plot, their plots are explained just as much through visual style and potentially become subservient to it. As Peter Wollen comments when discussing *Rope*, a film that employed a multitude of strategies to mask the edits:

> My own experience has been that watching the camera movements becomes more gripping over time than watching the action. Gradually *Rope* changes into another type of film altogether. Instead of being a polished thriller, it becomes an experimental film, more like Michael

Snow's camera-centred *Wavelength* (1966) or *Back and Forth* (1969)
than a Hollywood product. (Wollen, 1999: 79)

Even Hitchcock's more heteronormative films (it is dangerous to place any in
this category, but perhaps *Rear Window*, or *To Catch a Thief?*) contain perverse
irruptions; as a highly perceptive former student asked in his dissertation on
Rear Window: 'When is a pervert not a pervert? When he solves a murder'.
L. B. Jeffries is saved from perversity through solving a crime, as his obsessive voyeurism of his backyard becomes the tool with which he achieves this
(although what he is doing with a collection of old slides of the flowerbeds –
taken before he suspects Thorwald – is never quite explained away). Hovering
on the brink of perversity is where many of Hitchcock's heterosexual men find
themselves, a precarious symbolic position consolidated by Hitchcock's alternation between a flatter, more functional style and his penchant for visual excess:
the distended shadows in *Rebecca,* the scarlet haze that engulfs the screen in
Marnie, the use of the subjective inverse zoom in *Vertigo*. Normality and perversity are, in Hitchcock's films, natural bedfellows and, contrarily, the latter is
frequently deployed to recalibrate and stabilise the former instead of vice versa.

Most of David Cronenberg's films, especially his portrayals of men, are
shot through with polymorphous perversity which frequently makes them
disquieting viewing experiences. He is also uncommonly interested in captur-
ing and expressing masculinity at the moment of its disintegration and/or
self-destruction, rather as Hitchcock was intrigued by the moments when men
inadvertently revealed perversity. Cronenberg evokes this on and through
the body of the text, as well as on and through the body in the narrative. As
Shaviro observes, his films 'display the body in its crude, primordial material-
ity' (Shaviro, 1993: 127); the director 'is a literalist of the body. Everything in
his films is corporeal, grounded in the monstrous intersection of physiology
and technology . . . the body is the site of the most violent alterations and of
the most intense effects' (128). Cronenberg's obsession with the transforming,
permeable and mutating body is illustrated in early films such as *The Brood*,
Videodrome or *The Fly*, and finds its ultimate expression in *Dead Ringers*, his
disturbing masterpiece about twin gynaecologists (both played by Jeremy
Irons). In Cronenberg's body-fixated movies, the body is often revolting, in
both senses of that word: it is in revolt (the ravaged bodies in *The Brood*, for
example) and it becomes disgusting; but, as Cronenberg comments, 'the very
purpose' of his films is 'to show the unshowable, to speak the unspeakable'
(Rodley, 1992: 43), something he does in a disconcertingly non-figurative way.

This concretising of fantasy and fixation in Cronenberg's films is the basis
for their polymorphous perversity: as we watch, we do not necessarily know
why the films are so upsetting (of course, often this is very obvious) but,
nevertheless, they make us feel tense. Cronenberg's films are hysterical, in

that they collapse the differences and boundaries between fantasy and bodily symptom without, for the most part, delving into the psychological disorder hysteria – except in *A Dangerous Method* (2011) which is, ironically (considering its subject is the split between Freud and Jung which defined the course of psychoanalysis), one of the director's more straightforward and straightforwardly beautiful films. The dynamic relationship between an unsettling and clinical visual style and bizarre narratives in Cronenberg's films is similar to the literal treatment of fantasy found in those of Luis Buñuel. As Shaviro identifies, 'the radical passivity of visceral anguish' (Shaviro, 1993: 149) pervades many of Cronenberg's films.

The central fixation of the majority of Cronenberg's films becomes the moment of transition between two states, from reality to fantasy, from one body to another, from one identity to another [the obsessive preoccupation with reinvention and schism is omnipresent in most of his films up to *A Dangerous Mind*, including *A History of Violence* (2005) and *Eastern Promises* (2007)]. The ultimate transition is from the bodies on screen to the body of the text and with that, the move to making what is on the screen comprehensible on a reflexive, intuitive level, not merely on the level of narrative or character decipherability. Illustrative of Cronenberg's fascination with antimetaphorical, transgressive transition is Seth Brundle's transformation (following a teleportation experiment that goes wrong) from man to fly in *The Fly*. Predictably, the most interesting phase in Brundle's mutation are those moments of incomplete metamorphosis, when he displays the characteristics of both man and fly, his body the embodiment of hybrid chaos. As Cronenberg explains: 'There's true beauty in some things that others find repulsive' (Rodley, 1992: 66), and in Brundlefly's disfigured confusion there lurks an unconventional and uncomfortable eroticism. Many of Cronenberg's characters repulse and attract in equal measure, so it seems corny but accurate to say that his best films get under your skin; so often preoccupied with the body, they effect a bodily response from their audience, not just through character and narrative but also through the complexities of their *mise en scène*.

Cronenberg has recounted how one man, who attended one of the first public screenings of *Dead Ringers* in Toronto, asked him: 'Can you tell me why I feel so fucking sad having seen this film?' To which the director replied: 'It's a sad movie.' Upon then hearing that someone else had 'cried for three hours afterwards', his views on *Dead Ringers* became crystallised:

> That's what it is. That's what I wanted to get at. I can't articulate it. It's
> not really connected with gynaecology or twinness. It has to do with
> that element of being human. It has to do with this ineffable sadness
> that is an element of human existence. It's a distillation of that. (Rodley,
> 1992: 149)

Cronenberg's films provoke physical responses in their viewers, often of horror; I remember distinctly clamping my arms around my front for most of *Dead Ringers*, I presume in a subconscious, reflexive attempt to protect my womb. Part of the sadness at watching *Dead Ringers* is the result of its coldness, that for such an intense cinematic experience in terms of narrative, Cronenberg's glacial visual palate – the repeated use of blue sets, costumes and lighting, alongside the film's clinical editing and camera style – is contradictory, and perverse.

The cold, medicinal blue that pervades *Dead Ringers* seems to stand for the Mantle twins' veneer of normality and respectability and their successful suppression of perversity (their fetishisation of women's reproductive organs and their overidentification with each other). Conversely, red suggests passion and desire, fulsome emotions that upset the repressed equilibrium of their sterile world. The first, ostensibly inconsequential, appearance of red occurs in the scene between the twins when Beverly returns to their shared apartment after having had sex with the actress Claire Niveau (Geneviève Bujold). Up until Claire, the twins have shared women, but Bev is falling in love and does not want to share her. The imbalance about to be created by this desire for separation is signalled via the puncturing of the lifeless and slick blue-grey of their apartment by Elliot's uncharacteristically bright-red cardigan. Two scenes later, red returns in the guise that anyone who has seen *Dead Ringers* is most likely to remember, namely Beverly's voluminous blood-red operating robes and hoods that recall the garb of Catholic cardinals. While Bev and his assistants perform the operation, on the other side of a glass wall Elliot, in silky, unctuous tones, talks an audience through the procedure. That the on-screen space is literally split between the coldness of Elliot's blue space and the relative passion of his twin's red operating space resonates with reasons for why the red is problematic: the twins are now differentiated and desire has begun to threaten their symbiosis, a symbolic function that emerges when Beverly has a nightmare about separation from Elliot.

Beverly imagines himself lying beside his brother, linked to him (like Siamese twins) by a corrupted umbilical cord, a rough, gnarled strip of external tendon and tissue that extends from both their stomachs. Lying beside him is Claire who, smiling, bites into the band of stretched tendon, at which point Beverly falls out of bed and wakes up screaming. The arrival of Claire has precipitated the twins' separation and, as this develops, red becomes more prominent, suggestive, for example, of not just desire (as opposed to perverse repression) but also of feminine sexuality and the womb in particular – the internal organs that have consumed the Mantle twins' professional attentions. In an attempt to flatter Claire (who is the Mantles' patient because she has a trifurcated cervix and womb) Elliot suggests that there ought to be 'beauty contests for the insides of bodies'. From when red starts to take over, the probing and exposure of the internal body becomes more pronounced, from the set of grotesque, fantastical gynaecological instruments (first seen as drawings in the red title sequence) Beverly has asked a professional artist to make up for him in gold to the twins' deaths. The root of the twins' perversity is their endless transgression of boundaries: between professional acceptability and violation; between private and public lives; between each other. That the Mantles do not grasp this need infantilises them, renders it impossible for them to attain adult masculinity, and the insistent and clear preponderance of the clearly differentiated colours in the *mise en scène* emphasises this lack and the self-destructive perversity that ensues.

Ostracised and alienated (after Beverly tries to perform a real operation with his gold instruments and Elliot's substance abuse is discovered), the twins retreat into their sterile apartment, estranged now from both Claire and medical practice. Now the connotations of the colour red (womb-like, blood-like, feminine, dangerous, passionate) that had hitherto operated on the surface of the film, begin to function on both a superficial and a metaphorical level within the *mise en scène* of *Dead Ringer*'s final sequence, as Beverly (who, in a reversal of roles, is now the dominant twin) pumps Elliot with painkillers before, with his new surgical instruments, cutting open his twin's abdomen at the point where a womb might be. Here, in the final rupturing of the twins' safe blue environment, blood oozes from Elliot on to the surgical chair and drips on to the floor. A short while later, Beverly kills himself. A funereal tracking shot takes in the detritus and the rich obscenity of their chaotic apartment. Then, a series of dissolves mesh together images of the dead twins, one folded over the other like a disturbed Pietà, a characterisation emphasised by the draping of the twins' flawless, notably unbloody, naked bodies in surgical sheets, artfully pleated in a manner reminiscent of classical sculpted versions of the grieving Madonna cradling her dead son. This is *Dead Ringer*'s concluding corporeal moment as the bodies *on*-screen and the body *of* the screen collide in a narrativised reversal of Beverly's nightmare of separation. Red came to represent a side of masculinity (passion and individualism) with which the Mantle twins cannot cope. This final Pietà is one of cinema's most evocative images of masculinity, not just on the point of disintegration but *as* disintegration, fragmenting hegemonic masculinity's perpetually reinforced belief in its own wholeness and strength. The source of sadness in the spectator of *Dead Ringers* is perhaps the film's bleak suggestion that marginalised masculinity can hold itself together and function in society only when totally repressed and in emotional denial. The minute emotions (redness) start to intrude the respectable facade of professional masculinity crumbles away.

The films analysed here are not exceptions to the rule that Hollywood deals only in hegemonic masculinity. The 'deal' might be that Hollywood is overwhelmingly straight and its films made for a predominantly straight audience but mainstream films nevertheless hold a residual fascination and appeal, even for non-mainstream sexual groups. As Doty explains when attempting to explain the allure of the mainstream: 'One thing that might be worth thinking about is that taking lesbian, gay, bisexual, and queer pleasures in these "mainstream" works constantly reinforces the idea that queer is everywhere' (Doty, 2000: 14). Following on from this, another way of looking at the complex pleasures of mainstream films is to say that hegemonic masculinity, by virtue of being almost invariably shown not in opposition to but in *relation to* its 'perverse' others, is both dysfunctional and so rare as to be a perverse refinement rather than a normative presence. In the examples looked at in this chapter, perversity, however strenuously denied or disavowed, comes to haunt the text and emerges on the surface of the films through their visual style and within the *mise en scène*, so forcing a redefinition of Hollywood's portrayal of, and narrative attachment to, hegemonic masculinity. The particular story, therefore, that *mise en scène* tells in this context is that dominant, classical masculinity rarely exists on its own but is defined by its relationships to non-hegemonic masculine subject positions and models. The effect of this reassessment occurring on the levels of *mise en scène* and visual style is that 'masculinity' becomes a more mutable concept, accessible to a diverse range of spectatorships or points of view. By extension, on the levels of sense and emotion, the fluidity of these multiple and flexible patterns of identification and feeling is inevitably beginning to erode assumptions about gender fixity, sexuality and masculinity in particular.

NOTES

1. Cf. my article '*The Cobweb*', *CineAction*, No. 63, winter 2004.
2. Cf. chapter 2, Bruzzi *Bringing Up Daddy: Fatherhood and Masculinity in Post-war Hollywood*, pp. 40–50.
3. In 'Tales of Sound and Fury' Elsaesser misremembers the portrait as being of Jim's father, Frank Stark (p. 56).
4. Cf. Paul Schrader (1990) 'Notes on Film Noir', in Paul Schrader and Kevin Jackson (eds) *Schrader on Schrader and Other Writings*, London: Faber and Faber, pp. 80–93.
5. Samuel Taylor Coleridge's description of Iago in *Othello*.

CHAPTER TWO

Towards a masculine aesthetic

INTRODUCTION

The previous chapter examined examples of masculinity and men's stories being evoked via *mise en scène* and film style. Here I want to extend that argument by offering analyses of specific sequences in selected movies that are among the seminal antecedents to the more recent films discussed in Chapter 3, in that they do not merely describe masculinity but, using non-narrative means, are also starting to formulate the 'language' of men's cinema. *Once Upon a Time in the West* (Sergio Leone, 1968), *The Wild Bunch* (Sam Peckinpah, 1969) and *Dirty Harry* (Don Siegel, 1971) are three key moments in the evolution of a mainstream cinema masculine aesthetic but their historical placement is also important and not entirely coincidental in that they were also made at a time of radical change both to gender relations and within Hollywood. To return to some of the issues raised in the introduction to this book, these three films deploy various stylistic features (Leone's circular tracking shot, for instance, or Peckinpah's slow motion) which both elicit complex responses from their audiences, that go beyond straightforward 'identification', and have since also been endlessly recycled, repeated and modified. Because of the ways in which they deploy style and spectacle expressively, all three films, the narrative centrality of men notwithstanding, affect their audiences and offer up diffuse, fluid and affective forms of identification not inextricably bound to gender or identity. Judith Butler writes in *Undoing Gender*:

> I want to suggest that the debates concerning the theoretical priority
> of sexual difference to gender, of gender to sexuality, of sexuality
> to gender, are all crosscut by another kind of problem, a problem
> that sexual differences poses, namely, the permanent difficulty of

determining where the biological, the psychic, the discursive, the social begin and end (Butler, J., 2004: 185).

In their discursive prioritisation of style, *mise en scène* and spectacle, *Once Upon a Time in the West*, *The Wild Bunch* and *Dirty Harry* all, in remarkably diverse ways, reflect upon the difficulties of difference and identity listed here. While watching *The Wild Bunch*, for example, the extreme stylisation of the final Agua Verde sequence cuts it loose from its fixed narrative moorings, so to interpret those minutes simply with reference to the male characters and violence is to underestimate their more visceral effectiveness.

During the course of an undergraduate module on melodrama I was teaching some fifteen years ago, I asked a seminar group of predominantly men what made them cry. The term before, they had appeared singularly resistant to the charms and effects of the melodramas (even the male-centred ones) of Max Ophuls, Vincente Minnelli and Douglas Sirk, and so I wanted to discover what, if anything, might provoke them to tears. Probably I was envisaging an ironic answer along the lines of the scene in *Sleepless in Seattle* in which Tom Hanks and a friend pretend to be moved to tears as they recount the ending of *The Dirty Dozen*. Instead, the answer I got was unexpected and brilliant as one of the group's many male cinephiles responded, with little hesitation, 'the crane shot in *Once Upon a Time in the West* as Claudia Cardinale arrives at the station'. I am eternally grateful for this inspirational answer as it proved the starting point for both my teaching of 'men's cinema' and, now, for trying to define mainstream cinema's masculine aesthetic. Firstly, by responding emotionally to a crane shot and not a character (further complicated by the character also being female), the student raised substantial issues about identification and why conventionally gendered assumptions about how films 'move' spectators have been superseded. Secondly, he was responding to one of the foundational tropes of 'men's cinema', as swooping camera movements in conjunction with male action recur frequently in evocations of masculinity.

Once Upon a Time in the West, *The Wild Bunch* and *Dirty Harry* are not so much the urtexts, the Adam and Eves of 'men's cinema' as they are the films that have most clearly crystallised much of my thinking about what constitutes men's cinema by having visibly influenced the subsequent development of a masculine aesthetic. Men's cinema is by no means entirely homogeneous and *Once Upon*, *Wild Bunch* and *Dirty Harry* catalyse quite different strands within it: whereas *Once Upon* consists of only some twenty scenes, the first three of which, as Christopher Frayling has noted, take over a quarter of the film's screen time (Frayling, 2006: 212), the average shot length in the final sequence of *The Wild Bunch* is around half a second. While sharing certain generic characteristics with the other films, *Dirty Harry* heralded a much rougher, scrappily energetic visual style, at the heart of which lies Bruce

Surtees's realist hand-held images, whip pans, crash zooms and lurching crane shots. The genealogy of men's cinema is complex, as elements from all three might well find their way into the same later films: Scorpio's hijacking of a school bus and Harry's pursuit of him clearly find their way into Jan de Bont's *Speed* but, arguably, when it comes to the action sequences, so does Peckinpah's frenetic montage style.

The three films also possess similarities alongside their shared preoccupation with performing masculinity. They share generic similarities, for instance, as even *Dirty Harry* is, as Robert B. Ray remarks, one of Hollywood's 'urban westerns, briefs for the continued applicability of the reluctant hero story to contemporary life' (Ray, 1985: 307): Harry Callahan's final act of throwing away his cop's badge recalls *High Noon* – just as *Once Upon a Time in the West* had pastiched the opening to Zinnemann's classic western – and is in turn recalled in Kathryn Bigelow's *Point Break* as Keanu Reeves throws his FBI badge into the Australian ocean. And all three are also, in diverse ways, notably anti-interiority or introspection, as words or the dramatisation of thought processes are kept to a minimum, an absence more than compensated for by their emotive, psychologically expressive visual styles. As a trio, they offer a potent snapshot of the evolution of masculinity in cinema at a significant and transitional moment in its history, when western masculinity was on the verge of breakdown and undergoing rapid change. Most of all, the films share an eloquent, evocative ambivalence towards masculinity which finds its ultimate expression in the evolution of aesthetic styles that transmit a variety of emotional responses from nostalgia and admiration to despair and dismissiveness.

ONCE UPON A TIME IN THE WEST

Sergio Leone's stylistically innovative *Once Upon a Time in the West*, a film Frayling has dubbed 'the first truly postmodernist movie' (Frayling, 2000: 266), remains one of the most iconic texts in the history of masculinity and film. Leone plays around with convention, genre and aesthetics and, in *Once Upon a Time in the West*, created one of the most eloquent cinematic illustrations of the performative basis of masculinity. To discuss first the crane shot as Cardinale arrives at Flagstone, referred to above. There are many factors that make my student's response entirely explicable. For one, Tonino Delli Colli's soaring crane shot possesses a satisfying wholeness, full of arching grace and balletic athleticism. Then there is Ennio Morricone's lush, romantic, majestic score which complements and enhances the moment's visual beauty. Frayling recounts how Leone, during filming, relied for atmosphere on playing tapes of the music and how 'Everyone acted with the music, followed its rhythm, and suffered with its "aggravating" qualities which grind the nerves' (Frayling,

Figure 2.1 *Once Upon a Time in the West* (Sergio Leone, 1968). Jill McBain leaves the station: the start of the crane shot.

Figure 2.2 *Once Upon a Time in the West* (Sergio Leone, 1968). Half way through the crane shot.

Figure 2.3 *Once Upon a Time in the West* (Sergio Leone, 1968). The end of the crane shot: Jill McBain rides off.

2000: 280). Morricone then remembers specifically how 'Sergio regulated the speed of the crane which follows Claudia Cardinale when she comes out of the station, in time with the musical crescendo' (quoted in Frayling, 2000: 280–1). The completeness of this shot, not just its surety, is what makes it arresting but its epic sweep is not necessarily allied to femininity and appears to function more as an abstract rendition of masculinity – a masculinity that engulfs, overwhelms Cardinale (as Jill McBain) – as well as more abstractly connoting Leone's own hypermasculinist 'authorial presence interposed between the audience and action' (Kitses, 2004: 255). As Kitses also observes:

> Much has been made of the amoral world Leone depicts, but it is the director's style that gives his work its radical edge. Comic-book-like, exhibitionist and narcissistic, Leone's films celebrate, critique and ultimately transform the Western. The style keeps the audience off balance, making the familiar genre strange. (Kitses, 2004: 253)

An earlier crane shot of Cardinale's train pulling into Flagstone station comes to rest and then a series of cuts takes one to her dismounting from her carriage, expectant and still ignorant of the fact that her family has just been killed. Put out by there being no one at the station to greet her, she goes in search of a ride, and the second crane shot begins through the window of the station building, before rising over the roof, in synchronisation with the lushest, most fulsomely, classically orchestral of Morricone's musical leitmotifs and the one repeatedly played in support of Cardinale. The music rises (Edda Dell'Orso's wordless soprano and string accompaniment) and hits its peak just as the strong, assertive crane shot reaches full height; Cardinale is, by now, insignificant and small, almost lost amid the dust and the crowds. The unstoppable fluidity of this shot takes us aback and also, importantly, precludes the possibility of fighting against it. It draws us in. So what was it about this image that had made my student cry? Simply its awesome beauty? There are factors, I think, that make tears an unlikely rather than a predictable response, such as the realisation that the crane shot is not rooted in conventional character identification. This is our first encounter with Cardinale so, despite having just witnessed the massacre of her family, which necessarily prompts some indirect sympathy for her, specific identification has not been built up. The sequence thus plays with certain key disparities in audience and character knowledge and makes use of the strength and visual elegance of the crane movement moving in time to the music to assert an alternative form of knowledge and power, one that enables us to engage with *Once Upon a Time in the West* on the level of sensibility.

This image is contradictory in that it both sweeps us up with it and conversely compels us – by brazenly flaunting its artistry – to acknowledge its constructedness and the existence of the off-screen space around it which impinges so forcefully on to this paradoxically sensuous Brechtian moment. Critics (notably Frayling and Kitses) have noted Leone's Brechtian alienation strategies: that his films recycle, parody and intellectualise, and are 'too self-conscious and too obviously "arranged" for some critics' (Kitses, 2004: 212). Both aspects of Leone's style, though – the ability to overwhelm emotionally and the tendency towards alienating formalism – need to be taken together, as the 'unrestrained quality of Leone's *display* in *Once Upon a Time in the West*, which sets the film apart as the finest synthesis of his attempts to transcribe the Hollywood Western' (213). The film's 'unrestrained quality' is also an integral part of its machismo and its insistent evocation of masculinity. As the film progresses, Leone establishes the connection (frequently made in westerns, in which swooping panoramic shots taking in the expansive landscape are relatively commonplace) between strong visual elegance and masculinity in a number of key scenes. One reason for this might well be (here and in his earlier westerns, as well, but to a lesser degree) that expressiveness has to come from somewhere and the men in *Once Upon a Time in the West* express very little verbally. I tend to think that the shedding of tears at movies comes from an awareness of lack as well as from an engagement with emotions, gestures or moods that are visible and present. The impact of grand visual gestures, such as Leone's in *Once Upon a Time in the West*, function hysterically in that they have the effect of accentuating what is being masked or absent (perhaps ordinary, functioning masculinity) as well as what is there (omniscience and sensibility) via the very expressiveness that remains incompatible with the distance between style and character the scene generates.

There is, in the crane shot, a particular collusion and a particular beauty which centre on, or are evocative of, the film's emotional attachment to masculinity, indicated by its gestural similarities to other uses within the film of the smooth, moving camera, not just other crane shots but also the circular tracks and pans. Alongside the arrival at Flagstone, there are two sections of *Once Upon a Time in the West* that explain and contextualise this affinity: the film's opening and the final shoot-out between Frank (Henry Fonda) and Harmonica (Charles Bronson). The infamous opening twelve minutes or so of *Once Upon a Time in the West* are mesmerisingly (maybe irritatingly) slow and in them nothing much either happens or is said,[1] testifying to the fact that speed and action are not by any stretch the only means by which cinema conjures up masculinity. As three of Frank's henchmen arrive at the station, menace the station master and then wait for a train that brings Harmonica into town, there is no music and very little sound, beyond the squeak of a hinge and the buzz of a fly. The men do not respond logically to the small things that do happen in these languid minutes of screen time: the one being irritated by the fly does not simply bat him away with his hat, just as the one being plagued by water dripping through the ceiling does not move away but rather shields his head by putting on his hat, later drinking the water that collects in its brim. The excessively composed *mise en scène* augments the film's extreme self-consciousness: the slow pans, for example, or the close-ups of faces positioned to the side of the widescreen frame and juxtaposed – through Leone's obsessive use of deep focus – against the vast expanse of the big country behind them. Finally, there is the sound of a train approaching the station and Harmonica alights. The studied quiet surety of the past few minutes is suddenly scarred by the swift and noisy exchange of bullets that erupts between the four men and which Harmonica wins, shooting dead all three of his rivals. The convulsive puncturing of the prolonged silence is, of course, in part parodic.

This opening comprises many of *Once Upon a Time in the West*'s notable visual tropes: the jolting alternation of pace, the use of extreme close-up in the foreground of a deep-focus shot and the leisurely, fluid movement of the camera. It is only later, though, after Frank's arrival in the subsequent scene that these can start to be understood as part of the film's residual fascination, not just with stylisation but also with the reinforcement of masculinity through style and tone, as well as through narrative and character. After the music-less slaughter of the red-headed McBain family, Morricone's music intrudes at the moment when we first see Frank. At first, and led by a quintessentially late 1960s posturing electric guitar, the music is rather abrasively strutting; but, once the harmonica has been introduced, it segues smoothly into a paradoxically warm orchestral score (considering the extreme violence) but one perfectly in step with the aggressive, languorous strides of Frank and his men as they finally emerge from the scrubby bushes, their dustcoats undulating in the breeze. Filmed from a low angle, Frank and his men walk in the direction of the camera. The image then cuts to a long shot from behind them, the men walking in line, converging on the only family member left, the McBain son, at which point a tight 90-degree pan circles Frank and comes to rest, in close-up, on Fonda's face. The perfect synchronicity between score and camera move at this juncture is not just ironic: it is cruel, as if press-ganging us into wanting to be one of Frank's men. As the music peters out and a bell tolls, Frank pulls out his revolver (pointing in close-up at the screen) and fires, the sound of the shot becoming merged with the sound of the whistle from the train bearing Cardinale approaching Flagstone.

The image of a group of men walking – invariably slowly or in slow motion, frequently not quite in focus and almost always in widescreen – towards a low-angle lens has become, since *Once Upon a Time in the West*, an iconic trope of men's cinema. Leone's defining rendition of this (alongside Peckinpah's in *The Wild Bunch*) conveys so much: power, menace, group identity and camaraderie; its pace, coupled with the enveloping swoop of the pan that circles Fonda and comes to rest on his face, draws us into a complex form of identification, not with the men so much as with the feelings provoked by the synchronisation of the men's actions with the camera's angle and movement. In this, similarities with my student's instinctual response to the crane shot in the following sequence start to emerge. What characterises this and several other examples of men walking (such as the title sequence of *Reservoir Dogs*, discussed later) is the synchrony between action and visual evocations of masculinity through the gesture of a group of men walking purposefully, menacingly through space. (Synchronicity is likewise a persistent feature of men's cinema.) What adds to the richness of this narrative moment in *Once Upon a Time in the West* is that we, the spectators, find ourselves torn: we are irresistibly drawn to the momentum and power of Frank and his men invading the domestic scene (and as such find ourselves with the 'bad men' as our natural point of identification) while simultaneously sharing the McBain family's fear of Frank and thus forming an attachment with them. The feelings engendered in us by the virile, menacing gesture of Frank and his henchmen walking are, though, different from the mixed emotional responses to the men walking to their deaths at the end of Peckinpah's *The Wild Bunch* (discussed below) though I would posit that the pessimism embodied by the latter, as in *Reservoir Dogs*, is so richly affecting precisely because it recalls the majestic potency of the men-walking motif in its more triumphant form.

The climax of *Once Upon a Time in the West* is a duel between Frank and Harmonica, a long (8-minute) sequence that follows the by now familiar formal pattern of a slow build up to a brief, startling exchange of gunshots. The denouement begins as Fonda and Bronson enter what is almost literally an arena – the characteristic bullring backdrop Leone uses for various of his final shoot-outs. Fonda and Bronson walk slowly around the imaginary circle, eyeballing each other from opposite sides of it to the accompaniment of the same electric guitar and harmonica refrain that heralded the entrance of Frank before he and his men killed the McBains. Fonda's walk is distinctive; his legs are long and he takes few strides, like a racehorse ambling elegantly around the paddock. The phlegmatic but purposeful pace of *Once Upon a Time in the West* mirrors or perhaps was – in the same way that it was by Morricone's music – inspired by the way Fonda moves. Walk and music come together in Leone's repeated use of an inverse waltz rhythm for his shoot-outs, which begin lethargically, only to then conclude with unceremonious abruptness when the gunfire starts. The two distinct aspects of the film's pivotal sequences (the slow and the quick) also echo our ambivalent reactions to Fonda as Frank: here a brute but elsewhere the liberal spokesman of Lumet's *Twelve Angry Men*. The elegant Fonda finds himself compatible with the elegant, enervating side of Leone's visual style, while the masked violent side finds its expression in the brutal violence with which Leone concludes so many of Frank's scenes.

To return to the sequence of shots in the shoot-out: having observed the two men sizing each other up, the camera begins slowly to crane upwards and away from them. Todd Berliner remarked of the moment when the camera in *Raging Bull* cranes away from LaMotta as he walks towards the ring for his successful title fight that this retreat from the protagonist makes us lose the 'sense of privilege' we had previously enjoyed (Berliner, 2005: 51). It is not inevitably the case, though, that literal distance creates symbolic distance. Instead, it frequently feels that, particularly once a strong camera move (such as an upwards crane shot) has been established, spectator affinity could lie with the movement and the power that resides with the gliding, omniscient camera rather than with the figure on the screen. There is, in the climactic shoot-out in *Once Upon a Time in the West*, a residual rapport between male characters and camera movement, as the smooth pans encircle and enclose the action, creating another ring around and beyond the diegetic one. It is the circling camera move that cements this idea of compatibility between masculinity and visual expressivity while, at the same time, via its Brechtian intrusiveness, signalling that there are alternative points of identification. When the crane move stops, the high-angle shot is replaced by a different high long shot of the two men, and the imposition of some distance between us and the duelling men is made clear, just as it was at the end of William Wyler's *The Big Country*, as the tough men about to slug it out become as inconsequential as a couple of insects scrubbing about in the grubby sand.

There is subsequently a cut to a closer, ground-level shot from behind Fonda's booted legs. He discards his jacket, which falls in the foreground between him and the camera, perfectly in time with soundtrack's transition from the electric theme to the more classically orchestral one. As Frank starts to walk again and the camera reverts to a high angle, there is another cruel juxtaposition between the beautiful crescendo and a close-up of Frank's steely face. As this musical phrase reaches its conclusion, however, there is an edit to a close-up of Harmonica who, since Frank discarded his coat, has been cemented to the spot and, belatedly, we realise that we have been duped: power, after all, resides with Harmonica, not with Frank; power resides with the one who does not slavishly mimic the restless camera but has the authority to stand up to it. There then follows an exchange of close-ups, and Fonda looks apprehensive. Bronson, in contrast, looks serene. There are echoes of both formal dancing and chess here: Harmonica leads while Frank follows and he now executes his first decisive and aggressive move, which is to walk towards his adversary, thus breaking the duel's hitherto fluid yet cagey circularity. There is then another exchange of close-ups (yet another foreword to the shoot-out still to come) and a final zoom into Bronson's face, at which point a flashback starts.

This is an exaggeratedly significant interruption and one that explains what past events Harmonica seeks to avenge. The flashback begins with a shot we have seen twice before of a younger Frank walking towards us. The image started off blurred and indistinct and has gradually become clearer until our suspicion that Harmonica is recalling a previous meeting with Frank is confirmed as Fonda walks (in sharp focus now) towards the lens, takes a harmonica from his pocket and offers it in the direction of the camera. It is the flashback that is interrupted now as we revert to a close-up of Bronson's eyes and an extreme zoom into them, before cutting back to Fonda and finally returning to a reverse shot of Harmonica but this time as a boy in the flashback, having the harmonica rammed into his mouth. There then follows another of the film's grandiose crane shots, in tandem with the rising harmonica refrain, as the camera pulls up from Harmonica to reveal him standing under his brother with a noose round his neck, hanging from a brick arch, stranded in an expanse of dust. The younger Frank smiles and they swap yet another sequence of close-ups, concluding with the boy falling in slow motion to the ground, in time with another chiming bell.

For one last time, Leone lets speed and noise break the spell of a slow build-up as the young Harmonica hitting the sandy ground is followed by violent edit to the short, sharp shoot-out with Frank, which sends Frank reeling. The finale is Frank, a harmonica now shoved in *his* mouth, slumping in extreme and disquieting close-up to the ground. The predictability and harmony of this sequence, complemented by the fluidities of editing, camera movements and music, not just actors and action, are richly satisfying. After two-and-a-half hours, Leone has tutored us in how to read *Once Upon a Time in the West* and has guided our emotional, psychological and also physiological responses to his ornate visual and aural compositions. In many ways this is a cold film, signalled by our uncomfortable empathy with Frank, and one that siphons off emotion on to visual style and music – anything except character.

THE WILD BUNCH

It would be hard to overstate the influence of *The Wild Bunch*, Peckinpah's awesome homage to masculinity, violence and death. A man rolling in slow motion over the edge of something after being shot or in mid-pursuit (in *The Wild Bunch* this is usually a wall) is now such a staple of the action chase sequence that it made it into my local pantomime this year. Though we may now be immune to some of the effects of on-screen violence (especially the hyperbolic, stylised violence of *The Wild Bunch*), if we know nothing else about Peckinpah's films we at least know that they are violent and fixated on masculinity. The twinning of violence and masculinity is, for many critics, especially troublesome, as Joan Mellen, writing it should be remembered, in 1977 illustrates:

The male in the films of Sam Peckinpah, of which *The Wild Bunch* is a typically virulent example, is no better than the decaying corrupt world

> that is squeezing him out. Equating masculinity with sheer barbarism
> Peckinpah justifies his cynicism by mythologizing the obsolescence
> of manliness in civilized America. For Peckinpah a man is somehow
> violent because he possesses male genitals . . . the Peckinpah hero fights
> because it is in his genes. (Mellen, 1977: 270)

Mellen's extreme critique of a film she dismisses for being extreme is of its time but also illustrative of a certain tendency in Peckinpah criticism, namely to reject his movies as assaults on audience sensibilities and for espousing antiquated views on gender. Writing from a 1970s liberal feminist perspective (Peckinpah is out of tune with 'civilized America'), Mellen now seems equally out of step, for more recent discussions of Peckinpah's violence are far more likely to frame his fascination with it as audacious or his fetishisation of the moment of death and the slow-motion shot of a bullet entering the body as an innovation. For that alone, he would be in any hypothetical pantheon of the most influential men's cinema directors, as proved by the graphic death of Ray Liotta in Andrew Dominik's *Killing Them Softly* (2012) or the men who have just been shot in Tarantino's *Django Unchained* (2012) vomiting blood. Here I will look in detail at two of the film's most violent, enduringly significant and aesthetically complex sequences: the opening scene and the fatal concluding shoot-out in Agua Verde.

In early twentieth-century Texas, Pike Bishop (William Holden) and his 'wild bunch' of ageing outlaws ride into the fictional Texan town of San Rafael disguised as soldiers for what they think will be one last robbery but the men's plan is thwarted by Pike's former partner Deke Thornton (Robert Ryan) and his motley crew who are lying in wait for them. In ways not dissimilar to those of Sergio Leone in *Once Upon a Time in the West*, Peckinpah superimposes an undulating structure on to *The Wild Bunch*, alternating anticipatory lulls with furious storms of action and gunfire. The pre-storm calm of Pike and his men riding nonchalantly into town (often, in the western, a motif connoting surety), barely suppresses the scene's coiled tension, its only overt outlet, at this stage, being Jerry Fielding's soundtrack, which meshes tentative rather than triumphant drum rolls with an eerie wind and brass accompaniment. Marsha Kinder notes how, as we realise that just around the corner is a heady shoot-out, we become 'impatient' with the periodic interruptions of the title sequence by freeze-frames that 'temporarily suspend the action' (Kinder, 2001: 65). She adds that 'the pauses also lead us to become aware of our own complicity as spectators, for they make us realize how eager we are for the violent spectacle to be unleashed' (65). Though again using them quite distinctly from Leone, Peckinpah's dynamic distanciation techniques, such as his film's self-conscious constructness, serve both to lure us in as spectators and deny us full emotional involvement.

As a band of cheery, doomed members of the South Texas Temperance Union march by singing 'Shall we Gather by the River' (in a reflexive homage to John Ford who uses the hymn in several westerns, including *The Searchers* and *My Darling Clementine*), a heartbeat joins the soundtrack and the opening gunfight explodes into action. Intricately composed as well as brutal, this violent shoot-out contains most of Peckinpah's stylistic signatures: frantic editing; frenetic action interspersed with slow motion; bullets travelling through men's bodies causing blood to fountain out of them; cutting mid-action; and men in their death throes convulsing and pirouetting mid-air. The 'surrealist edge' (217) Kitses notes in Peckinpah makes this at once an assaulting, but also a hypnotic, sequence: a 'perverse ballet' (Langford, 2010: 142) in which the magnified aestheticisation of death is shaped into a magnificent dance. Perhaps the most theatrical moment of the sequence occurs as one of the outlaws gallops out of town in an attempt to avoid the unfurling bloodbath. Shot from behind, he falls into the glass window of a dress shop. The combined surreal effect of the glass shattering as rider and horse plunge in slow motion into the shop front, observed by a row of mute, headless dressmaker's dummies is audacious and, as previously in the sequence, the potentially cathartic – or, at the very least, concluding – impact with the ground is temporarily denied as Peckinpah again cuts away from the action mid-movement to things happening elsewhere, as he had a minute or so earlier when the death fall through the air of one of Deke's men is broken up into four segments. As with the somersaulting man, the smashing of the shop window is in slow motion, while the fragments of action with which it is intercut happen at full speed. From end to end the fall into the dressmaker's window spans eight seconds and is divided into five parts, culminating in three magnificent shots from inside the shop as man and horse plunge through the glass sending bonnets flying and causing the three headless mannequins to tumble like skittles. However spectacular, though, there is no dwelling on this colourful finale either, as Peckinpah, unlike Leone who rather milks his beautiful moments, cuts swiftly just after the dummies have keeled over to Clarence 'Crazy' Lee – the 'wild bunch' member left in charge of keeping members of the railroad office hostage – licking the ear of a middle-aged woman among them who had had the temerity, seconds earlier, to call him 'trash'. Actually, it is Clarence's walk over to the woman that tops and tails the shop-front sequence but, in the intervening few seconds, it is easy to overlook this.

Though most readily recalled for his fetishisation of death, or more precisely for his fascination with the moment of impact of bullet on body and the bloody emissions that ensue, it is arguably Peckinpah's editing of action and specifically his coupling of full speed with slow motion that have proved most influential (though Quentin Tarantino pays homage to the lot). Accounts of how many individual shots or edits Peckinpah includes in *The Wild Bunch* vary: the Internet Movie Database (IMDb) puts the number of edits at 'about 2,721', excluding the start and end credits;[2] the film's editor, Lou Lombardo, maintains that the original release print contains some 3,643 cuts;[3] while Langford puts the total number of shots in the film at 3,642, 'at a time when the industry average was around 700' (Langford, 2010: 142). Suffice it to say that there is a lot of them and that the average shot length at the height of its action sequences is about 0.5 second. Breaking up and slowing down a sequence, such as the failed robbery at the start of *The Wild Bunch*, is a curiously violating act of fetishism, not entirely dissimilar to a frame-by-frame analysis of Abraham Zapruder's film of the assassination of President John Kennedy, which might temporarily give you the illusion of getting closer to the truth of how JFK died and who killed him but which also unequivocally distorts and distances you from the brutality of the act itself. It is only when played at full speed that the violence – or, indeed, the narrative – of Zapruder's home movie, like the fictional violence of Peckinpah's battles, truly comes out.

The pace of Peckinpah's editing, the extreme brevity of the shots and the way in which he splices together fragments of unrelated action are all features that have heavily influenced subsequent men's cinema, especially how action sequences are cut. Peckinpah, as Prince observes, integrates diverse images into 'a synthesized collage of activity' (Prince, 1998: 66), constructing action sequences that follow an onion-like form: an action within an action within an action. This multi-tiered editing is, as Langford contends, one of 'the most dramatic innovations in montage cinema since Eisenstein' (2010: 142). Peckinpah's style has been adopted and adapted many times since, and has become the virtually official way of cutting men's cinema action, from the *Die Hard, Mission Impossible* and *Bourne Identity* franchises to *Gladiator* and numerous other individual films. Peckinpah dismantles and unpicks linear action into individual narrative threads – for example, Prince comments that, though in Peckinpah's papers the opening gun battle and the finale at Agua Verde are presented as 'linear and chronological list(s) of images', the director expressly instructed Lombardo to take 'every piece of action and intercut it with another' (66). The feeling of exhilaration engendered by watching these sequences stems from their pace, their visceral energy, but not necessarily from their comprehensibility at the level of detail; their emotional, as opposed to 'intellectual', impact is just as much a result of the fact that it becomes impossible, when viewing them at full speed, to take in what each individual image is about, a coupling of excitement and confusion that remains particularly influential. Kinder likens Peckinpah's editing of action in this opening sequence of *The Wild Bunch* to sex, arguing that the 'excessive violence' in *The Wild Bunch* 'is orgasmic rather than cathartic, erotic rather than revelatory, for Peckinpah positions the spectator to desire rather than fear its eruption' (Kinder, 2001:

66). For Kinder, this stylised violence is not frightening except in how it forces us to 'face our own visceral response' to it but is, instead, a 'guilty pleasure' that 'allows us no emotional distance' (66–7). The overwhelming, adrenaline-fuelled, orgasmic experience is again something that later action directors have sought to emulate.

Unlike some of his emulators, though, there is also a moral complexity that underpins Peckinpah's visualisation of violence and gives it added resonance. *The Wild Bunch*, for instance, was filmed in 1968, a turbulent, assassination-dominated presidential campaign year when the Vietnam War was at its height. Peckinpah commented in 1969 that violence is 'ugly, brutalizing and bloody fucking awful. It's not fun and games and cowboys and Indians.' Extrapolating from such statements, Prince surmises that there is a 'a clear link between him (Peckinpah), his films and the shocked, grieving America of 1968' (Prince, 1998: 32), just as Kitses breathlessly asserts '*The Wild Bunch* is America' (Kitses, 2004: 223). Peckinpah was allegedly disappointed that audiences came to 'dig' the violence of *The Wild Bunch* but, though not all later films that mimic Peckinpah's editing style are necessarily politicised to the same extent, the unsettling moral ambivalence of his shoot-outs is something else that has endured into the films of later directors such as Scorsese or Tarantino.

The final shoot-out in Agua Verde against General Mapache is both the most complex and the most significant of Peckinpah's violent action sequences. Here, the lull before the storm is supplied by the Wild Bunch's purposeful, fateful last walk from the brothel where they have been carousing. The male posse either riding abreast into town (as Pike et al. did at the start of *The Wild Bunch*) or walking slowly abreast has become, as identified in relation to *Once Upon a Time in the West*, one of the enduringly iconic motifs of men's cinema. However much of a cliché it has become through its use in later films, such as Ron Howard's *Apollo 13*, the elegant fluency of the Bunch's walk to their certain deaths still sends tingles up the spine – and, as with the synchronisation of crane and soundtrack in *Once Upon a Time*, this is not the result of straightforward character identification. Reputedly improvised on the day of shooting (the action was storyboarded to cut from the Bunch leaving the prostitutes to confronting Mapache), the walk was choreographed by Peckinpah and his assistant directors. As Pike musters the other remaining three, they ceremoniously take their rifles, cock the hammers and set off. To the accompaniment on the soundtrack of Mexican singing and a repetition of the ominous drum roll, the quartet file past Mexicans lining their road to dusty death, almost as if paying their respects to a passing funeral cortège. Part of the walk's effectiveness stems from its relative formal simplicity. The quartet's movement possesses an awkward, flawed, tragic heroism as Pike and the others, much as Macbeth does, belatedly rediscover their lost valour. Just as Macbeth exits to *his* certain death at the hands of Malcolm's army with the

Figure 2.4 *The Wild Bunch* (Sam Peckinpah, 1969). The Wild Bunch walk back to reclaim Angel from Mapache.

rousing lines, 'Blow, wind! Come, wrack! / At least we'll die with harness on our back' (5:5), so the Wild Bunch strides purposefully to theirs.

Pike et al. are returning to reclaim Angel from Mapache, and the apotheosis of the men's fated bravery is their grandly graceful rounding of the corner of a building just before stopping (or very nearly for, as always, Peckinpah cuts on the movement, in this case from the Bunch to Mapache). Perversely, the four men emerging in a fluently synchronised line from behind the building and then almost coming to a halt, is possibly as moving, as viscerally overwhelming, as the dramatic and abrupt beginnings to the action sequences. That not even their final walk is allowed to be completed is a supreme act on Peckinpah's part of sadistic denial which summarily thwarts once more our clichéd fantasies of heroism and closure. Though we have it coming (for the signs are already there that the Bunch's demise will be handled no differently from other momentous actions), the fragmentary restlessness of the journey to confront Mapache (shot from the front, the back, using mid-shots and close-ups, smooth camera moves and one jerky point of view) divests the men's final walk of the grace heaped on Fonda at the end of *Once Upon a Time in the West*. This is gritty rather than elegiac bombast, exemplified by Warren Oates's ungainly, rolling gait.

The gunfight which follows provides the by now conventionalised medley of furious, even chaotic, exchanges of fire, punctuated by the stylised slow-motion capture of figures (usually men) in their final energetic acts – reacting to being shot, flailing, blood spurting from them – before falling dead. The awful symmetry of beautiful death is encapsulated in the repeated image of men dying against the backdrop of a limpid, soft blue sky. Nature, this majestic sky intimates, continues regardless. Central both to the narrative and to the fight between the Wild Bunch and Mapache is the latter's newly acquired machine gun which functions neatly as a diegetic metonym for Peckinpah's

Figure 2.5 *The Wild Bunch* (Sam Peckinpah, 1969). Lyle takes command of the machine gun.

Figure 2.6 *The Wild Bunch* (Sam Peckinpah, 1969). Lyle guns down Mexicans across Mapache's table.

editing style of lacing together short and explosive individual shots. Exemplary in this respect is the bloodbath that follows Tector Gorch turning round and shooting a German manning the machine gun, whose wild, dying contortions cause lethal bullets to rain randomly on the Mexicans, before Pike finishes him off. A little later, Tector assumes control of the machine gun. He sprays shots at the Mexicans converging on him, a splash of blood violating the baby blue sky as he shoots one off the roof. Then, under an archway, another group silhouetted once again against the clear sky buckle forward in slow motion dead, their rifles arcing into the air. The anomalous, untouchable serenity of the sky is juxtaposed, throughout the Agua Verde shoot-out, with the dusty, agitated violence on the ground.

The peak of the sequence's machine-gun activity culminates in Lyle's death. Able to get back to the machine gun despite being repeatedly shot at, Lyle resumes firing – and screaming, which is notable because, amid the cacophony of bullets and blasts, the sequence has been virtually bereft of human sounds. Lyle peppers with bullets the Mexicans who, on the other side of Mapache's feast-laden table, are charging towards him. The choreography of these hyper-action moments is consistently telegraphed, not just by the spiralling dying shadows against the skies but also by the waves of Mexicans who, like surplus wild stock being forced through pens to their slaughter, charge into the machine gun's range. As they tumble through the doorway, another wave of Mexicans is caught by Lyle's bullets, as men writhe in slow motion in a murky cloud of spent gunpowder and dust, their shoots of blood interchangeable with the irrepressible jets of red wine spewing forth from a severed bottle. Peckinpah's aesthetic excesses tell us we are now very close to the end: on every level, there is little more to add and Deke's men are by now hovering outside town. If Kinder has identified correctly the eroticism of the violence in *The Wild Bunch*, then one has to ask how many 'orgasmic' 'eruptions' can the spectator 'hooked on a guilty pleasure' (2001: 66) take before insouciance sets in? If every act of violence in Peckinpah (or each death or near-death feat in later action films) produced the same high-octane, adrenilised, visceral response, then watching would not only be pleasurable but physically and intellectually debilitating. Part of the attraction of Peckinpah's repetitious style is not only its eroticism but also, by the time Lyle is gunning down the Mexicans across the table, its familiarity. One of the many enduring pleasures of violent action movies is that, after the initial assault, they stop surprising us, and being inured to brutality is part of the satisfaction.

The Wild Bunch's ultimate Macbeth-like moment comes as, shielded by an upturned table, Pike turns to Dutch and goads him into a last moment of action. With horror he witnesses Lyle and Tector staggering as they take yet more bullets, after which, with perfectly choreographed reflexiveness, it is, for the sequence's climactic twenty seconds, finally Pike's turn to take control of the machine gun. To a noise-track of ceaseless gunfire, the visuals for these few seconds are built around close-ups of Pike, grimacing as he sprays the town square with bullets, and the reverse high-angle long shots of the Mexicans writhing and falling. Just as Eisenstein built his montage sequences up to a fast-cut, final, almost patchwork of images, so Peckinpah here need supply only minimal narrative logic (such as Dutch smiling as it looks, fleetingly, as if Pike is making headway) to hold together his series of kaleidoscopic fragments. Their effectiveness lies in their shared histrionic abstraction: the hazy beauty of a Mexican falling backwards in soft-focus slow motion or even the clouds of billowing black smoke curling around horses plunging to the ground as Pike fires at Mapache's armoury of explosives. Morality, identification and attraction are now as randomly distributed as Pike's bullets, until the bathetic juxtaposition of Dutch's excitable 'Give 'em hell, Pike!' and the subsequent image of a boy sniper taking aim and killing him. As Pike succumbs, our responses once more coalesce. Suddenly the noise, which has been relentless, fades out in time with Pike crumpling to the ground (still clutching the talismanic machine gun) and Dutch joining him. As a series of slow-motion close-ups of the two veterans in their death throes unfolds, we might imagine that Peckinpah is finally going to permit us a moment of cathartic fulfilment. But compared to the final close-up of the dead Henry Fonda at the end of *Once Upon a Time in the West*, Peckinpah's wilful, abortive truncation of *The Wild Bunch*'s potentially cathartic finale is underlined by there being no last image of Pike dead at all, only a brief and awkwardly foreshortened one of Dutch. Immediately, Mexican townsfolk, sensing the battle is finally over, start to emerge from hiding, swiftly followed by a cruelly calm dissolve of Deke and his men riding into town. The ruthlessness of this conclusion stems from Peckinpah, unlike Shakespeare, denying us the classic tragedy's reward of time to contemplate a protagonist's death, though one could perhaps read Deke's decision not to claim the reward for bringing back the bodies of the Wild Bunch as the tragedy's gruff, monosyllabic eulogy.

Grønstad argues that the western is a genre in which 'violence has become a pure figure, or sign, and as such it belongs to the regime of the aesthetic and transtextual' (Grønstad, 2008: 137). Without catharsis, the bloody end of *The Wild Bunch* inevitably becomes pure spectacle, detached and extractable from the norms of action and identification. Of this scene, when Pike, Dutch, Lyle and Tector return to reclaim Angel, Grønstad goes on to say that it 'is one that eventually allows spectacle to supersede story' (Grønstad, 2008: 148), and it is the case – as it was to a lesser degree in the gun battle that opened *The Wild Bunch* – that the narrative moorings of the Agua Verde sequence have become, if not lost, then submerged under violence and excess. Spectacle transcends narrative in *The Wild Bunch*. Why, in this context, this is important is that it is through this recalibration of cinematic elements that we see straightforward forms of identification being marginalised in favour of instinctual, universalised responses to unshackled spectacle. That is, until Dutch and Pike die, which jolts us back into the narrative.

Peckinpah introduced several fundamental tropes and mannerisms to men's cinema. First, there is the fascination with, and fetishisation of, the moment of death whose physicality prompts an empathetically physical response in the spectator. Then, there is his penchant for overtly choreographed action sequences within which these individualised interludes are framed, linked to his innovatory editing, in particular the juxtaposition of excessively short single images frenetically spliced together and intercut with the slow-motion contortions of pain and death. Peckinpah's tendency is to use these snatches of slow motion specifically as a mechanism for singling out death though, in later men's cinema, the same technique often comes to be used, more generically, to draw attention to the hero, the intended focal point of what otherwise is orchestrated chaos. Collectively, these comprise the essential components of Peckinpah's aestheticisation of violence, which some (like Mellen) take to be an obscene glorification of masculinity. A counterargument might be to view Peckinpah's stylised dissection of the effects of violence as not an elegant apologia for masculine instinct but rather an equally elegant critique of those same masculine instincts, about which he is terminally equivocal. Though *The Wild Bunch* is about death, including the death of 'a certain form of masculinity' (Grønstad, 2008: 130), the irony remains that, while that 'certain form of masculinity' is moribund, the ways in which Peckinpah depicts and couches the multiple forms of death in *The Wild Bunch* are still influential and very much alive. The visual and formal intricacies levelled at the representation of these traits at once glorify and undermine his 'heroes'; the restlessness of Peckinpah's editing, for example, never allows us the unambiguous, de-equivocating moment of straightforward closure, as any 'pure' enjoyment of the fetishised spectacle of violence is immediately adulterated, compromised and intellectualised.

DIRTY HARRY

Though this book tends to emphasise films that use style and *mise en scène* expressively, arguably just as important, in terms of how Hollywood has tackled masculinity, and to its masculine aesthetic, is the minimalist antithesis to Peckinpah or Leone, exemplified by a movie such Don Siegel's *Dirty Harry*. The influence of spare films, such as *Dirty Harry*, is extensive throughout both cinema and television but is not talked about as much. From later cop cycles, such as *Lethal Weapon* or *Die Hard*, or television series from *Starsky and Hutch* to *CSI*, to the work of Walter Hill or Mike Hodges, to Jan de Bont's *Speed* or Doug Liman's editing of the chase sequences in *The Bourne Identity* (2002), the influence of *Dirty Harry* and contemporaries, such as *The French Connection* (William Friedkin, 1971), is evident. Synchronicity, as remarked upon several times already, is a significant feature of much of men's cinema, and, just as Leone's elegant aesthetic complemented the pedigree languidness of Henry Fonda, so Siegel's economical, functional aesthetic works well in tandem with Eastwood's giving-little-away acting style.

The casting of Clint Eastwood has necessarily influenced the cycle's reception and subsequent success (for, notwithstanding its later success and influence, *Dirty Harry* itself was not especially successful at the box office). Character-wise, 'Dirty' Harry Callahan conforms, like many of Eastwood's roles, to the clichéd 'strong, silent' stereotype (earlier, in Sergio Leone's 1964–6 *Dollars* trilogy, he had been 'the man with no name'). Callahan is a loner who, since the death of his wife, lives alone and, despite being allotted a partner, prefers to work alone. Numerous actors were approached for the role, including Paul Newman who, believing the character was too right wing for him, reputedly suggested Eastwood for it. Often discussed negatively is *Dirty Harry*'s underpinning ideology: that, alongside *The French Connection*, it was one of 'the major conservative films of 1971' (Ryan and Kellner, 1990: 41) and Callahan one of the 'official heroes' (Ray, 1985: 315) of the Right whose catchphrase [from *Sudden Impact* (Clint Eastwood, 1983)] 'Go ahead – make my day' was quoted by US President Ronald Reagan in a 1985 speech on taxes. There is also Harry's target in *Dirty Harry*, Scorpio, an effeminate, long-haired lone sniper who both wears a belt buckle in the shape of a peace symbol and, as Ray observes, recalls the 'stock Right position that the JFK assassination . . . was the work of a single aberrant individual' (308). Snobbism imbues many readings of *Dirty Harry*. Its ideological position is right wing, certainly but it does not take Harry's brand of strong, silent machismo entirely seriously, and the film's critics at times disregard the cycle's more self-conscious ironies: for instance, when Ryan and Kellner remark upon Callahan's concerns that a doctor treating him for a bullet wound early in the film will have to cut his expensive $29.95 pants exemplify his 'particularly pathetic' brand of 'lower middle class' conservatism (1990: 44). A glance up at Eastwood's delivery of the line is sufficient to suggest it is at least in part ironic, just as Callahan's sardonically performative dimension comes out, for example, in the verbatim repetition of his speech about his .44 Magnum, first to the failed bank robber at the beginning of *Dirty Harry* and then to Scorpio at the end:

> I know what you're thinking: 'Did he fire six shots, or only 5?' Well, to tell you the truth, in all this excitement, I've kinda lost track myself. But being that this is a .44 Magnum, the most powerful handgun in the world, and would blow your head clean off, you've got to ask yourself one question: 'Do I feel lucky?' Well, do you, punk?

Despite the tweeds and elbow patches, Harry's hyper-masculinity or his conservatism are not to be read entirely straight, a tonal complexity that emerges particularly acutely on the level of style. As, superficially at least, *Dirty Harry* is less overt or flamboyant in its portrayal and evocation of masculinity than either *Once Upon a Time in the West* or *The Wild Bunch*, Siegel's film, with its controlled, unflashy aesthetic, lacks the hysterical fear of masculinity's potential fragmentation that threatened to overwhelm the earlier texts. *Dirty Harry* is not as hyperbolically expressive but it does not automatically follow that its belief in hegemonic masculinity is any more secure.

Joan Mellen visits as much criticism on Eastwood as Dirty Harry as she had done on Sam Peckinpah, but for different reasons. She hated how, in Eastwood's characters, 'male silence has been sanctified with almost religious fervor' (Mellen, 1977: 13); then she loathed his loner ideology and that 'the glorification of the vigilante male has become the dominant masculine myth of the seventies' (Mellen: 295); and she is firmly of the stereotypical belief that Harry's revolver is his 'surrogate penis' (297). Ironically, Mellen's otherwise crude critique contains an unexpectedly evocative, nuanced description of Harry as '. . . tall and slim with thick brown hair adding sensuality to his otherwise ascetic appearance, at once muscular and taut, Harry is like a panther always ready to leap on his prey' (295). Just as Eastwood is a refined actor, however, so *Dirty Harry*'s minimalism is a subtle means of evoking early 1970s anti-counterculture masculinity.

Dirty Harry's pre-titles sequence opens with a pan down the names inscribed on a memorial plaque to the members of the San Francisco Police Department killed in the line of duty. With a sharp edit, the image cuts to an extreme, close-up, low-angle shot of a silencer and gun, which we soon learn is being aimed by the serial killer 'Scorpio' at a woman swimming in her rooftop pool. A muffled shot rings out and the woman writhes and dies. Though the distorted close image of the barrel of a shotgun recalls the familiar, similarly distorted and foreshortened image of Harry pointing his Magnum revolver downwards at a criminal he is about to dispatch (used, for example, on the publicity poster for *Dirty Harry*), the cycle's opening sequence becomes markedly less mannered once Eastwood enters the frame. Generally, Bruce Surtees's crisp camera style juxtaposes static, tripod-mounted medium shots and gritty, hand-held pursuit sequences, with a sparing use of vertiginous angles which are often saved for the more unstable characters (as here for Scorpio's first murder or, later, for the man threatening to commit suicide by jumping off a building). The film's otherwise pervasive minimalism complements the phlegmatic straightness of Callahan's sartorial look of suits, ties, tank tops, tweeds and leather elbow pads.

In the scene following Callahan's rooftop discovery of Scorpio's note with his demands for money, the mayor assigns Callahan to the case. As Harry is leaving, the mayor reminds him that he does not want a repeat of a previous case when he had killed a man during a chase. Without changing tone or expression, Harry explains (in one of *Dirty Harry*'s most frequently quoted passages of dialogue) how that occurred:

> HARRY: 'Well, when an adult male is chasing a female with intent to commit rape I shoot the bastard, that's my policy.'
> THE MAYOR: 'Intent? How did you establish that?'
> HARRY: 'Well, when a naked man is chasing a woman through an alleyway with a butcher knife and a hard on, I figure he isn't out collecting for the Red Cross.'

Callahan's unruly but authoritative machismo is underlined not by the film's style drawing us in but by it keeping us at a distance, like Jean-Pierre Melville's treatment of the similarly cold Jef Costello in *Le Samourai*. Detachment is still part of mainstream cinema's lexicon of masculinity, though with all the flashy, hyperactive editing and computer-generated gimmickry around now, it has increasingly become marginalised in favour of a form of men's cinema centred on affect and spectacle.

Soon after Harry has been assigned a new partner, Chico, the two drive out at night in pursuit of Scorpio, bemoaning the fact that their helicopter-bound colleagues had earlier in the day managed to lose him. The sequence opens with a classic two-shot from the bonnet of the car and through the windscreen, framing the pair driving and talking. A diverse, but generically important, series of shots then conveys their progress through a San Francisco red light district. First, there is a travelling point-of-view image of the neon-clad shops and club fronts through the passenger window which leads into a straight-on reverse-angle shot of Chico in profile still looking out, his features partially obscured by reflections of the neon signs chasing across the windscreen. Then, there is an edit to a two-shot into the car again but this time from the passenger window with both men in profile as they listen to a detailed radioed description of the 'rooftop prowler', which continues in the background during the ensuing sequence.

As the image reverts to further swerving, urgent point-of-view shots of the streets, so the street sounds and a montage of synthesised snippets of music become increasingly distorted and menacing, briefly taking on a hallucinatory quality which is stabilised and suppressed (as the musical montage fades away) by the reverse close-ups of Harry looking either side of him as he drives. Over an alternative two-shot of Harry and Chico, this time from the back seat of the car, looking over their shoulders and out through the windscreen, Chico suddenly says to Harry that he sees a man carrying a suitcase who fits the description on the radio. In among a fast, efficient sequence of shots (hand-held close-ups of the two cops intercut with comparably rough and urgent point-of-view images of the streets) Harry comes close to running over a couple attempting to cross the road. Naturalistic lighting, like the bumpy hand-held camera, is a distinctive feature of *Dirty Harry*'s chase sequences and here, through the light-studded gloom, both he and Chico see the man with the suitcase again, at which point the camera swivels 90 degrees. This produces an odd moment, and one that feels distinctly 1970s as opposed to 2010s, as the fast pan to the right, looking up a side street as if already in pursuit of the man with the suitcase, pre-empts Harry's rather slower pursuit, as he has to wait for the car to lurch to a halt. These days, Jason Bourne would have found a way of leaving the moving car – or Doug Linam would have simply edited him out of the car sooner and not worried about the parking. Chico remains in the car as Harry, in tweed jacket and with Magnum cocked, stalks the man with the suitcase. Apart from the police radio and the distant tinkle of a streetcar bell, the

Figure 2.7 *Dirty Harry* (Don Siegel, 1971). Harry and Chico searching for Scorpio.

Figure 2.8 *Dirty Harry* (Don Siegel, 1971). A reverse shot of the red light district.

Figure 2.9 *Dirty Harry* (Don Siegel, 1971). Harry and his Magnum pursue the wrong man.

sequence is now tensely silent. The gleaming nose of the Magnum emerges round a sharp concrete corner, followed by Harry, as the man he is pursuing slips away. Harry chases him to his home but, in a moment of ironic bathos, realises he has been following the wrong man as, caught peering in through his window, he finds himself accused by neighbours of being a peeping Tom. This is another deflating, undermining ending to a sequence, which implies we are not supposed to take Harry's masculinity entirely seriously.

So what do the aesthetics of that sequence achieve? Firstly, it is common for chase sequences in *Dirty Harry* and its sequels, or pursuits in similar buddy movies, to make use at some point of the flat, establishing two-shot through the car windscreen, showing the mutually supportive bond between the two policemen, a camaraderie that is subsequently just as frequently embellished by the searching shots of the streets outside from the points of view of either or both of them. Added to this, the sequence's rough stylisation – for instance, Surtees's use of a hand-held camera, the jerky pans and inelegant zooms or reverse zooms, the distortions on the soundtrack that mean that the police radio has a battle to be audible over the snatches of warped, truncated street sounds – projects the instinctive machismo of, in particular, Harry, hence the aptness of Mellen's anomalously poetic description of him as 'like a panther always ready to leap upon its prey' (1977: 295).

This chase offers a very clear example of *Dirty Harry*'s roughly hewn and ungainly style. Its style certainly does not scream out to be looked at in the way Leone's grandiloquence did although its unobtrusive edginess suggests and informs a different kind of masculinity. Harry Callahan is the cool presence at the core of *Dirty Harry* and, as was the case with the introductory scene (Scorpio shooting the woman swimming), the film's more showy visual stuff is generally reserved for other characters, especially unstable ones. After the chastening chase described above, Harry is called to the imminent suicide attempt of a man who has got on to a high roof from which he is threatening to jump. At junctures such as this, when Harry is confronted with unstable masculinity (the pre-titles, for instance, or the slightly wild and wayward crane shot away from the football pitch when Harry has first caught up with Scorpio), *Dirty Harry*'s visual style becomes jumpier and more intrusive. Conversely, when Callahan is in control, the camera tracks him far more simply as when, early in the film, he saunters over to the scene of a bank robbery, still chomping on his hotdog, his .44 Magnum in the other hand. When confronted with the potential suicide case, the visual style is an amalgam of the two and is more expressively urgent, jerkily following Harry as he ascends in the fireman's ladder. As Harry calmly tries to talk him out of killing himself, the raggedly subjective shots downwards at the assembled crowds equate to the man on the roof struggling to think through his decision. Clint Eastwood directed this sequence (and performed the stunt himself), and it is far more ostentatiously raw and edgy than the preceding chase, full of jumpy, hand-held camerawork and replete with the kinds of vertiginous high- and low-angle point-of-view shots down to the street and up towards the roof that have now become virtually indispensible to action films.

Dirty Harry exemplifies several important tropes in the argot, or shorthand, of men's cinema but it is interesting how motifs, such as the swerving roller-coaster-ride shots down from the rooftop, have been adapted as well as assimilated. Whereas in *Dirty Harry* these desperate, unstable images are prompted by the instabilities of the potential jumper, in contemporary action movies, by contrast, it is nearly always the most heroic of the heroes who scales the sheer rock faces or sides of buildings (*Mission: Impossible*, the *Bourne* series, *Skyfall*) in sequences whose thrill is that they seemingly propel us over the edge too. The villains are almost invariably more tentative or incapable. Most straightforwardly, such images come to express the male characters' 'derring-do', their instinctual physicality, but they also signal their precariousness and, by extension, the relative fragility of the dominant masculinity they embody. These sequences – like the heightened moments in *Vertigo* enacting Scottie's phobia of heights – handcuff us to the action and possess the buzzy frisson of nightmares, unconscious reminders that one stumble and all our feelings of authority and security will perish. The stylistic flourishes and tropes that *Dirty Harry* brings to men's cinema, such as the hand-held following shots or the subjective whip pans in the heat of the chase, fundamentally build a rapport between the spectator and the pursuer and/or subject of the chase (in this instance, Harry, but to a lesser extent Chico who indeed, if the angry look up towards his partner on the fireman's ladder is anything to go by, resents his supremacy). The by now (to any audience of action cinema) intensely familiar editing of the chase sequence, however bathetic in the end, is symptomatic of this rapport.

Dirty Harry's visual style exemplifies in many respects the post-classical embellishments of classical Hollywood's 'excessively obvious style' (Bordwell et al., 1988: 1) and demonstrates just some of the ways in which Hollywood's naturalism, its concealment of 'its artifice through techniques of continuity and "invisible" storytelling' (3) have been adopted and adapted by men's cinema. *Dirty Harry*'s is not Cowie's 'styleless style' though neither is it the style equivalent of George Cukor's idea of bad costumes that 'knocked your eye out' (Gaines, 1990: 195), as its visual flourishes do not draw attention to themselves at the expense of action, nor do they interrupt or overwhelm scenes as, arguably, Leone's crane shot did in *Once Upon a Time in the West*. Despite this, *Dirty Harry*, in its gritty anti-stylisation, amassed some of the tropes and motifs that are now among the most enduring of men's cinema. As Harry is a man of few words, who lets his big revolver 'do the talking', thoughts and thought processes are often articulated, perhaps even formulated, in *Dirty*

Harry via visual style. Bordwell's 'invisible' style ultimately proved incapable of evoking Harry's malaise or his frustrations with legal procedure, the police and institutions more broadly: the internalised manly tussle between what Harry can achieve by sticking strictly to police rules and what he thinks it is right to do (shooting the rapist or killing Scorpio) is subliminally enacted on the surface, the body of the film. The relative flatness of the scenes in the San Francisco Police Department building or the District Attorney's office alerts us to this, though part of the lexicon of men's cinema and of how Hollywood frequently couches masculinity through such insipid 'styleless style'. In these buildings, Harry is trapped and loses his individuality, swamped and oppressed by his institutional surroundings. Dirty Harry becomes stylish only once he gets outdoors.

For all its gritted-teeth, macho bravura, *Dirty Harry*, however, concludes with a reminder of Callahan's inconsequentiality as, after throwing away his badge, the film's closing image is an atypically smooth aerial zoom out showing him up to be a virtually invisible speck against the rugged backdrop of the quarry in which his final duel with Scorpio had taken place. Eastwood's virtual disappearance behind the final credit roll works as a poignant rendition of the notion that dominant (white, middle-class, heterosexual) masculinity has been, like the classical Hollywood style, just assumed to exist, and has been too rarely actively thought about or defined. The rapport between on-screen masculinity and a film's visual style recalls Lacan's arguments about the phallus. Though the 'most tangible form' (Lacan, 1977: 287) for conveying the phallus is assumed to be the male, the man and the phallus are not equivalent, as elsewhere Lacan posits that the woman's *'jouissance'* can be 'raised to the function of the phallus' (284). As Lacan outlines, according to Freudian doctrine, the phallus is neither 'a phantasy, if by that we mean an imaginary effect', nor 'as such an object', and 'it is even less the organ, penis or clitoris, that it symbolizes' (285). The phallus's power is as a signifier but one that 'can play its role only when veiled' (288); if unveiled, the frailties of both the phallus and masculinity would be exposed.

In trying to understand and define 'men's cinema', I am adapting Lacan here to support an argument for an emotive and unspecific form of spectatorship whose responsiveness to what is occurring, in terms of *mise en scène* or visual style, overrides and surpasses specific, stable forms of identification with the figure of masculinity on the screen. The identifiable location of this, however – as with the symbolic symbiosis in Lacan between masculinity and the phallus – remains the figure of masculinity on the screen. In a film such as *Dirty Harry*, a comparable relationship between signifier and potential object is more evident than it was in *The Wild Bunch* or *Once Upon a Time in the West* because its visual style is not so extravagant that spectacle comes to supersede story.

When discussing the complex ideologies of Hollywood films of the late 1960s and 1970s, Robert B. Ray categorises the era's most prominent films as either 'Left' or 'Right'; he predictably puts *The Wild Bunch* into the 'Left' cycle and *Dirty Harry* into the 'Right', though he also concluded that, the numerous overt differences between the two groups notwithstanding, films from both cycles were, in fact, 'capable of being taken two ways' (Ray, 1985: 327), and of satisfying both sets of audiences. Following on from this, it is possible to contend that the three contrasting individual movies discussed in this chapter, when it comes to their conceptualisations and evocations of masculinity, can be seen to be working in similar ways to create a dynamic symbiosis between men, *mise en scène* and aesthetics. The development of a 'masculine aesthetic' differs from the deployment of stylistic elements to express masculinity; it is a language, a set of underlying principles, a mode of communication and a series of signs, tropes and aesthetic features that collectively assists an understanding or definition of 'masculinity' in cinema. Though (as articulated in the introduction) a source of inspiration was Silvia Bovenschen's essay 'Is there a feminist aesthetic?', my conceptualisation of Hollywood's 'masculine aesthetic' is not as a straightforward, regendered equivalent, most fundamentally because Bovenschen (writing in the mid-1970s) evidently saw the development of a 'feminine aesthetic' as a conscious political act, as not just standing for 'aesthetic awareness and modes of sensory perception' but as signalling that 'women artists will not let themselves be kept back anymore . . . so let us take a look at what they are doing' (Bovenschen, 1985: 49–50).

Though around masculinity there has built up a comparable idiomatic coherence, Hollywood's 'masculine aesthetic' has not formed consciously or deliberately; instead, it has grown up in a haphazardly associative way, more akin to the unpredictable genealogy of DNA than a linear Darwinian model of evolution. In men's cinema's version of a double helix, tropes and motifs from one film mutate and are taken up by others which then, in turn, might metamorphose into a regular feature of a 'masculine aesthetic', without its chromosomal antecedents being reflexively acknowledged or even necessarily known. The glass lift shoot-out in *Skyfall* (Sam Mendes, 2012) can be traced back to the final shoot-out in Orson Welles's *Lady From Shanghai* (discussed in Chapter 1) although the action sequence does not reference this source directly, and the slow encroachment of Henry Fonda's posse on the doomed McBain family in *Once Upon a Time in the West* or Peckinpah's insertion of slow-motion shots into otherwise fast-cut action sequences in *The Wild Bunch* are liberally echoed in later films, such as *Reservoir Dogs*, *Die Hard* and *Gladiator*, though the lines from earlier to later films are, again, not necessarily direct. The intention of the next chapter is to analyse the development of 'men's cinema' and Hollywood's masculine aesthetic from the perspective of more recent films.

NOTES

1. As Frayling observes, despite its length, *Once Upon a Time in the West* consists of only about twenty scenes, the first three of which take over a quarter of its overall screen time (Frayling, 2006: 212). So little happens in *Once Upon a Time in the West*, in fact, that the triple 'story' credit for Dario Argento, Bernardo Bertolucci and Sergio Leone plus separate 'screenplay' credits for Leone and Sergio Donati are a touch absurd.
2. http://www.imdb.com/title/tt0065214/trivia.
3. Ibid.

CHAPTER THREE

Men's cinema

In this chapter the focus will be on selected films in which are exemplified some of the key characteristics of men's cinema. Consistencies and repetitions are always intriguing, and I shall look at some of the repeatedly used tropes, motifs and style features that contribute to an identifiable 'masculine aesthetic'. These motifs and tropes are of different varieties, and the analyses of individual films frequently extend beyond them but they nevertheless share the fact that they speak eloquently about masculinity. Inspired by the films discussed in the last chapter, I shall also consider examples that elicit from their audiences emotive and more instinctual responses, the implied relationship between image and audience opening up the possibility that the expressiveness of a film's style and *mise en scène* can be mobilised to urge or compel spectators to become part of the expressivity of men's cinema, to respond physically and emotionally to the films' conceptualisation of masculinity. I have arranged the chapter chronologically by film, for men's cinema is in part historical and developmental, whose tropes and motifs, over time have been rehearsed, modified and modernised. Many of the films discussed in this final chapter display a knowingness and a reflexivity that imply an awareness of these established cinematic conventions but which have been acquired subliminally as well as consciously. Each film or sequence analysed below identifies or furthers the discussion of particular tropes, motifs or style features and, in diverse ways, picks up from the previous chapter's review of *Once Upon a Time in the West*, *The Wild Bunch* and *Dirty Harry*, as well as introducing new elements to the masculine aesthetic, primarily those that reflect and engage with recent significant technological advances.

RAGING BULL: CRANE SHOTS, BEAUTY AND LOSS

In many of Martin Scorsese's films there exists a strong correlation between style, meaning and masculinity. There is, for instance, an auteurist uniformity about his portrayal of the moment when the male protagonist first spies the woman with whom he is about to fall in love. Whether (to cite three Robert de Niro examples) it is Travis Bickle spying Betsy for the first time in *Taxi Driver* or Jake LaMotta seeing the underage Vickie by the pool in *Raging Bull* or Ace spotting Ginger playing the tables in *Casino*, this event is marked first by its specified relation to the male protagonist's lusting gaze and second by the mobilisation of a series of stylistic tropes that serve to fetishise, eroticise, objectify the (mute) woman, such as: slow motion, close-up or a zoom or track into her body. In *Raging Bull* (1980), Jake is still married to his first wife when he asks his brother Joey who Vickie is. The point at which he falls in love with her is marked not just by action and dialogue but by how it is filmed: the slightly slowed image of Vickie's legs moving to and fro in the water, the sensuous ripples caressing her young flesh as Jake imagines he would like to.

Raging Bull is a nostalgic film, and the languidness of these shots of Vickie hark back to classical examples of male infatuation, such as the moment when Jeff's voice-over in *Out of the Past* says dreamily, 'And then I saw her . . .', as he first sees Kathie Moffatt coming into a bar in Acapulco. The dreaminess of Mitchum's vocal tones, however, in tandem with the dreaminess of the chiaroscuro screen image, as Kathie emerges from the external brightness into the bar, is used, in a conventionalised way, to eroticise specifically the female form. In *Raging Bull* the domains of masculine and feminine are not always so sharply demarcated for, either side of the short sequence of shots of Vickie at the pool, there is the fleeting use of close-up and sensuous slow motion in specific conjunction with images of Sal and other mafiosi friends, a far less conventional eroticisation of the masculine form that Scorsese uses a number of times in this film and elsewhere, most notably in the opening sequence of *Goodfellas*. The use of slow motion for the gangsters in *Raging Bull* is indicative of two forms of intertwined desire, for Vickie and, far more ambivalently, for the world of power and privilege inhabited by Sal and his friends. Whereas in *Goodfellas* it is categorically Henry Hill's attraction to Paulie Cicero and the other mafia guys who own the taxi rank across the street that is indicated by the specific conjunction of his introductory voice-over and the fetishistic and lackadaisical close-ups of their gaudy accessories and flashy shoes as they emerge from their cars, this affinity between male protagonist and desire for the Mafia is, in *Raging Bull*, far more tentatively defined. Jake resists the Mafia's attempts to steer his career until relatively late on. It is not simply that he yearns for that milieu; instead, a comparable eroticisation of the mafiosi to that found in *Goodfellas* – via the use of similar visual tropes, such as the gentle, caressing close-ups of Sal and his friends' hands, sunglasses or clothes – here remains equivocal. Jake, these moments of eroticisation suggest, is, unlike Henry Hill, not straightforwardly attracted to the Mafia lifestyle; instead he views it with obsessive jealousy. Jake is jealous of them because of their friendship with, and assimilation of, Vickie; he assumes they hold an attraction for Vickie that he is unable to match. These slow-motion interludes therefore signal Jake's weakness and his fear that he, despite his boxing successes, will forever remain peripheral. To return to the initial eroticisation of Vickie: the conventional conclusion here might be that Jake is here claiming ownership of Vickie as the objectified woman of his imagination; the actual inferences, conversely, are that this eroticisation of Vickie – that follows the same pattern as the eroticisation of Sal and his cronies – confirms her to be perpetually out of reach and the fragility of Jake's subjectivity.

Frequently, Scorsese's male protagonists feel confident and in control early on, only for the remainder of the films to chart intricately their demise. *Raging Bull* offers one of the most painful examples of this as the transition from one state to the other occurs only a couple of minutes in as, hot on the heels of the elegiac beauty of the title sequence, there is an abrasive cut to the older, fatter, uglier 1964 Jake preparing dreary anecdotes and gags for 'An Evening with Jake LaMotta'. *Raging Bull* exemplifies the supremacy-to-defeat narrative structure as it is propelled by the struggles between victory and failure, between personal happiness and jealousy and so on. It also plays out these struggles, not just on the level of narrative but also on the level of *mise en scène*.

The ease and beauty of the film's title sequence have been remarked upon many times and its fragile elegance lures us in. In soft, grainy black and white[1] and to the accompaniment of the intermezzo from Mascagni's *Cavalleria Rusticana*, Jake LaMotta shadow boxes around a ring dressed in his trademark leopard-print robe. The images – captured largely through the ropes along one side of the ring – are slightly slowed down, making this otherwise ugly pugilist (LaMotta was no Ali) seem almost dainty as he dances around the ring and swings at the air, an air filled with smoke that shrouds the ambiguous figure of Jake in mystique, even majesty. The music, the fluidity of the movements (both Jake's and the camera's) and the soft monochrome stock all suggest these titles form a eulogy rather than an opening, but for what? Pam Cook, in still the most emotive and moving article on *Raging Bull*, argued in 1982 that the film's tragedy centres on masculinity and loss: that 'masculinity is put into crisis so that we can mourn its loss' (Cook, 1982: 40). Certainly, the juxtaposition of beauty and loss is enacted starkly at the outset, as the lithe, fit and idealised Jake of the titles is swiftly replaced by the prosthetically deformed Jake of 1964, in his too-tight shirt and dinner jacket, rehearsing under the unsubtle, crude dressing room lights. The flat ugliness of this latter image also contrasts significantly with the depth and beauty of the title sequence.

Later, amid her discussion of *Raging Bull* and cinephilia, Cook remarks upon the film's 'visual pleasure',

> . . . the excitement of the *mise-en-scène* which alternates between long, reflective shots which allow us to contemplate the scene in safety, at a distance, and explosions of rapid montage which assault our eyes and ears, bringing us right into the ring with the fighters. Sometimes we almost literally get a punch in the eye. I don't like boxing; but the illusion of 'being there', the risk involved, is a real turn-on. The film moves and excites by making the past immediately present, by making us present in history. For women, perhaps, this illusion of presence is doubly exciting, since we are generally represented as outside history. But the price of that pleasure is an identification with masculinity on its terms rather than our own. (Cook, 1982: 40–2)

Cook is worth quoting at length here, as it is important for my commentary on the film to get from the diverse pleasures of *Raging Bull*'s style to issues of excitement and identification. I am less concerned – no doubt in part because I am writing thirty years after Cook – with matters of gender and difference and more interested in questions of how a film conveys masculine subjectivity (both Jake's and that assumed by the film's *mise en scène*) and how such subjectivity flourishes, thereby prompting the instinctual and non-cerebral audience identification Cook touches on. Unlike Cook, who differentiates not only between Scorsese's 'long, reflective shots' and the 'explosions of rapid montage' but also between their differing effects on the audience, I tend to see the vast array of visual tropes and editing styles as all part of *Raging Bull*'s overriding preoccupation with the essence of masculinity and how to evoke it in all its inconsistency, its fragmentation, its complexity.

One of the key shots in the film is the ninety-second Steadicam shot of Jake LaMotta walking from his dressing room to the ring to fight Marcel Cerdan in Detroit, in 1949, for the middleweight title (which LaMotta wins). The shot charts Jake's final preparations in the dressing room, his journey through the corridors and tunnels that lead to the arena and his eventual emergence into the crowd awaiting the start of the title fight. In 1980, the Steadicam, a system that enables the camera operator to obtain smooth tracking shots using a hand-held camera and without the need for tracks, dollies or cranes, was a relatively recent invention, first used commercially by Haskell Wexler in *Bound for Glory* (1976). Scorsese and his cameraman on *Raging Bull*, Michael Chapman, also used the small, lightweight Arriflex 35 BL camera. Todd Berliner draws comparisons with the generic follow-the-star-on-to-stage shot used in so many music and performance documentaries [*Don't Look Back* (1967)[2] and *The Last Waltz* (1978), for example] and parodied so effectively in Rob Reiner's *This is Spinal Tap* (1984), as Tap get lost trying to find the stage. It is also reminiscent of the long hand-held tracking shot in *Primary* (1960), Robert Drew's documentary following John Kennedy as he makes his way through swelling crowds into a hall where he is due to make a speech. That shot at the time was, in technical terms, a show-off, macho, 'look at what I can do with the new lightweight cameras' moment that befitted its subject matter: the rise and imminent victory of John Kennedy, the fresh, dynamic new face at the time of American politics, about to clear out Eisenhower's 1950s Republicans by defeating the incumbent vice president, Richard Nixon. The Steadicam shot in *Raging Bull* makes, initially at least, a similar impact: encapsulating and allowing us to revel in Jake's big moment of success. The straightforwardness, however, of this relationship to the *mise en scène* is short-lived as the shot's implied linearity is rendered more complex by how the sequence goes on to end and by how it is contrasted with the subsequent scene.

The Steadicam track in *Raging Bull* is particularly compelling and satisfying as a result of the synchronisation of gesture, sound, meaning and camera movement. Though Berliner remarks, as cited earlier, that when the 'backward tracking shot becomes, with hardly a pause, a forward tracking shot' we, the audience lose our 'sense of privilege' and become merely one of the fans (Berliner, 2005: 51), shifts in direction do not invariably interrupt fluidity or alter tone. It seems more important, in this instance, that this shot's smooth grandiloquence exists beyond the immediate confines of narrative and character, and is used instead to connote or translate the intermingling of triumph and masculinity. Contrary to Berliner, it seems to me that, when the camera peels away from LaMotta, starts to soar and encircles the ring as he continues through the roaring throng, it is a moment of maximum adrenalin and heightened identification. Our point of identification is not so much LaMotta as the rush of power he is shown, via the camera, to be experiencing. That is, until it stops. Unlike the music, which keeps going, the soaring camera move is unexpectedly cut short before it has reached any natural end and is replaced by the relative mundanity of the referee in the centre of the ring introducing Jake. This technique of interrupting a shot or camera move with a sharp edit, which occurs elsewhere as well, signals reasonably clearly the deflation of whatever idealisation of masculinity precedes it.

Cook likens the structure of *Raging Bull* to tragedy, and these brusque truncations could be viewed as interruptions to our cathartic enjoyment, all part of the film's preoccupation not with masculine success but with masculine disintegration. In keeping with this, when LaMotta finally wins the middleweight championship at the end of the bout with Cerdan, his crowning moment is resolutely undermined by an edit even more cruel than the transition from title sequence to 'An Evening with Jake LaMotta'. Jake's triumph is conspicu-

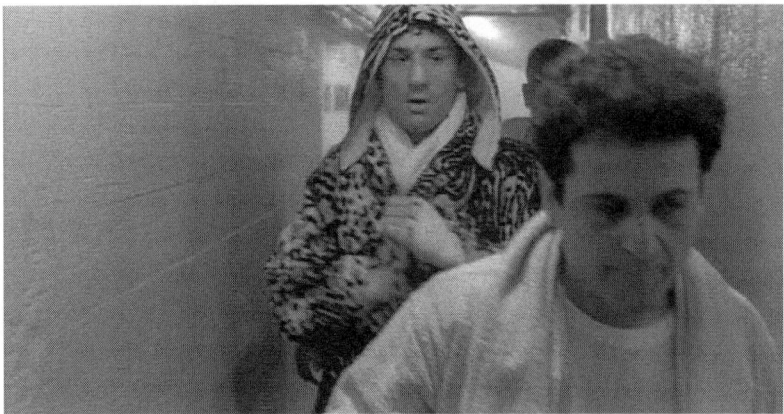

Figure 3.1 *Raging Bull* (Martin Scorsese, 1980). Jake's fight for the world title: the start of the tracking shot.

Figure 3.2 *Raging Bull* (Martin Scorsese, 1980). Jake's fight for the world title: near the end of the tracking shot.

ously disjointed and short-lived. Cerdan being unable to continue, the referee comes over to LaMotta to declare him the winner. The sound becomes muted and dream-like, as the referee's words drift away and Jake raises his arms, goes over to Cerdan's corner and is then held aloft, images of victory intercut with shots of a sea of press cameras, flashbulbs popping with arhythmic speed. Jake is then lowered to the floor and, with his gloved fists once more aloft, looks down (in a medium shot) to the World Champion's belt being put around his waist, distant chants resonating in the background. There is a cut to a tighter shot that has Jake to the right of frame, his arms around the men beside him and tears in his eyes. This has been slowed down slightly, and the slow motion is held over into the next shot, a repeat image of the belt being put on Jake, this time from a lower angle. The muffled fizz of the flashbulbs continues over a final image, a close-up of the belt around Jake's middle, the last bulb's soft thud coinciding with the edit to the next scene and the subtitle 'Pelham Parkway, New York 1950', the introductory image of which is a ballooning LaMotta in opened shirt and shorts scoffing a sandwich and bashing his television set in a vain attempt to obtain a picture.

This edit from crowning glory to bloated ugliness is, like the cut from dancing pugilist to oafish entertainer at the outset, a moment of sadism. *Raging Bull*'s masochism has often been remarked upon, largely in relation to the pummelling Jake's body endures during the boxing bouts. That at times he just absorbs his adversaries' blows re-enacts the loss of any stable notion of the masculine subjectivity so mourned by Cook. Equally resonant are the sadomasochistic tendencies that characterise the film's style: interrupting a flowing camera move, the disjointed editing or denying the spectator a straightforward cathartic response to the boxing bouts. *Raging Bull* is frenetic and disjointed; pockets of fluidity reside within an overall aesthetic that is fractured and wholly antithetical to the ponderous predictability of more traditional boxing movies, such as *Rocky* (1976), which Scorsese consciously did not want to emulate. Shots, particularly ostentatious ones, are not permitted to remain unqualified; the big aesthetic moments in *Raging Bull* are not show-stopping tours de force, like the final triumphant shots of *Rocky*, perhaps.

One place in which the film's intellectual coherence (as opposed to its disjointed visual style which various critics have remarked on) comes out is in the parallel between body and film so that, what is happening on a narrative level, principally to Jake's body (the violence, the pain, the masochism) is also being transmitted and felt on the body of the film, the surface of the text. This is what renders *Raging Bull* moving and effects, if anything does, some form of catharsis. It also offered a form of catharsis to its director, Scorsese, who said that he 'put everything I knew and felt into that film and I thought it would be the end of my career. It was what I call a kamikaze way of making movies' (Christie and Thompson, 2003: 77). Another aspect of the coherent incoherence of *Raging Bull* is the physicality of the representation of LaMotta being matched by the physicality of the viewing experience. In *Carnal Thoughts* Sobchack hopes that what her book will engender

> is an appreciation of how our own lived bodies provide the material
> premises that enable us, from the first, to sense and respond to
> the world and others . . . charging our conscious awareness with
> the energies and obligations that animate our 'sensibility' and
> 'responsibility'. (Sobchack, 2004: 3)

The tight relationship between Jake's corporeality and our visceral response to the movie's spectacular masochism is our main point of access and understanding.

One fight that many, including Scorsese, have focused on is the film's last – the third bout with 'Sugar' Ray Robinson when Robinson wins back the middleweight crown. Berliner picks out the slow-motion shot of Robinson winding up for a punch, his body surrounded by smoke or steam, as one of the film's many 'implausible images' (Berliner, 2005: 41), then commenting that Robinson's stance is 'ridiculously awkward . . . like a third-grader pretending to be a fighter' (41). The degree of critical distance Berliner is exercising here, though, marginalises the sequence's affective power, for the illogicality of the shots encapsulates both our mixed, equivocal responses as spectators and Jake's own internalised contradictions. Towards the end (Round 13) of this terrible fight LaMotta takes a barrage of punches from Robinson of which the wheeling, expressionistic punch described above is just one. LaMotta is on the ropes, goading Robinson to have another go at him ('Come on Ray'). Silence descends briefly and Robinson, centre frame, surges towards both LaMotta and, via the point-of-view angle, the camera; then there follows a reverse shot of Jake and another of Ray, the splicing together of 'implausible images' thus mirroring the assault LaMotta is enduring. During these gruesome close-ups, the destruction of his body is emphasised not only via the tight images of blood and other liquids spurting from him but through the tempestuous collisions on the level of *mise en scène* and sound: the mismatched angles, the amplified noise, the slow motion, the dark, unpopulated backdrop to Ray's killer punch.

In this final fight there are the consecutive close-ups of Jake's bloodied and bloated face, taking Sugar Ray's punches; the images defy sense, are from conflicting high angles and have swung round 90 degrees. In a Soviet, notably Kuleshovian way, the sequence is made sense of by the spectator as its internal dynamics ignore spatial, temporal and generic logic. Robin Wood, for one, challenges the criticism of Scorsese by Andrew Sarris and others that his films 'lack a sense of structure' (Wood, 2003: 223). I would extend this by arguing that the ostensible illogicality or fragmentariness of *Raging Bull*'s style, in addition to its narrative structuring, has a specific role within the film's pervasive masochism, as the disjointedness of the film's visual construction definitively interrupts and interferes with our potentially more straightforward responses to its emotional core. Thus, Jake's pleasure at finally becoming world champion is fleeting, just as the beauty of the title sequence cuts rudely to the overweight, disfigured Jake rehearsing his clunky nightclub gags. We are offered cathartic potential only for this to be disconnected or taken away. At the end of LaMotta's losing fight with Robinson, Chapman's camera makes similarly elegant, swooping, circular moves around the ring to the ones we have seen before but, this time, the pan circles elegantly only then to come to rest on a close-up of blood dripping from the ropes as Robinson is pronounced world champion. Scorsese mentions how he had asked himself why LaMotta simply takes the punishment, deducing: 'He takes the punishment for what he feels he's done wrong' (Christie and Thompson, 2003: 80). In many ways 'tragic', *Raging Bull* is also so overwhelmingly draining because, unlike most tragedies, the emotions its images generate in us are so frequently at odds with what we want to feel. Here, I would posit, the slow, dejected, wary pan across the ring to the bloody rope makes us mourn LaMotta's painful demise but without permitting us also to identify with it or with him.

THE RIGHT STUFF: SYMBOLS AND THE PHALLUS

The penis and its relationship to the phallus will always be somewhere close to the heart of any representation of masculinity, though not always as overtly as it is in Philip Kaufman's film adaptation of Tom Wolfe's book about the Mercury 7 US space programme of the late 1950s/early 1960s. Richard Dyer, in ' Don't Look Now', commented that 'the penis isn't a patch on the phallus' (Dyer, 1992: 116); later, in 'Male Sexuality in the Media', he argued even more strongly for the demystification of the relationship between the penis and the phallus:

> One of the striking characteristics about penis symbols is the discrepancy between the symbols and what penises are actually like. Male genitals are fragile, squashy, delicate things; even when erect, the penis is spongy, seldom straight, and rounded at the tip, while the testicles are imperfect spheres, always vulnerable, never still . . . It is not flowers that most commonly symbolize male genitals but swords, knives, fists, guns. (Dyer, 1985: 30)

In contrast to the majority of critics of masculinity and film, Dyer dwelt not on the phallic potential of the male body but on the reductiveness of such an attachment which wrongly equates masculinity with the penis. The affiliation between the penis and hard phallic imagery, Dyer suggested, was not only unerotic but also separated men from the source of their erotic pleasure by promoting the notion that the penis had 'a life of its own' and was an object over which the man had 'no control' (1985: 31). Denial of the erotic potential of the male form is, of course, the underlying theoretical rationale for several of the other critiques of masculinity on film referenced in the introduction.

The conclusion of Dyer's essay discusses certain significant parallels between 'basic storytelling grammar' and male sexuality. He suggests, provocatively, that 'virtually all narratives, regardless of what medium they are in, reproduce the way male sexuality is organized' and continues:

Male sexuality is said to be goal-orientated; seduction and foreplay are merely the means by which one gets to the 'real thing', an orgasm, the great single climax . . . It is no accident that the word climax applies to orgasm and narrative. In both, the climax is at once what sex and story aim at. (1985: 40–1)

This proffers a manifestly heterosexual view of 'male sexuality' but one which will, indeed, be familiar from many films. Jan de Bont's *Speed* (1994), for instance, concludes with an ostentatiously phallic subway train bursting through to street level as Keanu Reeves and Sandra Bullock embrace and then kiss. *Speed* has included two other such narrative 'climaxes' (the lift, the bus), however, both in tandem with first a homosocial and then a heterosexual moment of post-climactic tranquillity. So, even in the most overt and obvious examples, male sexuality is ambiguously defined.

The Right Stuff (1983) offers one of the clearest Hollywood critiques of masculinity and symbolism (represented as the struggle for supremacy between the magnificent men and their flying machines) while, like Dyer, remaining positively attached to masculinity itself. What I want to explore in particular here is the relationship in *The Right Stuff* between the debates (on the level of *mise en scène*) surrounding masculinity and phallic symbolism and its evocatively rich visual style. The film contains various moments of 'pure spectacle' (as Neale might put it) though they are not invariably linked to the exploits of the male body. The effect of these stylistic excesses is particularly marked in the 70 mm, six-track stereo version of this three-hour film. *The Right Stuff* opens with a monochrome sequence composed of faked and genuine archive footage of an X-1 (a small, experimental plane used by United States Air Force test pilots in attempts to break the sound barrier) being released from a B-29, mixed with specially taken, point-of-view shots from inside the X-1 as a pilot tries and fails to break the sound barrier. The plane judders as the pilot's dial goes further and further up the Machmeter, reaching 0.99, at which point there is an explosion, not caused by 'the supersonic boom, but the test plane crashing to the ground' (Charity, 1997: 34). At the point of the plane's impact with the ground, the film, with a single brash edit, explodes into colour, and the image ratio jumps from square (1:1.33) to wide (1:2.33). As Charity continues:

The audacity of this cut (reminiscent of the first cut in Welles' *Touch of Evil*) heightens the impact of the explosion and marks the end of the preamble. This dramatic crash is the movie's take-off point. The sudden shift to colour and widescreen heightens our appreciation of these aesthetic pleasures. It's a bold announcement of the scale of this picture. (34)

As is suggested through numerous films, the construction of idealised masculinity through the synchronisation of different elements of style, narrative and *mise en scène* is a recurrent feature of 'men's cinema'. The effect of this widening of the screen at the beginning of *The Right Stuff* to the accompaniment of Bill Conti's triumphant, soaring soundtrack (the music subsequently used for Chuck Yeager's repeated, successful test flights) is dramatic and intense, especially in the stretched 70 mm version. It is also specifically related to masculinity in that it is the first of many moments in *The Right Stuff* when we, as spectators, experience and therefore understand the pilots' adrenalin rushes, glories and fears; conventional, character-driven forms of identification are supplanted at the start of *The Right Stuff* by a more abstract identification pattern rooted in an instinctive and emotional, even primal, audience response to the non-narrative textual elements. This identification with aesthetics, which transcends character and gender, is an essential trope of 'men's cinema'.

Kaufman's use of non-narrative elements, such as colour, ratio and music, in this instance is expressive, serving to transfer to its audience the emotions that drive the interpersonal and historical struggles the film's story narrativises. The construction of masculine identity in *The Right Stuff* centres on the ultimately intangible and unrealistic notion of 'the right stuff', a symbolic construction (frequently comically conceived) that links the battle to be the 'best pilot' of them all with increasingly abstract notions of authentic and heroic masculinity. Most of the film is dedicated to the Mercury space programme of the 1950s and early 1960s, from the first successful single-manned flights of Alan Shepherd and Gus Grissom to the orbital flights of John Glenn and Gordon Cooper prior to the Apollo programme taking over. *The Right Stuff* starts, however, with Chuck Yeager, the hero of both Wolfe's book and Kaufman's film, who remained a test pilot rather than become an astronaut because he failed to conform to the government profile for the job (he did not go to college, for example). Unlike the astronauts' flying, Yeager's is instinctual and strenuous; history – and the middle portion of *The Right Stuff* – might marginalise Yeager and give preference to the space programme but this programme of testing diminishes the Mercury 7 rather than building it up. 'The right stuff' and authentic masculinity is, ironically, exemplified most concretely by Yeager – the one omitted from the Mercury programme – rather than by the endlessly tried and tested astronauts.

The film's equivocal attitude to the phallus is repeatedly and comically illustrated by the series of tests the would-be astronauts have to endure during the Mercury programme selection process: they have to ejaculate into a small, metal, penis-shaped container; they are walked down the corridor with a catheter up them; they are wired to machines in a claustrophobic capsule; and they have to see for how long they can keep a table tennis ball afloat in a tube filled with water without taking a breath. The tests that ostensibly prove their suitability as astronauts are demeaning and belittling, more adept at accentuating their mortality and frailty than their heroism. The Mercury pilots were beaten into space not only by cosmonaut Yuri Gagarin but by a chimp and, when the NASA scientists are testing the various incarnations of the rocket that will finally launch an American man into space, the earlier models' performances are distinctly Monty Pythonesque.

There is, in fact, a *Monty Python* sketch 'Erotic Films' (part of Episode 5, Series 1, 'Man's Crisis for Identity in the Latter Half of the Twentieth Century') in which a couple in their underwear (the man is Terry Jones) kiss heartily before falling back on to a double bed. A montage of film clips starts up that includes: a tower being erected, water crashing against rocks, fireworks, a rocket launch, a train entering a tunnel, an udder being milked, a plane crash-landing on water, a tree being felled, the tower from the start of the sequence being demolished. These images supplant the sexual act and most (the image of Nixon grinning being the exception) make comic reference to it. At the end of the montage the woman is sitting up in bed having a cigarette complaining about being made to watch films, while Terry Jones – crouched next to a portable projector – assures her there is 'just one more, dear'. In *The Right Stuff* there is a comparable sequence as NASA, in the wake of the USSR's first successful Sputnik flight, test a series of their own rockets, only for these to explode on the launch pad, shoot up a few feet then shrink back into the earth, leave the ground only to dive-bomb back to the ground, and refuse to launch at all. Throughout *The Right Stuff* rockets, and being able to tame them, are at the heart of how masculinity becomes defined. These are not just failed rockets.

In direct contrast to the way in which the astronauts and rockets are filmed, Yeager, though nearly defeated, is never humiliated. Unlike the early space missions, which are filmed from inside the claustrophobic, cramped capsules, the astronauts' discomfort mirrored by the oppressiveness of the close-ups, Yeager's flights are captured largely from outside, his plane hurtling through perfect clouds hanging in infinite blue skies, intermingled with a few shots of Yeager inside the cockpit straining to keep an X-1 under control. The images' liberation and exhilaration and the scenes' fast editing opens up the potential for identification with Yeager, not a straightforwardly narcissistic identification as envisaged by Neale but a more nebulous response both to him and to his at oneness with the skies, with the movement and music and with the dimensions of the image. The importance of the scale of the image to the film's articulation of masculinity is made clear in its last, prolonged sequence, in which Yeager testing the air force's latest X-1 (just as the pilot test programme is to be scrapped) is intercut with a night of lavish Texan entertainment laid on for the Mercury astronauts by Texan vice president and head of the United States space programme Lyndon Johnson (just as *their* programme is about to be superseded).

Figure 3.3 *The Right Stuff* (Philip Kaufman, 1983). Yeager crashes.

Figure 3.4 *The Right Stuff* (Philip Kaufman, 1983). Yeager survives: 'Is that a man?'.

The difference between Yeager and the Mercury pilots is enforced on various levels and exemplified by their overall situation: as the astronauts eat pork and beans from disposable plates while watching a fancy fan dance, Yeager is hurtling solo through the skies. Rising Icarus-like into the upper atmosphere, he first temporarily loses consciousness and then control of his aircraft, just managing to eject himself in time. As his fellow test pilots drive to the crash site, one, having spied a glint of silver amid the black smoke, turns to

Figure 3.5 *The Right Stuff* (Philip Kaufman, 1983). Yeager burnt but alive.

the other and asks 'Sir, over there – is that a man?' As Yeager emerges, striding towards them defiant and angry, his face blackened and burnt, the other
replies with the wry smile of shared pride in his buddy's macho exploits 'Yeah,
you're darn right it is!' This last image of Yeager in *The Right Stuff* is, for all
the ostensible supremacy of the astronauts and the space programme, the
film's triumphant narrative 'climax' and 'among the most transcendent images
in contemporary cinema' (Charity, 1997: 84).

   Why is Yeager's masculinity never in question? It is partly because, unlike
the astronauts strapped up to endless machines or stuck immobile in their
capsule, Yeager never relinquishes independence or control. Also, his masculinity is neither questioned nor compromised because of the manner in which
the conjunction of stylistic elements (camera, editing, music) reinforces his
mastery. In the final sequence there exists a contrast between the crowded
interiors of the Texan celebrations and the expansive exteriors of Yeager's last
flight. Crucially, both the astronauts and Yeager are rendered insignificant by
their respective environments but, whereas the astronauts are swamped by
and lost amid the throngs milling around them, Yeager, after the crash, is a
solitary and tiny glint of silver on the vast screen. While the astronauts find
themselves undermined, Yeager's reputation as the one with 'the right stuff'
is consolidated: the 'best pilot', as Gordon Cooper dubs him,[3] and the best
man. While *The Right Stuff*'s use of phallic symbolism (often crude, usually
ironic, sometimes adolescent) undercuts the astronauts' ostensible claims to
masculine supremacy, the majestic image, the soaring music, the vast, flat
desert landscape and the open skies, conjure up a nostalgic attachment to

an older, more stable and traditional image of masculinity exemplified by Yeager.

Yeager and the other test pilots in the late 1940s characterised Mach 1, or at least what resided on the other side of the sound barrier, as 'the demon in the sky'. Just as the demon remains both imaginary and unattainable, so the pursuit of idealised masculinity, the film (even in the case of Yeager) seems to be saying, will ultimately be futile. *The Right Stuff* and so many other films celebrate the pursuit of masculinity as opposed to the possession of it. The abstractness and elusiveness of idealised masculinity is what Kaufman's expressive use of the widescreen image evokes: the expanse of luminous blue skies, for example, that Yeager dissects with his plane. The urgent need to 'break' an intangible barrier and the infinities of sky and space serve as appropriate metaphors for man's attempt to 'break' and understand masculinity and then to understand that it will remain unobtainable, unknown and out of reach. *The Right Stuff* makes us both yearn for, and through that yearning almost believe in, the intangible essence of masculinity; it also, however, treats the striving for masculine perfection ironically, and to this not even Yeager is quite immune: shot through with romanticism and nostalgia, Kaufman's rendition of him, for all its old-fashioned heroism, is nevertheless imperfect, for Yeager ultimately *was* left behind and *was* superseded by the pilots selected for the space programmes. This contradictory relationship with what masculinity might mean or be can be characterised, using other terminology, as the enforced distinction between consciousness and more repressive instincts: what you would like to be, what you are and what you would like to forget you could ever be.

This attachment to such an unrealisable ideal of 'the right stuff' serves to make sense of Lacan's conceptualisation in 'The Signification of the Phallus' of the phallus as a symbolic construct, 'the privileged signifier . . . chosen because it is the most tangible element in the real of sexual copulation, and also the most symbolic in the literal (typographical) sense of the term' (Lacan, 1977: 287). Lacan's radical proposition is that, unlike the penis ('the tangible element'), the phallus 'can play its role only when veiled' (288), that, like other symbols, to see or name it would be to divest it of its potency. As Lacan later goes on to argue, if seeming to possess symbolic power replaces really having it, then the phallus is at its most powerful if 'veiled', masked or absent from view. Rather as Dyer identifies, once seen, the discrepancy between the hard, frightening, potent symbol and the penis (which the phallus is mistakenly assumed to represent) becomes abundantly clear. Masculinity is thus predicated upon a false attribution of phallic power to the male as a result of the misplaced assumption that the symbol (the phallus) has its correlative in the body (the penis). This is all neatly and effectively enacted in *The Right Stuff*, as hard, phallic rockets and planes dissect limpid blue skies or float in space, searching for Mach 1 or the moon, only for their pilots to be rebuffed, injured or killed by the invisible phallic power that in their imaginations is reduced to 'the demon in the sky'. The most effective evocation of the 'right stuff' is not the pilots but the stretched 70 mm image.

TOP GUN: HOMOSOCIALISM AND THE SYNCHRONIES OF MUSIC AND EDITING

An essential component of the 'right stuff' as evoked by Kaufman's film was the synchronicity between image and music, for Bill Conti's score was definitely one way in which in *The Right Stuff* masculinity was aesthetically transposed and evoked, seducing the film's audience into falling in love with masculinity as opposed to simply the embodiments of a masculine ideal by actors and characters on the screen. The issues raised in relation to desire and/ or identification come from a similar theoretical position to that adopted by Jackie Stacey in relation to psychoanalysis-based feminist film criticism of the 1980s. In 'Desperately seeking difference' Stacey argued that 'The rigid distinction between *either* desire *or* identification . . . fails to address the construction of desires which involve a specific interplay of both processes' (Stacey, 1987: 61). Though Stacey here is proposing an ambivalent, eroticised form of identification with, specifically, an on-screen figure, what I am particularly interested in developing is the comparably ambivalent form of identification with, and desire for, masculinity proffered by certain tropes and motifs within a film's *mise en scène* and style. It is not the case, for instance, that the purpose of Chuck Yeager's walk towards his colleagues at the end of *The Right Stuff* is merely to persuade the spectator to identify with or desire him or to be him; the effect is more diffuse than this and revolves around the conceptualisation of a film's aesthetics as the route to making the spectator desire or identify with an abstract notion – in this instance masculinity – as opposed to its configuration.

The discussion now moves to the action film, a genre that, especially with the demise and reconfiguration of the western, has become Hollywood's main arena for exhibiting masculine physicality. Again, however, I am less interested in talking about the representation of masculinity than in how that masculinity is conceived through, or embodied and enhanced by, style and *mise en scène*. When discussing masculinity in the action film, Tasker's *Spectacular Bodies* centres on issues of representation but the genre has also lent itself, through its fascination with spectacle, to the analysis of visual style. One critic to have concentrated on the visual style of contemporary Hollywood action cinema is José Arroyo who, when writing about Brian de Palma's *Mission: Impossible*, remarked upon how such 'high concept cinema . . . strives to offer a theme park of attractions: music, colour, story, performance, delight and the sense of improbably fast action' (Arroyo, 2000: 22). Arroyo then asserts that the aim of the collision between all these elements is to 'seduce the audience into surrendering to the ride' (22). In a similar vein, Dyer writing about *Speed*, makes the point that 'To go to an action movie is to sink back in the seat and say, "show me a good time"' despite the pervasive cultural and political anxiety generated by passivity, especially in relation to masculinity (Dyer, 2000: 20). For Dyer, the 'delicious paradox' of action movies is that the films promote an 'active engagement with the world' while also promoting a passive sense of enjoyment as they 'come to you, take you over, do you' (21). The conclusion to his argument for action cinema as sex is the assertion that 'for the male viewer action movies have a lot in common with being fellated' a position that compromises masculinity because

> it's the other person . . . who's doing the work, really being active. So it is with action movies. In imagination, men can be Arnie or Keanu; in the seat, it's Arnie or Keanu pleasuring them. Now that's what I call speed. (21)

A refreshing element of Dyer's analysis of the pleasures of action cinema is its attention to the physical act of watching the films. In contradistinction to Dyer, however, I will here argue (in relation to the development of a masculine aesthetic in the action film as a mechanism for generating pleasurable viewing) for an amorphous association of imagination, identification and jouissance more in keeping with Stacey's idea of erotic identification and less wedded to the idea that watching action movies is physically a passive experience. As a result of the physical responses of excitement and so on generated by this, emotion created by identification not only with character but also with spectacle and movement does not have to feel passive. Eroticism does not simply stem from things being done to us but from the transference of that power from what is happening on the screen to those watching via multiple resonant conjunctions between *mise en scène*, image and sound.

I should now like to initiate a discussion of some of the key persistent tropes of action cinema and to discuss them as illustrative of this active spectatorial response. When writing about *Mission: Impossible*, Arroyo commented:

> Applying the Frankfurt School's critique of mass culture to this type of film-making would not be hard: *Mission: Impossible* is not very original; the structure of the whole doesn't depend on details; it respects conventional norms of what constitutes intelligibility on contemporary film-making. It could be seen as an example of pseudo-individuation, that which seems different but is in fact the same, whose object is to affirm capitalist culture. (Arroyo, 2000: 23)

Arroyo might be right about the action cinema's sameness and its unconscious ideological allegiance to capitalism; the genre's homogeneity, however, is also dependent on an understanding of the films' detail or at least on an analysis of their intricate construction, hence my desire in this book to focus closely on specific stylistic elements.

The ensuing discussion of Tony Scott's *Top Gun* (1986) centres on a specific issue in relation to the analysis of detail, namely the film's most significant subtext: its homosocialism and suppression of homosexuality via, specifically, the film's often numbing synchronisation of music and editing. The relationship of action cinema to homosexuality has been frequently noted, and one component of its affirmation of capitalist culture is, *predictably*, its repression of homosexuality. However, and with this I wish to recall once again Freud's polemic in 'The Sexual Aberrations', certain action films (such as *Top Gun*) are specifically constructed, it would appear, around situations that are inherently and defiantly homosocial and explicitly afford images of masculinity that invite the erotic gaze (male or female) towards the masculine body that Neale, for instance, found so troubling. As Wood argues (again with reference to Freud's ideas about perversity), repression is not

> necessary for the development and continuance of human civilization in any form; it is necessary only for the continuance of *patriarchal* civilization, with its dependence upon a specific, rigid and repressive organization of gender roles and sexual orientation. (Wood, 2003: 221)

Top Gun's exaggeratedly upbeat and macho style (lots of rivalry, shouting by men in uniforms, whooping and high fiving) directly supports this zealous attachment to straightness though, ultimately, it proves impossible to repress the queerness that threatens its hysterical protestations of machismo. *Top Gun* remains both a seminal action movie and one of the campest films in the canon. Available on the Internet are endless (and redundant) queered versions of *Top Gun* but *Top Gun* is hardly in need of queering, defeated as it already is by the strain of its own futile rearguard actions against its perverse core. The synchronisation of music, rhythm and energy works both to construct the archetype of the (straight) young action hero and then to suppress the more indeterminate fears of his, and the film's, queerness, a strategy exemplified by a series of sequences that intermingle recreation and intensive fighter pilot training, starting with the sweaty game of volleyball in which Pete 'Maverick' Mitchell (Tom Cruise) and his co-pilot 'Goose' take on 'Iceman' (Val Kilmer) and his co-pilot 'Slider'. In terms of the theme of masculine rivalry on which *Top Gun* pivots, Maverick and Iceman are the only two real contenders for the 'Top Gun' slot (the best pilot of a cohort), a competition that underpins all the film's competitive exchanges.

The introductory chords of Kenny Loggins's 'Playing with the Boys' (specially written for *Top Gun*) start up, over the concluding frames of a classroom spat between Maverick and Slider, functioning as the bouncy overture to the volleyball match, one of a series of big performances of larger-than-life masculinity, an upbeat sequence in which machismo is defined through the classic conjunction of brash music and fast editing. The generic blandness of Loggins's thumping and insistent mid-1980s exercise/dance number complements the sort of generic unoriginality Arroyo detected, and enjoyed, in *Mission: Impossible*. We the audience for *Top Gun* are, by this narrative juncture, familiar with the film's routine packaging of masculinity, and this familiarity informs and defines our enjoyment. After the edit-out of the classroom scene, there is a sequence of short close and medium close-ups establishing the now infamous and much parodied game of volleyball, commencing with a tight shot of a pilot's (Iceman's) sweaty back, the ball spinning on the forefinger of his partially bandaged hand. The iconography is crucial: sweaty bodies adorned with that most masculine of accessories, the soldier's metal identity tag, Iceman's protective bandage and the aviator sunglasses *Top Gun* made so fashionable and desirable. From Kilmer's strapped hand the image cuts to Cruise, who checks his watch, shouts 'let's go' to Goose and claps a motivational, manly sort of a clap. Iceman serves, Maverick receives and Goose hits back to Maverick; the song's lyrics have started in time with Maverick's first strike of the ball, and thus the complementarity of music to editing effortlessly sucks the audience into specific synchronicity with Cruise, making him the sequence's pivotal force.

Then, following this establishing montage of hypermasculine close-ups, the camera cranes out to a high-angle shot of the sandy court, a move of strength, certainty and ostentation. The game itself is not as important, this move indicates, as the rivalry between Maverick and Iceman being played out in this arena. A series of medium shots and close-ups ensues, revolving around a barrage of serves, flamboyant stretches to retrieve the ball and high fives, creating a composite image of competitive masculinity. A couple of these – for example, Iceman receiving serve – are slowed down slightly, the alternation between fast and slow creating the rippling effect common among post-classical Hollywood action films. Slider's pumped-up celebration coincides with the beginning of the song's chorus, the most repeated, and hence most familiar, section of the music for which the catchy homosocial lyrics are:

Playing, playing with the boys,
Staying, playing with the boys.
After chasing sunsets,
One of life's simple joys
Is playing with the boys.

The images and sound accompanying the chorus are cut in time to the beat and tell their own mini-narrative: Slider whoops as he wins a point, a sound in danger of being dwarfed by the song's parallel crescendo; a reverse image of Maverick looking annoyed; Goose placing his arm around his buddy's back as they walk away from both camera and net; Goose looking back over his shoulder as the image reverts to Slider who, three-quarters on, strikes a bodybuilding pose, tightening his stomach and arm muscles; Iceman spinning the ball on his finger again, this time front on; Tom Cruise sounding another motivational clap to indicate he is ready to receive; finally, there comes the climactic rally comprising various close-ups of Kilmer gritting his teeth, Slider lunging for the ball and, on winning the point and Cruise high fiving again, a celebration timed exactly to coincide with the climax of the chorus. The volleyball game ends as Maverick, bathed in the golden light of late afternoon (fully emphasised by Scott's overattachment to pink filters), leaves the court, puts on his obligatory white T-shirt, jacket and aviator shades and roars off on his Kawasaki motorbike to dine with Charlie (Kelly McGillis), now to the altogether more romantic and heterosexual strains of Berlin's 'Take My Breath Away'.

Throughout *Top Gun* masculinity emerges as a performance, a show put on for an imaginary watching crowd. Constantly to be inferred is that masculinity comes into being only when performed for others and that, divested of the need to put on a show, such brash, confident masculinity would cease to exist. The performative elements of *Top Gun*'s images of masculinity are not only emphasised by, but also constructed through, the deployment of music and editing: the songs are obviously performances in themselves, and that the renditions of masculinity they accompany are likewise performances is underlined by the synchronous editing. The energy dedicated to the display of masculinity draws attention to the potential lack and emptiness at its core and to the men's barely repressed instabilities. For all their posturing, the 'top gun' pilots are vulnerable, a vulnerability confirmed by the awkward contrast between their exuberant performances (the high fives, the fists pumping the air, the glistening muscles) and what these might be repressing, such as the spectre of queerness that lurks behind all these excitable homosocialist exchanges.

Some ten minutes later comes a test-piloting exercise, the prelude to which is Maverick getting fired up after being told that Iceman, already ahead in the 'top gun' competition, has won another exercise. In flying gear, walking towards the camera and towards their jet, he turns to Goose and delivers the entrée to the film's most famous line 'I feel the need . . .', before his co-pilot duly supplies the second half of it: '. . . the need for speed'. The obligatory high fives ensue, before a hard edit to a jet roaring across the screen. The first part of this sequence is without music but the boom of the first jet performs a similar starting gun function to the first beats of the song that announced the volleyball match, heralding the commencement of a battle of the skies to the accompaniment of Harold Faltermeyer's soundtrack music. Maverick soon decides to depart from the planned exercise and goes after Viper instead. Following a close-up of Cruise, there is a tighter shot of his hand on the control stick and a purposeful 'click' as he changes the settings on it, proclaiming, much as a cowboy cocking his trigger might do in a western, his readiness for a fight, an intention underlined with another brief shot of him shunting the stick again as if going up a gear in a manual car. (Surely there is more to piloting a fighter jet than this? Having said that, though, an unexpectedly large number of 'men and machine' films feature similarly purposeful gear-stick shunting as preludes to high-energy action). Scott then cuts from these tight interiors to a wide aerial exterior of two planes, the first being Maverick's as it breaks out of formation to soar almost vertically upwards.

Once more, there is the simple but affecting synchronisation of narrative trajectory, character, image, and, this time, a drum- and bass-led instrumental track. The music becomes more pulsating and strident, complementing the fast-cut chase sequence comprising (as all the flying sequences do in *Top Gun*) a medley of close interiors of tense pilots and expansive exteriors of planes zipping across limpid blue skies, failing to convey precisely what is going on but suggesting, nonetheless, the strain and effort such nebulous antics entail. The potential for likening such adrenalin-fuelled sequences to the single-minded trajectory of the male orgasm is, in *Top Gun*, great but here, just as Maverick, fraught and excitable, thinks he has his man and is about to 'fire' at Viper, consummation is denied as an instructor's radar locks on to him from behind. Maverick, had this been a real exchange, would have been killed; as it isn't, he simply gets told off. Throughout *Top Gun* such parallels between action and sex come to the fore, only to be undermined either by being interrupted or by the reiteration of the homosocial context.

The synchronisation of music and editing is used consistently in *Top Gun* to, most overtly, frame mood but also to proffer a dynamic construction of masculinity whose intention it is to repress such potentially disruptive forces. Cutting a sequence to the rhythm of a fast, beat-driven soundtrack superficially, at least, irons out nuances and complications. In relation to masculinity, such a transparent, synchronic editing style has the effect of imposing oversimplified notions of masculinity, men's actions and men's motives; it also generates a comparably straightforward, uncomplicated and physical response in the audience. Much of the enjoyment of watching an action movie, such as *Top Gun*, depends upon our physical, active, and not merely cerebral and passive, engagement with it. It might seem overly simplistic to suggest that the pounding beat of the soundtrack (slightly faster than an adult heartbeat) makes our heart race and adrenalin levels rise but this is largely the feeling *Top Gun* induces.

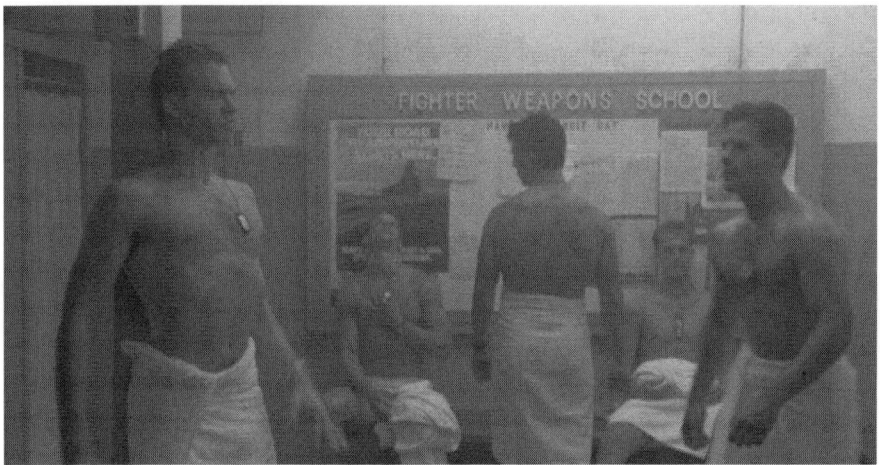

Figure 3.6 *Top Gun* (Tony Scott, 1986). Posing in the locker room.

In hot pursuit of the near-orgasmic training session is *Top Gun*'s tumescent locker room scene, a scene of minimal narrative purpose except for providing a backdrop for Maverick's admonishment for his reckless, though magnificent, flying. Camper even than the volleyball game, it is made up of little more than a series of tableaux of wet, half-naked men posing in dinky, identical white towels pulled tightly around their taut waists. The spectacular superfluity of this locker room scene is underlined as Cruise, who had been posing against a pillar, moves away after his dressing down, to be replaced (as if by another suitor in a Regency dance) by a dripping Val Kilmer, who takes up pose and residence for even less discernible reason, at exactly the same spot. In case we have not understood that the two ace pilots (or is that torsos?) are being compared, Scott has the camera track smoothly round from distance to close-up, a move perfectly timed with the instructor's exit bottom frame left, Cruise walking away from camera and Kilmer arriving at the pillar from screen right. The emphatic harmonisation of these various elements ironically draws attention to, rather than detracts from, the fact that very little happens in this scene bar posturing and men putting themselves on display (an example, in miniature, of the way in which the film obsessively tarmacs over the fissures created by queerness straining to get out). As Pauline Kael, in her characteristically pithy review observes, in *Top Gun*, 'It is as if masculinity had been redefined as how a young man looks with his clothes half off' (Kael, 1986: 117).

Though *Top Gun*'s narrative concludes with the superficial stability of the heterosexual romance between Cruise and McGillis, the definitive affirmation of heterosexuality comes too late. As Kael noted, *Top Gun* is defined by its homosocialism – its attachment to, and prioritisation of, the bonding between men that derails the normative heterosexual union. In the end, the pumped-up action sequences are spectacular but they are also the hysterical, fraught manifestations of the pervasive tensions between normality and perversity which the film never quite manages to reconcile. These action sequences thus function in tandem, rather than at odds, with the far more blatant camp of moments such as the locker room scene. The polarities – the macho and the closeted – come together, for instance, during the volleyball game, as masculinity becomes not merely pure spectacle but pure performance. It is, however, too easy to use *Top Gun* as proof that all men's action cinema is queer at heart, so now this discussion will be balanced by a discussion of *Die Hard*, an altogether straighter example of the masculine aesthetic – or, at least, an example in which distinctions between heterosexuality and the perverse are more neatly demarcated.

DIE HARD: THE ACTION SEQUENCE AS MASCULINE RECUPERATION

In *Die Hard* (John McTiernan, 1988) distinctions between heterosexuality and perversity are drawn overtly on the level of narrative and representation, for example, via the differentiation between action hero John McClane (Bruce Willis) and narcissistic villain Hans Gruber (Alan Rickman), resulting in latent perversity being linked to 'bad' men, with a penchant for expensive couture and flowing hair, while 'good guy' McClane remains the film's stabilising figure: a white father and cop in functional clothes. *Die Hard* establishes the relationship between sexual/marital fulfilment and success as an action hero very clearly. As the film begins, McClane is an estranged husband working as a cop in New York, going to Los Angeles to see his wife and children for Christmas. His wife Holly had left New York six months earlier to take up a job in California where, as deputy in a large Japanese corporation, she works, much to McClane's annoyance, under her maiden name of Gennero. *Die Hard* centres on McClane saving his wife and most of her fellow Nakatomi Corporation employees from a German terrorist group, headed by Gruber, which has infiltrated and immobilised the building. At the end of *Die Hard*, McClane is reconciled with Holly who, when asked by a member of the LAPD what her name is, replies 'Holly McClane'. That success as an action hero restores McClane to his patriarchal role could not be more explicitly demonstrated though, by *Die Hard 2: Die Harder*, (Rennie Harlin, 1990) their marriage is again in difficulty and, by the later films, Holly has disappeared altogether.

Though many of the films discussed in this book invoke the sexual act metaphorically, very few feature sex explicitly; sex frequently emerges as a counterforce that could, if permitted a more dominant role, destabilise the

action and its hero. That masculinity in cinema is so often predicated upon
sexual frustration is one notable paradox of men's cinema. With so many
heroes having to prove their masculine worth via conflict or battle, the action
film's expressive and conventionalised *mise en scène* and visual style frequently
become the means by which desire and sexuality are most actively expressed,
with eroticism coming to be displaced on to action. Within this context, the
demise of Gruber, the witty, intellectual German who heads a homosocial
band of psychotic brothers, is essential to the restoration of heterosexual
equilibrium. The beginning of the end for Gruber and deviancy comes in
the form of an extended exchange of machine gun fire between McClane
and Gruber's men, a sequence that starts just as Gruber had thought he had
regained the upper hand by fooling McClane into thinking he was an ally.
McClane had handed Gruber a gun which, as it turns out, is not loaded.
McClane remarks (after Gruber has fired the gun): 'No bullets. You think I'm
fucking stupid, Hans?' Gruber had, however, summoned his henchmen and
a bell announces the arrival of the lift. There is a cut back to Gruber who asks
smugly, 'You were saying?', at which juncture the soundtrack music begins
and the camera starts to move, signalling the imminence of an action sequence,
just as a song beginning over the end of the previous scene had done in
Top Gun.

Die Hard's action sequences mirror the straightforward symbolism and
linearity of the film's overall narrative. In terms of how the *mise en scène* is integrated into this dynamic, the spectacular visual style of the action sequences
is driven by, and has as its focus, John McClane. One of the signature generic
features of the modern action film (in homage, no doubt, to Sam Peckinpah)
is the construction of extended sequences around the coupling of short shots
and fast editing, a stylistic trope that fuels, and is an integral factor in, a film's
pervasive, indefatigable breathlessness. Another element of many an action
sequence is noise and, here, atmospheric sound is provided by gunfire and
the repeated loud crackle of shattering glass. Just after the stand-off between
McClane and Gruber, the camera tracks swiftly towards the lift door as two of
Gruber's long-haired cronies emerge, immediately spraying with bullets the
office into which they enter. There follows a reverse shot of McClane returning fire as he runs past the lift door, his machine gun emitting fluorescent
clouds. Each shot is extremely short (under or around a second) and tilted
which is one of *Die Hard*'s recurrent visual affectations and one that adds to
its sense of impatience and urgency. The sloping angles are ways of signalling,
firstly, the prominence in *Die Hard* of the point-of-view shot (often from the
perspective of McClane in hiding, trying to work out what Gruber is doing)
and, secondly, that all is not as it first appears. There follows the briefest
exchange of shots/reverse-shots between McClane and Karl, the blondest and
most psychotic of Gruber's men, including two differently framed shots of

Figure 3.7 *Die Hard* (John McTiernan, 1988). The action sequence: canted frame.

McClane running by – one wider, one substantially tighter, both canted – and the repeated splintering of glass as Karl's bullets whistle by him. Then there is a cut to another tilted, low-angle frontal shot of McClane running around a corner, an agile Steadicam in pursuit.

Repetition is an intrinsic structural component of such a frenetic sequence, and, as the two terrorists emerge from around the same corner, the camera tracking speedily into them, there is yet another slanted reverse shot of McClane running, holding his gun aloft as he dives left into an anteroom, bullets raining around him. After a quick close-up of Willis crouched on the ground (a familiar position by now), there follows a floor-level point-of-view shot of a third terrorist making his way towards him. From the same low angle we see the terrorist's legs being shot through with bullets, and a wider shot shows him falling through more glass. The mutual firing continues unabated between McClane and the other two, though there is the briefest of respites as Karl slithers behind a desk. Overall, however, visual instability reigns as machine guns blaze, the average shot length decreases and framing angles multiply.

There is another short hiatus as Gruber (now also crouching behind a low piece of office furniture) and Karl talk in German. We may not understand this, but then neither, it transpires, does Karl, at whom Gruber then has to snarl in English to shoot at the glass which is shielding McClane. Via a further sequence of canted point-of-view shots, the sequence is stripped to its bare essentials of noise and fragmenting glass, its conclusion arrived at as McClane, fearing he is done for, spies the inviting luminous green of a nearby 'Exit' sign. Karl, wanting both to smoke out McClane and finish him off, rolls a newfangled grenade towards him (the anteroom in which McClane has been is, of course, his modern-day hideout) and, as Karl and Gruber look for but cannot see him, they presume they have won the battle. As Gruber finds the bag of detonators McClane had taken, he says triumphantly 'We're back in business'. An edit to a television screen marks the conclusion of the sequence.

Victory, it transpires, belongs to John McClane who, though in pain from the shards of glass embedded in his feet, escapes via the emergency exit. This sequence's uncluttered linearity, its pace and its inevitable propulsion towards a decisive and predictable narrative climax are all features that, though they fall short of directly connoting the male sexual act, remain obliquely suggestive of it, down to the climactic ecstasy of freneticism and noise and the sharp withdrawal from it into the meta-world of television coverage of the siege. Action in these circumstances (especially within a narrative in which heterosexual union and marital contentment are, at the outset at least, distant possibilities) supplants, rather than merely augments, the sexual act. In *Die Hard*, McClane's successes as action hero then provide the route back into Holly's affections, so the perversity of the action sequences ('perverse' because their frenzied action becomes an eroticised substitute for the sexual act) is eventually repressed by the couple's rapprochement. This serenity, though, is only superficial as the urgent, passionate exchanges even in *Die Hard* occur between men, whether antagonistically, as between McClane and Gruber, or supportively as between McClane and Al, the black cop who has maintained a radio dialogue with him throughout the siege.

I have discussed here an indicative action sequence but, in terms of what *Die Hard* tells us about masculinity and how, on a stylistic level, it operates to enforce this, the relationship between action and narrative is especially important. Energetic, heated conflicts and the protracted battle between McClane and Gruber are ostensibly the way for McClane to regain Holly; the action sequences in *Die Hard* (the all-male zones), however, are always more exciting, spectacular and enjoyable than the quieter, more tentative moment of the couple's reunion. I remarked earlier that, unlike Dyer in his discussion of *Speed*, I do not necessarily believe the action spectator occupies an exclusively passive position, however pleasurable, in relation to the action itself. Passivity in *Die Hard* resides quite explicitly with Holly, held captive by the terrorists and able only to admire her husband's bravery from afar, and with the feminised Al who, likewise, can only look on and hope while McClane risks his life. Conversely, we, the spectators, are permitted to identify with *Die Hard*'s active forces by being propelled through its action sequences alongside McClane. In turn, these scenes are lent both coherence and excitement via this proximity. So, ultimately, the short shots and fast edits engage us by making it possible for us to invest physically in the action sequences while their punctuation with point-of-view shots cements our collusion with McClane. Gruber and his men are always one step behind; we are not.

MASCULINITY, MUSIC AND SONG

This is the only section of this chapter that focuses on more than one or two films. Music is a vital element of men's cinema but, to express this, it felt most appropriate to examine several films together, the main ones being *Backdraft*, *Blue Collar* and *Master and Commander*. Synchronicity and repetition are significant elements of the masculine aesthetic at the heart of men's cinema, exemplified by the compatibility between Bruce Willis's movements, camera and editing in the action sequences in *Die Hard* or the synchronisation of music, editing and close-ups of Tom Cruise to denote his centrality to the volleyball sequence in *Top Gun* and to the film as a whole. Music is a potent component of this homogeneity, and there are various notable examples of music being used to amplify or cement the coalescence between hero and film. *Backdraft* (Ron Howard, 1991), a film about two fire-fighter brothers, Stephen (Kurt Russell) and Brian McCaffrey (William Baldwin), has significant limitations as a film but offers an illuminating example of music's centrality to the development of a film's underpinning theme – in this instance, what being a man, a son, a fireman entail. Howard's film is replete with several showcase sequences that are in themselves mini-narratives about masculinity. One such is an extended montage synchronously edited to the truly awful 'The Show Goes On' by Bruce Hornsby and the Range. The sequence conforms to the predictable structuring formula of the three-minute narrative pop song, using its collection of easily readable composite images not just to illustrate what 'being a fireman' is about but also, more broadly, to demonstrate what is entailed in 'being a man'. The music starts over the end of the previous sequence, as it had done in *Top Gun*, and the montage's images exemplify its heavily telegraphed symbolic intentions. They mix the dramatic (Scott Glenn trying in vain to revive a woman just pulled out from a blaze; firefighters silhouetted against the flames; a fireman saving a smiling boy; a fireman on a high crane fighting a blaze; a man being cut out of a wrecked car), the recreational and cooling off (a game of basketball replete, as ever, with high fives; slow motion shots of tired, hot fireman hosing down their faces), the routine (Brian kicking a street mains pump in frustration as he tries and fails to attach a hose to it; two episodes of training) and the comic (the unit trying to rescue several escaped chickens; Brian being woken by the unit's dog). That the representative identity being constructed here is a cohesive and integrated one is signalled by the somewhat slavish synchrony with both tune and lyrics – that when the unit is playing basketball, for example, the lyrics are 'he's the one keeping the score'. Even more hackneyed is the editing of the car crash to Hornsby singing 'the show must go on'. So far, in both film as whole and in the montage, the one off beat, as opposed to on the beat, narrative constituent has been the sibling friction between Stephen and Brian, which naturally concludes the montage. The music falling away coincides with them crashing through a fire door and on to the roof of a building, having battled it out during a training exercise of racing up a fire escape carrying a hose. This sort of music-led montage has become a Hollywood genre movie staple and often functions as a sealed unit, in this case to temporarily obliterating alternative visions of masculinity, so that it is harder than one might imagine to resist being swept along by its momentum or to maintain much critical distance from it.

Music is frequently used in men's cinema to reflect energetic masculinity and, simultaneously, to engender energised responses in us as we watch. In both *Backdraft*, for the 'being a man' sequence, and *Top Gun*, for the volley-ball game, narrative is choreographed both to the rhythms and to the lyrics of a non-diegetic song. In the two examples, familiar music, which lies outside the parameters of the narrative, functions as a commentary on the action and so, as Ian Garwood observes, possesses 'autonomy from the image' (Garwood, 2003: 110). As Garwood goes on to say, however, 'this quality of "distance" can still be exploited for a specific narrative effect' (110). The narrative effect of the synchronisation to the song track is to offer a synthesis of themes that would otherwise take longer to explain (namely being a fireman, brother and man) at the same time as cajoling us into falling in line with, and feeling sym-pathetically disposed towards, them. Music, as Dyer notes, 'acts on our bodies' (Dyer, 2012: 7). When, though, music – and, more specifically, the song – is seen to act on the bodies of men in films, the conjunction of enjoying, dancing to or singing along is frequently problematic as far as the establishment of strongly heterosexual masculinity is concerned.

There are certainly exceptions to this, such as the last scene of *Master and Commander* (Peter Weir, 2003) in which Russell Crowe and Paul Bettany play violin and cello together in a delicate moment of non-homosocial rapproche-ment between the ship's captain and its doctor. Perhaps the 'problem' is singing? Already discussed briefly in Chapter 1 is the scene in *The Deer Hunter* in which Christopher Walken dances and sings along to Frankie Valli's 'Can't Take My Eyes Off You' while playing pool. Another example of a man singing along and dancing occurs early on in *Saturday Night Fever* (John Badham, 1977) as Tony is getting ready to go out to the strains of the Bee Gees' 'Night Fever' – choosing his colourful shirt and slicking back his hair as Farrah Fawcett-Majors smiles down on him from the poster on his wall. In Paul Schrader's *American Gigolo* (1980) a bare-chested Richard Gere as the epony-mous gigolo is getting ready for an assignation and choosing from a selection of Giorgio Armani shirts and jackets, while prancing and singing (it has to be said, rather self-consciously, which adds to the sequence's charm) to Smokey Robinson and The Miracles' 'The Love I Saw in You was Just a Mirage'. In all three examples the men are enjoying themselves, wrapped up in their images, bodies and what they are doing; their dancing and singing along to a song offer a hiatus, a moment of spectacle or a break in the narrative that, in turn, sheds significant doubt on their heterosexual credentials.

When, however, the relationship between music and men is reversed so that the music responds to male characters but they, in turn, do not respond to the music, the implications can be quite different. This is often the mode of title sequences in which the male characters are introduced to the accompaniment of a non-diegetic song; in these instances, the track commonly augments, for example, their swagger – as in *Shaft* (Gordon Parks, 1971) or *Reservoir Dogs* (Quentin Tarantino, 1992) – or the hypermasculinity of their environment, as at the start of Paul Schrader's *Blue Collar* (1978). In *Shaft* Richard Rowntree 'struts the street' and 'seems to do so in time to the beat of the music' (Dyer, 2012: 160) which is Isaac Hayes's specially written 'Theme for Shaft'. The synchronicity between Shaft walking, the streets of Manhattan, and the soundtrack has the affirming effect of making Shaft belong to his urban world and us to feel at one with it, too. In *Reservoir Dogs*, there is less specific character/music alignment, as the heist group walks through a car park to the strains of 'Little Green Bag' (George Baker Selection). The lyrics are largely incidental ('Lookin' back on the track for a little green bag'); what, conversely, is much more important is the languid cool the song manages to wrap the narrative action in, complementing perfectly the (misplaced and misrecognised) swagger of the suited heisters. Their effortless cool (Susan Fraiman, for example, begins her book *Cool Men and the Second Sex* by referring to having been 'confronted by coolness' [2003: 1] as she started to write about Tarantino) is echoed by the definite but, at the same time, playful bass intro of 'Little Green Bag'. Tarantino's soundtrack music – as meticulously selected as Scorsese's – is as cool as the men it accompanies.

Another title sequence that immediately sets a defiant, macho tone is that of *Blue Collar*. The assertively butch titles are synchronised to Jack Nitzsche's 'Hard Workin' Man', performed by Captain Beefheart, with lyrics by Nitzsche, Ry Cooder (also on guitar) and Schrader. A heavy, blues beat starts up over an establishing image of the 'Checker Motors' factory car park, cutting to a vertical aerial shot of the machine-filled factory floor beneath, dissected by a couple of hard-hatted men. To the accompaniment of drum, bass and now a wailing electric guitar, there is a different view of the factory: an eye-level track looking through a row of giant rolls of sheet metal, followed by a shot of welders working on a car. Then, directly in time to the music, a worker yanks two arms of a machine backwards as Beefheart's guitar plucks a strangulated high note. At the end of the musical phrase there follows the first in a series of freeze-frames as, starting with Richard Pryor, the main cast members' names come up on screen. For the duration of each freeze-frame, the minimal, underlying blues rhythm keeps up, sounding particularly industrial, like the clank of tools on metal. Moving images resume and, alongside

Figure 3.8 *Blue Collar* (Paul Schrader, 1978). The 'hard workin'' welder.

Figure 3.9 *Blue Collar* (Paul Schrader, 1978). Freeze-frame of a 'hard workin' man'.

a fluid, low-level track along some machinery, the song's lyrics begin: 'Got a two-ton hammer . . . I'm a hard workin' fuckin' man / Six-foot solid from the ground'. *Blue Collar*'s title sequence continues like this – half-lit images of the working factory floor to the accompaniment of 'Hard Workin' Man' (written specially for the film), regularly interrupted by freeze-frames and the main credits – until it concludes by bringing together its three narrative strands of the song, Schrader's director credit and the arrival on to the inspection platform of a pristine, finished car. Layers of insistent repetition draw us into this tough, blue-collar world; momentum builds up around the conglomeration of rough lyrics, the insistent, bulky beat of the bass track, the whining guitar and the gritty, almost documentary-esque images of unfinished car skeletons and the bulky frames of the men at work on them silhouetted against a wall of dingy windows. This is largely the opposite of *Shaft*'s man-in-the-city opening, dark interior images of a strenuous and boring dead-end job that, as Nitzsche's lyrics remind us, is what men in the 1970s found themselves doing if they did not 'work as hard as you can' at school.

Blue Collar announces itself to the identifiably macho strains of a heavy blues, 4/4 beat in tune both with the men's hard working environment and their unreconstructed gendered identities. The rhythm of the Nitzsche track is a significant factor in its effectiveness but it is obviously not the case that 4/4 is the only masculine time signature. For *Gladiator*'s first battle, for instance, between the imperialist Romans and the under-resourced defenders of Germania, composer Hans Zimmer starts by using an altogether more delicate 3/4 waltz time (which Zimmer adopts at times for other film scores, such as *Sherlock Holmes*). Zimmer decided to base the first movement of this long orchestral piece on a classical Viennese waltz, initially lending the soundtrack an elegance and fluency that sit contrapuntally to the more primitive goriness of the battle imagery. This then gives way to the freer dissonance of the Gustav Holst-like theme,[4] until finally there comes the more standard 4/4 time signature which signals that both the Roman victory and the end of the sequence are imminent. Much of Zimmer's soundtrack for *Gladiator* is pacy and rousing; this final stage of the battle score is instead slow and stolid, set to slow-motion images of battle, such as Maximus (Russell Crowe) sinking his bloodied sword into a less well-equipped foe. The orchestral strains gradually become more prominent over a final flurry of slowed, underexposed shots of soldiers slugging it out in World War I-like mud against the crepuscular gloom. Crowe stands up, surveys the carnage, raises his hand and declares victory at which point, the remaining Romans cheer, their swords aloft. This dignified and sombre leitmotif comes to rest, in synchronisation with the scene, over a close-up of a relieved but weary Marcus Aurelius (Richard Harris). I will return to this sequence later on.

Master and Commander displays an ambivalent, ironic attitude towards hegemonic masculinity, exemplified by the repeated diegetic playing of music, as Captain Jack Aubrey (Crowe) again and his ship's surgeon, Dr Stephen Maturin (Bettany), bond and unwind by playing violin and cello together. *Master and Commander* ends with such a duet. During the Napoleonic wars, Jack Aubrey commands a British frigate, HMS *Surprise*, which, through Aubrey's obsessive single-mindedness, becomes embroiled in the pursuit of a French privateer, the *Acheron*. By the end of *Master and Commander*, Aubrey thinks he has finally defeated the *Acheron* and, with his mission seemingly accomplished, he imagines he can finally grant Stephen his wish to return to the Galapagos Islands to study the flightless cormorant. Aubrey realises, however, that he has been duped and that the captain of the *Acheron* is not dead, as he had been led to believe, so he issues the order to go in pursuit of the enemy ship, once again dashing Stephen's hopes.

Captain and doctor are tuning their instruments. Jack (a brute in comparison with his more cultured and refined friend) is not insensitive to Stephen's disappointment at not being able, yet, to return to the Galapagos. Holding his violin, he turns to his friend and says 'well, Stephen, the bird's flightless? It's not going anywhere,' at which point, with a self-satisfied twinkle in his eye, he takes his fiddle and starts to strum bars from Luigi Boccherini's *La Musica Notturna delle strade di Madrid*.[5] Stephen, mollified, smiles back and sets himself to play his cello. The Boccherini is a perfect accompaniment to this moment of manly rapprochement: playful and tuneful at the same time as being an intrinsically competitive piece structured around alternating solos by different instruments. This competition is indicated in the 'well I'll show you what I can do' gestures and expressions Crowe and Bettany exchange as they swap the roles of soloist and accompanist. The harmony between Aubrey and Stephen as they 'jam', picking up on each other's riffs, interpreting each other's thoughts, is a crucial dimension of this exchange. The Boccherini's lightness and delicacy sit in counterposition to the narrative tension around it and, just as the duet sets off,[6] it continues over a frantically paced, speeded-up montage of sailors and crew preparing once more for a possible confrontation, as guns are loaded, sails prepared, positions resumed. The action returns to the captain's quarters as Jack takes up his bow and takes over the musical lead from Stephen. As he hits his stride, and as the energetic fifth movement of the Boccherini ('Passa calle') hits its concluding crescendo, the diegetic musical scene is replaced by an aerial shot of Aubrey's ship.

The tone of the conclusion to *Master and Commander* is, as it has been throughout, equivocal in its portrayal of masculinity as a mutable, unstable concept, a finely poised state that encompasses authoritativeness, warmongering and gentility. The decisiveness indicated, however, by the synchronisation of music and action (the sweep of Russell Boyd's aerial camera as it charts the *Surprise*'s course echoing the dancing violin up-bows) or the commanding certainty of the final aerial shot around the *Surprise* (seeming to imply that the end is just another beginning) sits equivocally beside the scene's initial suggestion that a 'real' man like Jack Aubrey would have been happy playing his fiddle all the way home. Throughout this book, scenes present themselves in which masculinity, or at least any circumscribed definition of it, is implied to remain beyond our grasp. The perpetual quest to find real masculinity also turns out to be, perhaps, the most apt metaphor for masculinity itself, that 'right stuff,' which like the horizon at sea, is destined to remain tantalisingly just out of reach. Aubrey has got bogged down in chasing the *Acheron* but that is, to recall Lacan, grossly to misrecognise masculinity. Playing music is one way in which *Master and Commander* demonstrates that there is more to being a man than hunting down the enemy.

BACKDRAFT: A FILM ABOUT FIREFIGHTERS; A FILM ABOUT MEN

Just as certain cinematographers could be credited with pioneering aspects of the style of men's cinema, so certain composers, pre-eminently now Hans Zimmer, have done the same. Of the films discussed in this book, Zimmer wrote the soundtracks for *Backdraft*, *Mission: Impossible 2*, *Gladiator*, *Sherlock Holmes* and *Inception* as well scoring related films, such as *Pirates of the Caribbean* and several other examples of masculine cinema. His rousing scores suit films like *Backdraft* particularly well, a Ron Howard film that abides by the Hollywood predilection for synchrony between music, action and narrative. A movie about firefighters, *Backdraft* is a strongly representative, 1990s, masculinist movie, 'masculinism' being, as defined so memorably by Robin Wood, the 'assumption of the rightness – the *naturalness* – of male *dominance* . . . the *cult* of masculinity' (Wood, 2003: xvii–xviii). 'Masculinism' is woven into *Backdraft*'s very fabric, its characters, narratives, *mise en scène* and overall aesthetic; though characters are flawed, the film's fundamental belief in 'the cult of masculinity' remains intact, as it does in so many of Howard's films.

Backdraft's pre-title sequence, set twenty years before the main story, contains many of the favoured ingredients of masculinist cinema: the recurrent Hollywood plot line of a son's equivocal veneration of the lost/dead father, the macho job and the synchronisation of character, action, music and visual style in the formation of an idealised, unapologetically traditional masculinity. At the film's core sits the unresolved sibling rivalry between the two McCaffrey brothers, both firemen and the sons of a heroic fireman whose death Brian witnessed in 1971. Brian had been taken by his father (played, like Stephen, by Kurt Russell) on a seemingly routine firefighting mission; marking their fire appliance's exit from the station, Zimmer's music begins, quietly but expectantly, before building in momentum, pace and depth to indicate that the men are about to be asked to prove themselves. Brian's father tells his son to give the rope that sounds the horn 'a good yank' as the fire engine is about to negotiate a busy interchange. Shots of the interior of the engine are intercut with shots of the street, the most memorable being the image of bystanders looking up admiringly as the appliance speeds by. There is then a fast track into the vehicle as it speeds round a corner, gleaming red while the music soars. They come to a halt near a burning building and Brian's father looks up at the fire and, with heady anticipation, declares 'there it is', a statement accompanied by a wobbly point-of-view shot of the fire that echoes Brian's perspective. As the music rises to its tumescent climax, it becomes clear that, in *Backdraft*'s terms, the moment at which men are tested is synonymous with the moment of triumph. Synchronicity between multiple cinematic elements at such a juncture is used for the purposes of disambiguation. The soundtrack cranks up again (the brass section is pre-eminent – appropriately enough, considering the luminous brass detailing of the pristine Chicago fire engine) as the firefighters go in to the blaze. Brian waves up at his dad, who is in the process of saving a baby girl, when the music changes abruptly to a minor and foreboding key (with strings prominent this time): the fire is unexpectedly fierce and, as an explosion sounds and flames rage, Brian despairingly calls up 'dad' as his father's helmet ominously tumbles to the ground. This establishing sequence concludes with a mute, slow-motion image of McCaffrey's distraught colleague, John Adcox (Glenn), comforting Brian who picks up his father's helmet as a vertical crane shot pulls out slowly from this tableau of trauma. This image becomes a *Life* magazine cover and immortalises the moment when Brian takes up the talisman that, in death, becomes the signifier for his father.

Like an operatic overture, this opening flashback functions as a prelude to what is to follow by neatly setting out the unity of iconography, character, narrative and stylistic tropes that will thereafter predominate. The use of slow motion to draw attention to heroic masculine exploits, for instance, returns very soon after the titles as firefighters walk into a door to attack a fire are silhouetted against smoke and belching flames. Slow motion again figures as Stephen emerges from the same door once the blaze is under control. The narrative of *Backdraft* has multifarious points of focus, both literal and metaphorical, which are repeatedly brought together, as in the pre-titles sequence: the symbolic connotations of fire; firefighting; an arson investigation; sibling rivalry; the testing and defining of masculinity. An essential component of the satisfaction *Backdraft* offers its audience is precisely its calculated accessibility: that it signals clearly not only where it is at but also where it is going, even if elements of the plot keep us guessing. The twin role played by *mise en scène* and visual style in cementing a strong sense of closure is fundamental. Against yet another backdrop of soaring orange flames, various plot strands are resolved: Adcox turns out to be the arsonist the firefighters have been mopping up after (for grossly misguided but not altogether reprehensible reasons) and the McCaffrey brothers finally reach a state of rapprochement, but only once Adcox, their surrogate father, has plunged to his death and Stephen lies dying.

So what is *Backdraft* ultimately about? The final fire's cascading ramparts, the uncontrollable, writhing hose spewing forth its unstemmable water and the violent flames that suck morally equivocal men to their deaths recall the

Figure 3.10 *Backdraft* (Ron Howard, 1991). Stephen falling into the fire.

iconography of hell. In *Backdraft*, however, fire is an ambivalent symbol. Though firemen refer to the need to tame it and not to let it sense their fear (thus implying that fire could share certain traits with femininity), they also evoke its complex affinity to masculinity: one fireman commends Stephen for taking 'that fire by the balls'; Adcox welcomes two rookies to 'the world of old man fire'; and the arson investigator, Rimgale (Robert de Niro), tells Brian that 'the only way to beat it is to think like it . . . the only way to kill it is to love it a little'. Stephen, especially, demonstrates, until the very end, the sort of equivocal, tortured response to fire that suggests fire, rather like the 'right stuff', is a subliminal, ultimately unknowable masculine force.

Most clearly resolved via the convoluted imagery of these final scenes is the brothers' relationship. Stephen implausibly survives (for a while) the fall that kills Adcox by landing on a platform jutting out into the cavernous warehouse's flaming abyss and, though Brian does tend him, he then leaves his brother in favour of finally finding the hero inside by instead helping to stem the fire. Brian who, until this point, has been overly sensitive and a little toughness short of a real man, looks up at the marauding blaze with a mixture of attraction and awe, belatedly understanding the ambivalent rapport with fire that, as he knows, good firefighters possess. He grabs the convulsive hose, brings it under control and aims it at the blanket of flames. Something resembling Russian marching music starts up, the camera cranes upwards and, in slow motion (of course), Brian demonstrates that he is, after all, a man, as Stephen looks on and exclaims exultantly: 'Look at him, that's my brother, goddammit'. Stephen dies in the ambulance holding Brian's hand but, as he (perhaps because he) loses a brother, Brian finally reaches a state of manhood.

In *Backdraft* the strain of masculinity, its equivocation, its fear of contradiction, comes out in the hysterical, protesting *mise en scène*, the flamboyant bombast of which is used to mask male doubts and fissures. Its insistent and uniform visual style becomes a hysterical overstatement of a belief in the integrity, straightforwardness and straightness of masculinity but, just as Freud's adamant reaffirmation of 'normal' sex ends up flagging just how 'abnormal' this prescriptive normality is, *Backdraft* also, with its powerful attachment to strong (hetero) masculinity as expressed through the simple stridency of its audio and visual styles, shows itself to be protesting too much.

After the most well-attended funeral since Annie's in *Imitation of Life* (1959), a fire station bell rings and a fast-cut series of images of men getting into a fire engine establishes that they are responding to an emergency call. Brian does not look as if he is going to join them but then, at the last minute, slides down the pole and jumps into the appliance as it moves off, just as he had done on his first day. As Adcox had done with him, so Brian takes a probationer under his wing. As the music reaches its zenith, a zoom into Brian shows him going from contemplative uncertainty to knowing serenity. The image then cuts to an aerial shot of a long straight road stretching all the way to the centre of Chicago with, at the end of it where smoke is sidling into the sky, a fire that needs quelling. The music is unambiguously triumphant again; Brian, the omniscient camera tells us, is on the straight and sure road towards manliness.

RESERVOIR DOGS: COOLNESS AND MEN WALKING

In terms of its cast, as well as its subject matter, *Reservoir Dogs* is a very male film. Though the macho swagger of Tarantino's first feature, and its notable lack of female characters, proclaim its masculinity, the film also possesses a more fragile, less macho side that emerges, for instance, in the emotional bond that develops between Mr White (Harvey Keitel) and Mr Orange (Tim Roth). The film's pervasive sensuality and ambivalent eroticism are rooted in its fluent and adrenalin-inducing visual style, as non-narrative elements are mobilised to express the narrative's inherent attitudes to masculinity. By way of trying to define, or convey, the excitement generated in its audience by its aesthetic style, I will focus on the post-title sequence of the 'reservoir dogs' walking in a group out of the diner.

The film opens with the male characters having breakfast, about to embark on a heist. They are engaged in one of Tarantino's trademark stream-of-consciousness riffs that culminates in an argument about the pros and cons of tipping and, especially on first viewing, *what* is being said is of secondary importance to *how* it is being said. With the first frame we enter the fast-talking banter mid-sentence; the camera, likewise mid-thought as it were, tracks slowly around a table at which is seated a group men, most of whom are dressed in black suits and white shirts except the boss, Joe, and his son (Chris

Penn) in a garish shell suit and adorned in bling. The track cuts from medium to close-up, but the strongly insistent circular movement continues virtually uninterrupted until the camera stops as Mr White snatches a notebook from Joe. After this brief hiatus, the circling camera movement resumes, stopping once again as Joe gets up to pay, which is when the tipping argument starts. Joe, these moves tell us, is the boss.

After he has persuaded the reluctant Mr Pink (Steve Buscemi) to make a contribution to the tip, a radio playing 'K-Billy's Super Sounds of the Seventies' intrudes. The image cuts to outside the diner, as the posse emerges in slow motion from right of frame, smoking, clad in undifferentiated mono-chrome suits and putting on their sunglasses. The framing and the angle shift as the men switch to walking in close-up towards the head-height camera, the titles going through each actor in turn, their names appearing under them. Tarantino has referred to Jean-Pierre Melville's well-dressed gangsters as wearing suits of armour,[7] and here there is a comparably strong sense of Tarantino's gangsters going into battle: instead of armour they have suits; instead of weapons they carry shades; and the slow motion accentuates the confident, nonchalant sashay in their step.

Once the main actors have been introduced, the close-ups are exchanged for a low-level long shot from behind; the jaunty chorus of 'Little Green Bag' plays on as the men walk away from the camera and the film title rolls upwards into frame, proclaiming that these men 'are . . . *Reservoir Dogs*', a collective identity that is enigmatic and impenetrable. There is then a cut to black for the remainder of the credits, towards the end of which we can just begin to pick out the gasps and groans of Mr Orange who has been shot and is bleeding profusely all over the pristine pale leather back seat of a car while being comforted by Mr White who, while driving, attempts to reassure him that he is not about to die. The 'dogs' have thus remained unblemished, virile and active symbols of functioning, superlative masculinity until precisely the end of the title sequence, and the ease, grace and confidence they ooze at the outset are resolutely undermined by the remainder of the film, beginning with this messy and bloody puncturing of Mr Orange's 'suit of armour'.

The allure of *Reservoir Dogs* was, at the time of its release, complex. Tarantino remarked: 'I've always said that the mark of any good action movie is that when you get through seeing it, you want to dress like the character' (Dargis, 1994: 17). It is intriguing that Tarantino equates the existence of desire- and narcissism-drenched identification with the action film, and I am arguing here for a correspondingly layered form of identification in relation to masculinity and *mise en scène*. Not that the films necessarily make audiences want to look like the characters but, rather, that they convey a sense of what it is to be them and feel like to be them, the essential elements of men's cinema spectator/film camaraderie. This is manifestly not a straightforward

Figure 3.11 *Reservoir Dogs* (Quentin Tarantino, 1992). The dogs walking.

Figure 3.12 *Reservoir Dogs* (Quentin Tarantino, 1992). Mr Pink puts on his shades.

Figure 3.13 *Reservoir Dogs* (Quentin Tarantino, 1992). The dogs walk away.

form of identification, and it is certainly not one that presumes the images of masculinity on the screen to be idealised ones. The ambivalence of our affinity to the 'reservoir dogs', however, is tied to Tarantino's use of stylistic elements, especially slow motion and music. Just as the men's swaggering majesty and unified coolness are soon betrayed as illusory, so the surety of the visual style draws attention to, rather than veils, the residual fear that masculinity might be insubstantial, fragile or the ultimate illusion. The aim, I think, of Tarantino's opening to *Reservoir Dogs* is to sweep us along with the momentum of the slow-motion walk, the culty soundtrack, the men's cool costumes and shades, and to make us then interpret the subsequently far less perfect representations of masculinity with this supremely confident opening always in mind. The cameraman on *Reservoir Dogs*, Andrej Sekula, commented that the 'dogs' stride out of the diner at the beginning of the film '*Wild Bunch* style' and with 'a sort of unnatural slowness' (Dawson, 1997: 62). *Reservoir Dogs* – the product of Hollywood's best-known film nerd – is knowing, ironic and reflexive. It defines itself in relation to past cinema as well as having become, virtually instantaneously, a trend-setting, definitive film in its own right. The dogs' cool is transferable and tangible.

A significant factor in the effectiveness of the men-walking-together motif is that it is recognisable and familiar: *Reservoir Dogs* works at framing and conveying masculinity not just because of what it does unilaterally but because of the fact that it recalls self-consciously past films such as *The Wild Bunch, Once Upon a Time in the West* or *The Right Stuff* and those films' use of the group of men walking purposefully to fight or to work. In *The Right Stuff*, just after they have stood up to the NASA scientists and become men as opposed to 'lab rabbits', by insisting on having a window inserted into the capsule design,[8] the Mercury 7 astronauts are, as Charity observes,

> rewarded with an iconic heroic image: the seven in slow motion, striding manfully abreast towards the camera through the long NASA corridor, with shafts of light rippling on their shiny silver space suits and Bill Conti whipping up the score. (Charity, 1997: 66)

Charity goes on to quote director Philip Kaufman on this scene, whose comments emphasise the peculiarly American, as well as cinematic, quality of such iconography:

> They have that swagger almost like they're a gang from *The Wanderers*, about to get into a battle with a neighbouring gang, in this case the Russians – that sort of American swagger . . . For me, that's freedom without viciousness, that kind of bonding and team spirit which, within proper bounds, I really like. (1997: 66)

Kaufmann here picks out the swagger and the bonding of men walking in unison, suggesting, as the walk does in *Reservoir Dogs* or *The Wild Bunch*, that its unity can conceal problems and issues.

A later astronaut movie, *Apollo 13* (Ron Howard, 1995), shows how conventionalised the group of men walking purposefully has become. Three Apollo astronauts are making their way to their capsule, about to be rocketed to the Moon; the sequence is short, perhaps, because its iconic familiarity means it does not require extended exposition. After a protracted, emotion- and tension-mounting build-up, audiences hardly needed the subtitle carrying the information about this being launch day but the sequence is about validation not surprise. The three Apollo astronauts emerge from the lift on to the walkway between launch tower and rocket. After brief close-ups of their legs striding to work, the image reverts to a classic medium shot of the astronauts marching towards both camera and capsule, staring into the middle distance and clutching their oxygen tanks as if they are briefcases: three commuters with Bibendum-like, as opposed to besuited, silhouettes. Their walk is almost imperceptibly slowed down and, in conclusion, there is a cut back to a high-angle crane shot of the walkway as the astronauts continue towards the rocket, the point of emphasis now being the magnitude of the task, as opposed to the men themselves. There are unity, symmetry and rhythm to the sequence that are evocatively comforting, as the camaraderie between the men is augmented and bolstered by a comparable synchronicity of aesthetic elements. James Horner's score, throughout *Apollo 13* an essential part of its strong homogeneity, here moves towards a well-worked climax, the last beat of the movement coinciding with the opening shot of the next scene: 'Mission Control, Houston, Texas'. The ultimate irony, of course, is that *Apollo 13* might lack Tarantino's ironic tone but it is not in the end that different from *Reservoir Dogs*, as disaster soon strikes *Apollo 13*'s mission and the men nearly do not return safely to Earth.

Our adrenalin builds as we find ourselves identifying with the group of striding men but often against our natural intellectual inclinations. This ambivalence is demonstrably shared by many of the more recent (and post-feminist) examples of men walking, whose pride invariably comes before a fall. There is something undeniably powerful in such images of bonding and supportiveness but, in many instances, what is ultimately exposed is the instability of a form of male bonding overly reliant on gesture and performance.

GOODFELLAS AND *THE AMERICAN PRESIDENT*: POWERFUL MAN WALKING

The group dynamic of men walking in tandem is a repeated trope of men's cinema but what about the single man walking? Is this comparably indicative of male confidence and power? The single man walking (if you include the lone man on horseback) is just as iconic and has just as long a history as the male group walking. In many westerns, for instance, the hero walks or rides into and out of town alone. The solitary male figure generally exemplifies a different kind of masculinity to his buddied counterparts: untouchable and lonelier but also more self-sufficient. The title sequence of *Shaft* provides a quintessential example of this, as John Shaft (Richard Rowntree) is shown to be at one with the streets, this time of New York City. After a high-angle, realistically grainy shot, and to the accompaniment of car horns and the generalised rumble of traffic, there is a partial zoom in to the neon fronts of the cinemas and theatres of Times Square, panning past them as if searching for someone or something. Then, emerging from the pavement as it were, comes the film's title *SHAFT* in bold red, to the opening percussive strains of Isaac Hayes's 'Theme from *Shaft*', followed moments later by the introductory twangs of a bass guitar, this time synchronised to the emergence from the subway of an African American man who strides confidently along the grimy street. The man in his dapper tweed suit, polo neck jumper and brown leather coat is private detective John Shaft. *Shaft*'s juxtaposition of long pans and shorter low-angle close-ups of its eponymous protagonist helps swiftly to establish the edgy, pulsing inner city environment as the optimal backdrop for Rowntree's strutting masculinity. Shaft does not stop walking (except briefly as, in one of the low-angle close-ups, he looks about him with the self-consciousness of a matinee idol having his picture snapped). He dodges between moving cars and flips a driver the bird who tries not to stop for him as he jaywalks across a street, eventually coming to rest in his local shoeshine parlour on his way to the office, where he gets into a fight with two gangsters lying in wait for him. John Shaft, his nonchalant walk declares, owns the streets.

I intend in this section to compare two distinct sequences that nevertheless share the trait of a man in a position of power walking in the company of a woman: Henry Hill (Ray Liotta) taking Karen (Lorraine Bracco) to the Copacabana Club, looking to impress her on their first date, in Martin Scorsese's *Goodfellas* (1990) and the opening scene of *The American President* (Rob Reiner, 1995) in which President Andrew Shepherd (Michael Douglas) walks to the Oval Office first thing Monday morning. The sequences display a similar fluidity, though one (Michael Ballhaus's for *Goodfellas*) is a single-take Steadicam shot whereas the sequence in *The American President* looks similar but is, in fact, made up of several individual shots edited together to make a comparably seamless impression. Both evidently required meticulous logistical planning which is emphasised rather than concealed.

The Steadicam shot in *Goodfellas*, a technical tour de force, shows Henry, a young Irish gangster, escorting Karen on their first date. Ballhaus manifestly influenced the film's camera style. Once one of Fassbinder's cinematographers,[9] Ballhaus has, of Scorsese's films to date, shot *After Hours*, *The Color of Money*, *The Last Temptation of Christ*, *The Age of Innocence*, *Gangs of New*

York and *The Departed*, all of which share a characteristically extravagant, expressive visual style. In addition, a flourish, such as the dynamic sweep of the Steadicam in *Goodfellas*, is reminiscent of Ballhaus's other work, such as the swooping aerial shot over the water into New York that opens Mike Nichols's *Working Girl* (1988). Henry has just picked up Karen from home. The single take commences, after they have got out of the car, with a medium close-up of Henry handing a parking valet his keys and is choreographed to The Crystals' 1963 single 'Then He Kissed Me', the opening chords of which sound just on the edit into Henry's hand and draws to a close just as Henry and Karen take their seats inside the club. The timing of the visuals to the Crystals' song is significant, not just because of what the song is about (a girl's old-fashioned, quaintly naive account of being kissed and proposed to) but because it renders the shot self-contained, dreamy, slightly detached from the rest of the film – as from Karen's perspective (as she eagerly lets Henry sweep her off her feet) it undoubtedly is. The classic perfection of the three-minute pop song is matched by the comparable perfection of this long, 'look-at-me' single take. The Steadicam in *Goodfellas* follows behind Henry and Karen until the very end and, unless remarked upon, their movement is continuous.

After handing over his car keys, Henry, with one arm protectively shielding Karen's back, crosses the street. Once on the other side, he takes Karen into the Copacabana Club by the back way ('better than waiting in line'), the long queue of those also trying to get in parting for them like obedient waves. They head down some stairs and, at the bottom, Henry opens a door before greeting and paying the doorman. The couple then turn right down a corridor, and Henry shakes hands with a couple of men and joshes with a couple canoodling in the corner ('Every time I come here! Every time!'). Henry is at ease here, a regular guest who is part of the fraternity, a 'made man'. The relaxed, elegant fluidity of the camera's motion conveys firstly Henry's mastery of the situation, that he belongs, and secondly the allure of this world to Karen, a nicely brought-up, middle-class Jewish girl for whom the Crystals' song is far more appropriate than a Mafia-run nightclub.

Henry and Karen weave through the bright bustle of the noisy kitchen and Henry tips another doorman as they finally enter the smoky pink club. The shot remains unbroken but Henry and Karen temporarily stop walking as a waiter talks to Henry about where he will position their table (which turns out to be right at the front). The camera begins to move again but this time it follows the table that has hastily materialised, carried aloft by another waiter who negotiated the tightly packed tables already in place, its billowing white tablecloth standing out amid the seedy gloom. A lamp is found, placed on the little round table and plugged in, at which point Henry and Karen come back into view and sit down but only after Henry has leant over to greet the people seated behind them. Karen removes her gloves and remarks on the peculiarity of Henry having liberally dispersed $20 tips.

Karen's white gloves resonate with her demure innocence and conventionality, totally at odds with Henry's ostentatious amorality. Just as Karen has removed the gloves and placed them in front of her (their pristine whiteness sitting easily with the tablecloth's unsullied purity), a hovering waiter presents Henry with a bottle of wine, from 'Mr Tony over there'. The camera then pans over to Mr Tony's nearby table, Tony acknowledging Henry's gratitude. As the camera pans back to Henry and Karen, 'Then He Kissed Me' winds down and, as it fades out, Karen asks Henry, 'What do you do?' to which he offers the familiar lie that he is 'in construction'. Karen remarks that his hands are too soft for someone in that line of work and Henry counters that he is a union delegate. The camera then pans over to the stage, where 'the king of the one-liners, Henny Youngman' has just arrived, a middle-aged, sexist comedian who opens his set with a weary dig at his wife ('I'm glad to be here – take my wife, please!'). The single take ends.

This continuous shot, for all its uninterrupted majesty, is about conflict or, rather, how conflicts can find themselves subsumed or glossed over, the most obvious of which is Karen's internalised struggle between desiring Henry and knowing that he is no good. Karen's disavowal is important to the Steadicam shot's effect: that she clearly knows what is going on and realises that Henry is a gangster but nevertheless is willing to suppress this knowledge because she is in awe of his lifestyle and evident power. The fluidity of the Steadicam's movement – the manner in which it sidles and shimmies with effortless ease through the corridors and kitchen or between the tables – connotes what it feels like to be sucked in willingly to all this and to enjoy both the lifestyle and the act of submission. Though executed differently, this act of succumbing to the allure of the Mafia has featured before in *Goodfellas*. Henry is Irish and, until he is 'made up' and enters the Mafia fold, he is an outsider, just as Karen is when she is ushered into the Copacabana. The sensuous slow-motion close-ups of Paulie Cicero's friends' shoes, clothes and accessories as they emerge from their cars at the beginning of the film capture the schoolboy Henry's fascination with, and desire to be part of, the gangsters' world while, later, the classic fetishising pan up the adult Henry's body, from his tassled loafers to face, as he leans against the bonnet of a swanky car waiting for a consignment to arrive at the airport, confirms that he has arrived. Just as the youthful Henry found himself irresistibly drawn to the world of Paulie Cicero so, as an adult, he is unstoppable in his seduction of Karen.

Karen's role in this, however, is not merely to be duped. Just as she realises that Henry does not 'work in construction', so the steamroller quality of the extended Steadicam shot enacts an elaborate negotiation between marking the violence, the criminality, and brushing them aside, pretending they no longer exist. This long take is also fundamentally erotic as Karen is not only being inveigled into the milieu of the mob but is falling in love with Henry and, though her refinement (the black dress, the white gloves) might imply she is looking for the straightforward chastity invoked by 'Then He Kissed Me', her glances over at Henry as they walk into the club and the eagerness with which she represses all knowledge of what he does for a living imply she would rather become the mobster's moll. Our seduction at the hands of the Steadicam's sensuous dynamism serves to reinforce how a 'nice' girl like Karen could fall for a criminal like Henry: it is not just Karen who is being swept into the bowels of the Copacabana but us via the unrelenting camera. As with Scorsese's use of an expressive camera style in *Raging Bull*, the overt synchronisation of camera and character is only partial. Echoing the sequence's inherent ambivalence (that Henry is attractive but also a criminal), it appears that our point of view is not synchronous with Karen's. The moment when Henry and Karen pause for the waiter to find them a table seems extremely important, as it is then (the resumption of the camera's and the characters' movements notwithstanding) that the critical distance between Karen's limited perspective and our greater omniscience is underscored. The gangsters' world is attractive and smooth, like Ballhaus's shot, but the short cessation of movement in the middle of the courting couple's journey to the best table in the house (magicked, as it were, out of thin air) serves as a reminder that the shot is a performative flourish that has been intricately woven and meticulously choreographed. With this critical distance comes the inevitable recognition that the club's and Henry's charms and glamour are merely superficial.

David Bordwell, in a discussion of 'the prowling camera', cites this *Goodfellas* single take and remarks that 'thanks to lighter cameras and stabilizers like Steadicam, the shot pursuing one or two characters down hallways, through room after room, indoors and outdoors and back again, has become ubiquitous' (Bordwell, 2006: 134–5). While undoubtedly correct in this, Bordwell is not especially interested in dwelling on what the effect of this prowling might be. The 'prowling camera' does not do just one thing or produce just one effect. In the opening sequence of the romantic comedy *The American President*, the fictional titular president, Andrew Shepherd (Douglas) is heading for the Oval Office at the beginning of his working week. *The American President* was scripted by Aaron Sorkin, and the film's opening sequence, though smooth and energetic in its own right, is especially noteworthy retrospectively as an early prototype for the 'power walk' which became a staple feature of the early series of Sorkin's later creation *The West Wing* and is still frequently parodied, such as on *The Graham Norton Show* when Martin Sheen, who played the series's fictional president Josiah 'Jed' Bartlet (as well as playing Shepherd's chief of staff in *The American President*), performed a mock 'power walk' through and round the back of the BBC studio. The *West*

Wing's renditions of the power walk used Steadicam which made them appear immediately slick and robust. What remains interesting about the incarnation in *The American President* of an ostensibly similar cinematic moment is that here the film's cameraman, John Seale, creates a comparable effect by using diverse editing and camera techniques.

The title sequence of *The American President* is a conventional, bland montage of the portraits of past American presidents displayed in the White House, languidly edited together using cross-fades, and captured by a camera that, though constantly moving, is leisurely and staid. The tone of these titles (accompanied by a lushly anonymous orchestral score) is sonorous and serious, and the sequence concludes with a classic wide shot of the White House exterior. A sharp edit marks the transition to the start of Shepherd's walk, a brusque contrast with the stroll through the icons of American presidential history that had preceded it. A security man whispers into a concealed microphone ('Liberty's moving'), announcing that the president is on the move. President Shepherd emerges with Jane, his PA, who is running through the day's schedule as they walk, briskly and purposefully, through the corridors of power, the sequence thereby collapsing, as subsequently occurs in *The West Wing*, literal and metaphorical signification. Shepherd strides dynamically towards the camera while Jane struggles a bit to keep up; they get closer to the camera and turn, the fixed camera panning round in unison. The meetings schedule Jane runs through includes one with American Fisheries at which the president will be presented with a prize fish. Shepherd tells Jane to remind him 'to schedule more events when someone gives me a really big fish' but the drollery is lost on Jane who is busy writing this instruction down. The use of humour is compelling because, though it temporarily interrupts the power *talk*, the quip does not detract attention from the power *walk*, as Shepherd does not alter pace, look or tone. There is no faltering, no let up. Nothing, this seamless progress convinces us, will make the president digress from his mission.

Shepherd and Jane enter a lift as the dialogue continues uninterrupted. The lift doors open to reveal Lewis Rothschild (Shepherd's press secretary, played by Michael J. Fox) waiting for them. Shepherd continues his walk to work and Rothschild joins him and Jane, expressing concern at the omission from a speech the president made the night before of plans to tighten gun controls. Leaving out a piece of liberal policy from a speech about 'the great society',[10] is an important indicator of Shepherd's political leanings (as well as his caution) but, however significant such a detail is, it again does nothing to arrest or stall him: Shepherd had started walking the second the lift doors had opened, this time away from the camera and flanked by Lewis to his right and Jane to his left. He then makes his way along a corridor and through another door, at which point there is an edit to a frontal shot, a switch in angle that coincides

Figure 3.14 *The American President* (Rob Reiner, 1995). Andrew Shepherd walks to his office.

Figure 3.15 *The American President* (Rob Reiner, 1995). Andrew Shepherd walking and talking.

with both the group's passage through a door and a changeover of security personnel.

Key to the effect of the sequence is that there is no break in momentum, not in Shepherd's tank-like progress towards the Oval Office nor in the pace of his conversation, the tone of his voice or the direction of his gaze which remains focused on the middle distance in front of him, often a look denoting determination and strength. The only thing that does change is the topic of conversation which is equally seamlessly co-ordinated with the walking. On passing through this second set of doors into the portico running alongside the garden, for example, the subject switches to Shepherd's high approval ratings, though there is also a secondary exchange going on in which the gardener addresses the president, Jane whispers to him that his name is Charlie, and Shepherd returns the greeting with no discernible hesitation in either the walk or the main conversation. The walk's purposefulness and momentum are generated throughout using a combination of Steadicam and fixed-mounted images, individual shot sequences being generally built up using a wider shot (usually showing the characters walking to camera), a profile close-up as the characters walk in front of the camera on their way past it and then a pan or Steadicam track round as they continue away from it. Unlike the single-take Steadicam shot in *Goodfellas,* various camera angles are intercut here but the seamless editing ('seamless' because the cuts almost invariably come as the direction alters, the characters go through a door or a character enters or exists the frame) creates a comparable effect.

Through a third set of doors, the presidential entourage enters the inner sanctum of the Oval Office and the network of offices that surround it. This sequence has got progressively busier and here, while Shepherd and Lewis continue their discussion of the 'great society' speech, aides and office staff bustle around them, a busyness signalled by switches in framing and camera angles as well as interlaced blocking. The rise in adrenalin produced merely by following this sequence is interrupted again by an amusing exchange between Shepherd and Lewis as the president asks his press secretary to reduce by half his morning caffeine intake, only to be informed that Lewis does not drink coffee, at which point the president advises Lewis to hit himself 'over the head with a baseball bat'. Once again the shift in the script's tone is not matched by, for example, a change in vocal register from Michael Douglas or a lapse in movement. After wishing one of his office workers 'happy birthday' (again with a subsidiary exchange with Jane going on, in which Shepherd checks he has sent her some flowers), the president swoops past his chief secretary, Mrs Chapil, who is holding out his mug of coffee in readiness, which he takes, again without pausing, before finally arriving at his office. The conversation between Shepherd and his aides about the rise in his approval ratings continues unabated over another edit. As Shepherd at last comes to rest so does the camera and, throughout the next scene (a Monday morning briefing between the president and his close staff), the editing and framing comprise a quieter and more conventional mix of mid-close-up shots/reverse shots.

Particularly in light of it being the film's opening scene, the rhythm of this sequence of *The American President* is especially significant. The effect is to plunge the audience straight into Shepherd's high-pressure world and consequently, while compelling us to marvel at his capacity to manage a situation that could easily (on a technical as well as a narrative level) unravel, to lure us into his life and the pace at which he lives it. The extended single-take in *Goodfellas* is more sensuously erotic but both evoke the simplified linearity of stereotypical male sexuality. While it may be that male sexuality, like *Goodfellas* and *The American President,* is not actually this simple, these goal-oriented sequences do posit the possibility, however ironically, that this is how men see themselves and their sexuality. The stridency and linear trajectory of the man-walking sequence mimic an oversimplified conceptualisation of the male sex act precisely in order, I would suggest, to problematise it. Though these two sequences are different in tone and offer different attitudes towards this masculine fixation with maintaining a powerful appearance, it has been illuminating to discuss the examples from *Goodfellas* and *The American President* in tandem because, though in both superficial smoothness is used to mask and elide ambiguities (as it had done in the title sequence of *Reservoir Dogs*), the two films have achieved a comparable effect by different means. The pace of these two men-walking sequences creates a quite specific relationship between meaning and style, as both are insistent but not urgent or rushed. There is a clear sense in both that the men are in control and that internalised ambivalences and uncertainties are being suppressed or brushed aside quite literally by the momentum of their walk. In turn, the spectator's ability to remain impervious to the effects of this momentum is limited. Coupled with the symbolic alliance to sexuality, both sequences coerce their respective audiences into falling in love with masculinity as well as with power.

GLADIATOR: MASCULINE CENTRALITY AND SLOW-MOTION HEROICS

Gladiator (Ridley Scott, 2000), via the mutual interaction of character, narrative, *mise en scène* and style, is exemplary of a certain tendency in men's cinema to weave a film around its protagonist (in this case Maximus Decimus Meridius, played by Russell Crowe) so holistically that signification emanates, almost exclusively, from the symbiosis between action and hero. In narrative terms *Gladiator* might be considered old-fashioned (it recalls *Spartacus*, for example, as well as, in turn, heralding a mini-revival of the blockbuster epic) but its prioritisation of visual spectacle, which arguably diverts identification and attraction on to the CG special effects and away from Maximus, is modern and less nostalgic. Of significant interest is how specifically *Gladiator* builds up the symbiosis between action and hero, in particular the juxtaposition, in battle and gladiatorial combat scenes especially, between fast cutting (including computer-generated images) and slow-motion close-ups of Maximus. I shall look in more detail at the battle at the beginning of the film against the Germanic barbarians and the final gladiatorial contest in the Coliseum.

Maximus is the most significant and dynamic of Emperor Marcus Aurelius' generals, a status emphasised at the outset of *Gladiator* before the battle against the barbarians has commenced. The film's opening shots are of Crowe's hand skimming heads of corn as he walks through them (an image that is repeated several times and which we later learn is Maximus' recurring fantasy about returning home to his family). He then echoes this action by walking through his lines of troops on the eve of battle, parting them as he had done the corn and inspiring them, as Henry V did his 'band of brothers' before Agincourt. Crowe bends down and grabs a handful of dust which he smells as he looks over at his wolfhound. He mounts his white horse and issues the comically brusque, jarringly inelegant encouragement to a fellow officer: 'strength and honour; unleash hell'. What is striking about this opening is the relationship between the masses (both the sheaths of corn and the Roman infantrymen) and their natural leader; in essence, the two move in synchronisation and have a feudalistic, patriarchal symbiosis, the many being dependent upon and commanded by one man. After Maximus has motivated his troops with an inelegant and flatly delivered speech brimful of old-fashioned platitudes ('. . . what we do in life echoes in eternity'), catapults are cocked and fired, flaming arrows are lit and sent flying into the enemy lines, and the orchestral score quickens in expectation.[11] This is the conventional prelude to the ensuing battle but also a rather more specific build-up to a battle that will confirm the action's concentration around Maximus.

The principal battle sequence begins with Maximus' dog (already established as the general's alter ego) hurtling through fire and trees into the fray, soon followed by Maximus charting a similar course. Swiftly established is the manner in which *Gladiator* will represent combat, that is, via a disorienting, kaleidoscopic series of incomplete staccato images (the average shot during the more frenetic passages lasts under a second) from a multitude of different perspectives and angles. As an action style, Scott's recalls Peckinpah's in *The Wild Bunch*, though this is very much a sanitised, deradicalised version, as Peckinpah's innovations, upon their assimilation into the slick homogeneity of the modern action film aesthetic, have, over time, been watered down. Still, as was the case in *The Wild Bunch*, each truncated image in *Gladiator* is an incoherent, inconclusive fragment which only comes to make sense, patchwork style, through contextualisation. The flamboyant entry of Maximus, charging down the hillside on his white steed to slice through the head and helmet of a barbarian slumped against a tree, is the narrative intervention to give these otherwise exhaustingly cut-up images a focal logic. Scott and John Mathieson, *Gladiator*'s director of photography, use a variety of techniques to achieve the effect of rush and violence: for example, alternating and changing shutter speeds while filming or later editing together truncated fragments of shots. The effect is to make Maximus, when he enters, appear unstoppable.

Having established such momentum, Scott, like Peckinpah, elects at crucial junctures to slow down the action, as when Maximus decapitates a barbarian foe. He then resumes the frantic splurge of breathless close-ups which eventually leads to another violent encounter, this time on the ground after Maximus has been thrown from his horse. The repeated interruption of this battle scene by brief, slow-motion interludes focused on Maximus' involvement serves to make the sequence cohere around him. These are crucial punctuations; the slow motion is slight, not excessive, but its effect is to draw us into Maximus. As the refrain from the dominant (4/4) orchestral piece of the soundtrack score rises, images are slowed right down, and the end of this monumental scene is signposted, as, in the fading golden light of the end of the filming day, torch flames trail in a messy blur across the screen, half lighting a Bosch-like scene of chaotic carnage. This finale is, again, topped and tailed by Maximus, ending with the amplified sound of his exhausted breath superimposed on to the soundtrack as he, once more in slight slow motion, raises his sword aloft in weary triumph.

Such a juxtaposition, as part of an action sequence, between short, almost violently abrupt shots and more leisurely, legato, slow-motion (usually close-up) images of the hero has become, since Peckinpah, a relatively familiar convention of men's action cinema. Arroyo talks of Brian de Palma's use of this contrast in *Mission: Impossible*, referring to sequences that involve 'quick cuts, to enhance the sense of danger and to give the impression of movement' and 'slow motion, to arrest and break down movement' (Arroyo, 2000: 25). For Arroyo 'the combined effect is that of the sublime' and he goes on to dissect this generic use of contrast:

> The slow motion is thrilling to watch, but it's also fascinating because such a technique, so typical of the contemporary action/spectacle film, reduces difference into equivalence while divorcing an object from its properties. Here a drop of sweat and a knife are equally dangerous. (25)

The juxtaposition between fast and slow close-ups is not just an aesthetic affectation; it also creates an affinity between spectator and hero amid all the active turmoil of the surrounding scene and, through this proximity, establishes the idea that the hero, able to stand back for a moment from the freneticism surrounding him, controls his environment. Maximus, while fully implicated in the violence and chaos of the battles, is also singled out to become the epicentre of the conflict, the figure around which it evolves and the character who, more broadly, dictates the film's course.

What *Gladiator* has over, for example, *Troy*'s (Wolfgang Petersen, 2004) use of a similar juxtaposition to emphasise the supremacy in battle of Achilles, is Maximus' symbolic as well as narrative centrality: for instance, that he is a good soldier, a good man and a good father, identified by Marcus Aurelius as his rightful successor (over his biological son, Commodus) following the triumph in Germania. *Gladiator* reveals its patriarchal core, making Maximus the epicentre of everything that is strong and good: he has an affinity with the men under his command; he was a loyal, loving father and husband; he is the protector of Rome and its temporarily lost republican morality; he is the leader and saviour of the gladiators and eventually becomes Commodus' nemesis.

The various facets of Maximus' narrative, formal and psychological significance come together in the lengthy gladiatorial combat sequence in the Coliseum which concludes with the confrontation with Commodus (who believes Maximus to be dead) that makes up the symbolic centre of the film. This sequence (which occurs a little over halfway into the movie) opens with the gladiators emerging from the dark bowels of the Coliseum, and starts in a strikingly similar way to the Germania battle, with Maximus going through his ritual of rubbing soil between his palms and smelling it. There follows a close-up of Maximus donning a helmet before the gladiators march up into the light of the arena, Maximus' helmet being the one that is picked out by the rays of the sun penetrating the shadows. As they emerge into the light and squint at the vast crowds, a circular Steadicam shot, echoing Sergio Leone's, corrals the gladiators and mimics the spherical arena, its elegant sweep strengthening the sense of solidarity between the gladiators and cementing the bond between gladiators and crowd. The camera then comes to rest at a slightly low angle, literally looking up at Maximus. As Cassius (David Hemmings) announces the re-enactment of the 'Second fall of mighty Carthage' in which the gladiators are to play the 'barbarian hoards', a trail of chariots emerges through a set of gates. There is a close-up of Maximus (once more recalling the opening battle) as he harks back to his days in the army and instils in his fellow gladiators the need to work as a unit, because 'if we stay together we survive'. Once again, via the convergence of dialogue, *mise en scène* and style, the idea of unity and camaraderie is built up around the notion that success will follow only if Maximus is there to lead and orchestrate it. After Maximus has given his 'troops' his pep talk as he had done in Germania, there follows a frenzied montage of short, dramatic shots from multiple angles depicting the hostilities between gladiators and chariots (a chariot crashes over almost into the camera; a female charioteer being sliced in half), interspersed with the familiar close-ups of Maximus telling his men to work 'as one'.

When the slow motion begins, its significance is not arbitrary or obscure. The re-enactment of the second fall of mighty Carthage is going better than expected for the barbarian hoards, and Maximus mounts one of the enemy's white horses. As this is his moment of renewal and affirmation, the fact that this horse recalls his horse in Germania resonates with significance. This image is, typically, slightly slowed and continues as Maximus takes up a spear. What follows is a series of racing point-of-view shots of the chariots with Maximus in pursuit, intercut with slower, wider action shots. More so even than in previous confrontations, the visuals revert to Maximus after each altercation as he replicates his battlefield exploits: charging in slow motion in a straight line through the legionnaires' defences, scything off heads, blood dripping from

Figure 3.16 *Gladiator* (Ridley Scott, 2000). Maximus in the Coliseum: the focal point of action and frame.

his sword. What occurs in the Coliseum in terms of the musical score parallels directly the layering of the different leitmotifs leading up to the victory in the opening battle. The first stage of the gladiatorial contest, as things hang still very much in the balance with neither side clearly in the ascendancy, is set to the less rhythmic, more meandering Holst-like themes. As, under the tutelage of Maximus, the gladiator slaves start winning and history is in the process of being rewritten, snatches of the waltz-time motif from Germania start to intrude upon the more abstract themes, but remain fragmented, thus complying with the visual anarchy of the images and the contest's still uncertain narrative trajectory. Then, finally, the lusher orchestral waltz-time motif asserts itself more definitely, the brass section of the orchestra comes higher in the mix and Maximus is thrown a sword by a fellow slave. Synchrony dominates as we are entering the decisive stage of the contest. As before, the 3/4 time alternates with the more precarious and unpredictable Holst leitmotif until victory, as it had been in Germania, is pronounced by Maximus, in slow motion of course, raising aloft his sword, at which point the 4/4 rhythm is once more emphatically reinstated, a sign that equilibrium is restored. This battle concludes with Commodus mocking Cassius as he asks, 'My memory's a little hazy, Cassius, but shouldn't the Barbarians lose the battle of Carthage?' before deciding to go down into the arena to meet the hero known to him simply as 'the Spaniard'.

Gladiator is a measured and symmetrical film, and what ensues is the middle of three big personal confrontations with Commodus, the first being after Commodus has committed patricide, rather than have Maximus succeed his father, and the last being the final scene in which a duel between them ends with both men dying (and Rome being restored, as Marcus Aurelius had wanted, to the Senate). Commodus descends from the royal box and enters the arena; he asks for the masked gladiator's name but Maximus refuses to give it, replying enigmatically (and with an allusion to *Spartacus*): 'My name is Gladiator'. It is here, in the moments leading up to Maximus' inevitable revelation of his face and name, that the overdetermined relationship between slow motion, close-ups, identity and subjective agency is affirmed, for Maximus' identity and power have been bound up with his face – with hiding it, revealing it, seeing its expressiveness. For all the film's innovative visual effects, *Gladiator* remains deeply traditional and Maximus its conventional hero. Maximus transcends the banalities of the narrative and plot construction much as the 'Barbarian hoards' defied history, as he is finally compelled to take off his helmet, turn around and face Commodus to deliver his and the film's definitive speech:

> My name is Maximus Decimus Meridius, Commander of the Armies of the North, General of the Felix Legions; loyal servant of the true emperor, Marcus Aurelius. Father to a murdered son, husband to a murdered wife – and I will have my vengeance in this life or the next.

Though there is no slow motion at this juncture, this is a comparably slow, powerful and portentous moment that segues into the momentous conclusion to the scene as the triumphal music, the cheers, the arms aloft and the circular pans around the spectators seated in the Coliseum all resume. The whole sequence is circular and closes as it began, with Maximus, once again the general, walking through lines of gladiators in the vaults of the Coliseum to the crowds' chants of 'Maximus! Maximus!'

Maximus' speech to Commodus lays out simply all that he embodies: father, husband, loyal servant, a man of morality and honour. The repeated use of certain stylistic motifs (especially the juxtaposition in the action sequences of fast editing and slow motion) coalesces to identify Maximus as the epicentre of *Gladiator*'s every aspect and to create a classic sense of unity between narrative, action, character, soundtrack and style. All aspects of *Gladiator* radiate out from Maximus and such at oneness with both the film's meaning and its style leads to an omnipresent collusion between masculinity, *mise en scène* and aesthetics. The contradictions or uncertainties manifested in some other films discussed in this book are replaced in *Gladiator* by an almost oppressive homogeneity, a consequence of which is the claustrophobic sense that off-screen space has ceased to exist: everything is conceived of as part of Maximus.

THE BOURNE IDENTITY: ACTION AND INTERIORITY

An element of *Gladiator* that marks it out as more 1990s than 2000s is the way in which male introspection and emotions are marginalised in it. This is the reason for the prioritisation in these discussions of *mise en scène*, music, editing and, more generally, visual style: they are often overloaded with information, much as they had been in the 1950s melodrama. Outwardly, Maximus represses emotion (the murder of his family, nearly being killed himself, being sold as a slave) and we get only fleeting glimpses into his interior state. In terms of men's cinema, since *Gladiator*, there has been a significant move towards male introspection and concomitantly the mobilisation of *mise en scène* and style to reflect masculine interiority, to capture more of the nuances and complexities and sensibilities of men and male heroes, even in identifiably masculine situations.

The Bourne Identity starts with Jason Bourne (Matt Damon) being saved by the crew of an Italian fishing boat off the coast of Marseille. Suffering from amnesia, the only clue to his identity is a tiny chip implanted near his hip, which contains the details of a Swiss bank account. Recovered, Bourne goes to Zurich and, in a deposit box, finds money, a gun and numerous passports, all containing his photo, and assumes the identity of one of them: 'Jason Bourne'. He is chased to Paris and gets embroiled in CIA-led manoeuvres (he used to be a CIA agent), until his boss, Alexander Conklin (Chris Cooper), tells him that he (Bourne) is 'US government property, you're malfunctioning $30-million weapon' who had masterminded an important ongoing operation. Over the course of this exchange, however, it transpires that, about to pull the trigger and assassinate the exiled African dictator he had been assigned to kill, Bourne had choked, run off, been shot in the back and thrown in the sea. Being questioned about this failed mission triggers a flashback which is told in largely indecipherable fragments intercut with images of the present, only really held together by Conklin's rational narration of events. Bourne's memories come to him as mental spasms in a series of short, frantically edited montages. In that most of the individual images are only a couple of frames long and, though not randomly selected, fly by too fast to be decipherable, their effect on us is largely subliminal. Conversely, their effect on Bourne is liminal. The splintered segments of flashback montages juxtapose glimpses of Bourne's arrival on the African dictator's boat, seeking him out and getting to the point of holding a gun to his head. Sharp, electronic clicks (like those of a camera as it snaps a picture) accompany the rapid-fire switches between images, connoting the present-day Bourne's act of running through the internalised photos in his distant memory bank. Each montage contains at least one blistering-white flash-frame – a shard of light, mimicked by Bourne when we return to him, as he blinks, grimaces, crinkles up his face or shakes his head, as if trying – but failing – to rid himself of these traumatic thoughts. For a few seconds (from when Bourne enters the ex-dictator Wombosi's cabin to when he decides not to assassinate him), the style of the flashback becomes more conventional and legible. Here, too, however, the linear action is punctuated with reverse close-up shots of Bourne, troubled, registering what he is there to do and recoiling from it. In terms of how they look, these are extremely similar to the images of him remembering the events in the present, so momentarily complicating the interrelationship between levels of consciousness, as Bourne's *conscience* two months earlier is here shown to react in much the same way as, in the present, his *conscious* does when repressed knowledge resurfaces. On both levels, the montage fragments are shards that puncture Bourne's consciousness, and the extreme rapidity of the editing, along with the flash-frames, enact the painfulness of his cognitive assimilation. The flashbacks conclude with Bourne, having been shot twice in the back, floating on the water at night (the scene from the start of the film).

Such forced reflectiveness has become a regular feature of several recent action films, though its most important source, the split male personality of so many old comic book heroes, is obviously not new. Related to it is also the ruse of successfully impersonating someone else, peeling away a mask, for example, to reveal the 'real' man underneath, as occurs at the start of *Mission: Impossible 2* (John Woo, 2000) as 'Tom Cruise' is peeled away to reveal Dougray Scott. But, with the rising popularity of the puzzle film, in particular, male- and action-centred versions of the split personality/fractured layers of consciousness themes have emerged to raise interesting questions about interiority and the action hero's compulsion to confront himself rather than 'act' his way out of an existential or personal crisis. In *The Bourne Identity*, Jason Bourne, at the end of the flashbacks, warns Conklin 'I don't want to do this anymore . . . Jason Bourne is dead, do you hear me?'

In *Skyfall,* the internal, psychological struggle is differently configured (surfacing, for instance, in the eloquently barren and brutal Scottish landscape around Bond's family home) and becomes a gloriously ludicrous Oedipal tussle between the orphaned 007 and Javier Bardem over their mutual surrogate mother, M. An interest in subjective introspection has an impact on the generic workings of the action movie, especially its standardised action sequences, and runs counter to many traditional assumptions about men and masculinity: that men 'do' or 'act' rather than think too much; that men are 'silent' and 'not good with words'; that they are 'unemotional' and suspicious of 'opening up'. Whereas classically repressed anxieties, of which either male characters were unaware or which they disavowed, surfaced in the *mise en scène* but remained at odds with what, on a conscious level, they knew about themselves, what occurs in the *Bourne Identity* flashback sequence is a coalescence between Bourne bringing his traumatic memories to the surface and the surface of the film. It is through the actual scarring of the film's surface (via the flash-frames and the extreme brevity of the shots) that we sense the strain of Bourne's act of remembering, so his memories rupture the *mise en scène* and suggest that the film, and not just Bourne's memory, is a preconscious meeting point between two states of being, the conscious and the subconscious. In turn, moments when repressed memories rupture both the hero's consciousness and the film's surface form an interesting relationship to the same film's totally implausible fantasy action sequences.

Robin Wood describes the action of an earlier fight in another Paris apartment earlier in *The Bourne Identity*:

> No shot lasts more than a second or two; we never see even the semblance of a punch actually landing, though most of them look violent enough to appear lethal. It is, in fact, almost impossible to make out what the two men are physically doing to each other – we are just allowed a very generalized sense of extremely violent movement. At the end, if I recall correctly, Damon has somehow managed to emerge without so much as a nosebleed . . . The fakery is so transparent that the readiness of spectators to accept it as 'real' shows a quite extraordinary eagerness to 'believe'. (Wood, 2003: xxxi)

Wood's account of the scene is, as ever, highly entertaining, drawing attention to the tensions between the hyperreality and the multiple implausibilities of the contemporary action sequence, as well as the physical impregnability of its fantasy hero. He concludes, however, by focusing on the wrong issue, I think: spectators rarely 'believe' in such heightened 'fakery'; rather the heightened fakery seems to be yet another example of the inverse ratio between psychological frailty and indestructibility, that the more traumatised the new action hero is, the more invincible he becomes. This is part of (post)modern masculinity. Immediately following the flashbacks, an armed man bursts into the CIA's Parisian safe house. Bourne floors him and steals his gun before trying (gangster- or cowboy-like) to shoot his way out of trouble (a gun in each hand, one held upside down). The fast and furious editing, rugged hand-held camera style and vivid array of shots all serve to make the scene echo the fragmentariness of the flashbacks. The first hit man resurrects himself but Bourne then dispenses with him more successfully, before shooting the two colleagues ascending the elegant Parisian circular staircase. The generically essential vertical shot down towards ground level is followed swiftly by a reverse shot of the top floor where Bourne is, the machine-gun fire causing debris to fly around him in, again, slow motion. There is a brief hiatus, Bourne hears the sound of a gun being reloaded and, in response, loads a fresh cartridge into his gun. A point-of-view shot over his shoulder reveals a man coming towards him. Bourne shunts the man he has just killed through the banisters and intentionally falls down after him through the central stairwell. Their drop is shown in slight, not exaggerated, slow motion. In an outrageous piece of hyper-realist fakery, Bourne, in mid-flight, fires at the man coming up the stairs, just before both he and his dead companion land on the hard tiled floor, the dead man cushioning Bourne's fall.

This coupling in *The Bourne Identity* of the hero's memory recall and the film's most fanciful action sequence, suggests largely that the hero's internal damage or frailty exists in virtually inverse proportion to any external damage he suffers. After plunging down a Parisian stairwell past several flights of stairs, Bourne is momentarily dazed and bruised but he is able to get up and go to find his lover Marie on a Greek island. The same rationale dictates the extended pre-titles sequence in *Skyfall,* as Bond, on or in a variety of fast-moving vehicles, gets embroiled in a chase through Istanbul. Though, post-titles, we see Bond in post-traumatic psychological meltdown (he is drinking excessively and does not attend to his appearance), Daniel Craig's grey suit for the Istanbul sequence, like Cary Grant's in the crop-spraying sequence of *North by Northwest* (Alfred Hitchcock, 1959), is as pristine after his travails with the jeep, the motorbike, the digger mounted on the train as it was in the first frame. Interiority and/or thinking in these action heroes, far from puncturing their armour, apparently add to their impregnability.

This, in turn, relates to spectacle which, by its very nature, interrupts any narrative's realist flow. Geoff King has returned more than once to the issue of spectacle – 'images at which we might wish to stop and stare' (King, 2000: 4) – and the role played by the spectacular in contemporary Hollywood. Though spectacle, he argues, may disrupt narrative, spectacular images can also 'sometimes help to move the plot significantly forward' (4) as, in fact, is especially the case in the action movie. In *New Hollywood Cinema* King subsequently suggests that 'Spectacle is a quality offered by Hollywood in its attempt to maintain the distinctive appeal of cinema, of the big screen event' (King, 2002: 178–9) and that the contemporary action spectacular (one example used is *Die Hard with a Vengeance* which King discusses at length) offers 'an altogether different economy of pleasure, in which the giddying blur of the high-speed chase and/or the gratifyingly spectacular release of aggressive impulse occurs at regularly recurring intervals' (King, 2002: 185). The 'different economy of pleasure' also entails transporting the spectator out of the realm of the real and the plausible; this is part of our detachment from *The Bourne Identity* and a variety of other action films for, if we believed its spectacle, we would be in a perpetual state of crisis and tension. As it is, we understand the hyper-reality's 'fakery' – that nobody would survive either the first ten minutes of *Skyfall* or Bourne's fall down the Parisian staircase more or less intact – and so can sit back and relish the spectacle.[12]

SHERLOCK HOLMES: THINKING AS ACTION

In *Sherlock Holmes* (Guy Ritchie, 2009) there is a noteworthy scene in which Holmes (Robert Downey Jr) participates in an insalubrious underground fight (part bare-knuckle boxing, part wrestling, part martial art). [13] From the outset, Ritchie's Holmes has proclaimed himself to be extravagantly different from his predecessors, most immediately in terms of appearance (the deerstalker hat is gone though the pipe remains) but also where personality is concerned. In both the Ritchie films and the BBC's contemporaneous series, *Sherlock*, in which Benedict Cumberbatch plays a modishly modernised version of the Victorian detective, the psychological dimensions of Holmes's idiosyncratic persona are emphasised. Both camps maintain that they are returning to overlooked features in the original Conan Doyle books but it nevertheless remains 'a significant departure for Sherlock Holmes adaptations to explicitly define Holmes as pathological' (Nicol, 2013: 125). In the Ritchie films, this pathology comes out especially in what the director has dubbed 'Holmesavision': the repetition of an action, first time as the slow-motion visualisation of the action he is about to execute, accompanied by an interior monologue, second time as the full-speed execution of the plan.

The boxing match can be interpreted as Holmes's attempt to exorcise physically the failure of his famed powers of deduction in the previous scene which had ended with Holmes eating alone, his face splattered with wine after offending Watson's fiancée Mary. The action cuts from Holmes dining (slithering a slimy piece of unidentifiable food sideways into his mouth) to him being thrown, bare chested and sweaty, against the wall of a grubby bear-pit-like arena. In front of a leering crowd, the fight is not going well until spying Irene Adler (his only potential female romantic interest) placing a bet spurs a bloodied Sherlock into resuming the contest. Images run in exaggerated slow motion, dynamically choreographed to Holmes's internal monologue outlining how the next phase of the fight will go. Augmenting the slowed visuals are the soundtrack's warped, elongated sounds which are intermittently interrupted by brutal, fast-motion images and amplified thuds and cracks as Holmes lands a punch, a comic book-esque stylisation, reminiscent of Guy Ritchie's earlier films, that also pays homage to *Raging Bull* and *The Wild Bunch*. In preparing us, via 'Holmesavision', for the fight sequence proper, Ritchie emphasises the ritualistic nature of cinematographic physical conflict and confirms the continued (even enhanced) effectiveness of that conflict once it is divested of its element of surprise. There are moments of graphic physicality and/or violence (in *The Wild Bunch*, *Raging Bull* or *Django Unchained*, for example) that possess genuine shock value but still a major part of why audiences enjoy the most brutal fights and the most dangerous action sequences is their predictability and the fact that they do *not* shock but, instead, possess a pervasive ironic, performative staginess. 'Holmesavision' harnesses this pleasure for it enables us to dissect the fight in advance of experiencing its rush. So, as Holmes's inner voice tells him to 'discombobulate', he, in slow motion, outstretches his arms, the muscles on which reverberate with the tension, before he swiftly and to the accompaniment of a magnified thump, clamps his hands on to his adversary's ears. When it then comes to Holmes, in exactly the way he had predicted, dispatching his opponent at jerky real-time speed (having predicted 'physical recovery six weeks; full psychological recovery, six months'), our adrenalin, which, like a coil being tightened, has been rising, is finally released.

Just as there are intellectual dimensions to the fight sequences of both Sam Peckinpah and Sergio Leone, so there is a very different intellectual dimension to Ritchie's contemporary reincarnations of Sherlock Holmes. Alongside its pathological aspects and Downey Jr's untraditional muscularity, is the emphasis on thinking, on the dynamics of interiority. This intellectualisation of Holmes reconfigures masculinity as a fusion between physicality and intelligence and, as such, frames a riposte to both ongoing preoccupations with men's silences, with the inabilities of men to articulate or verbalise their feelings, and the insistence on masculinity as represented by the body, its triumphs, its frailties, its musculature, its masochism, its brute force. Holmes's compulsion to intellectualise thus becomes a key facet of his physicality, as opposed to a force that undermines it; and, though it is a 'curse' as the detective puts it in the second Ritchie film *Sherlock Holmes: A Game of Shadows* (2011), his ability to 'see everything' becomes a crucial component of not just the narrative but the aesthetics and the experience of watching.

Game of Shadows contains a spectacular and exemplary train chase. Watson's plans to honeymoon with Mary in Brighton are thwarted when a band of assassins dressed as soldiers (co-opted by Holmes's arch-rival James Moriarty) and Holmes himself (disguised as a bonneted woman) board the train. Just after Holmes has thrown Watson's new bride off the train (timing it perfectly, he assures his friend, so she does not die), the two men fight but their tussle is halted by the carriage door being pulled back to reveal a bunch of assassins brandishing guns. Holmes and Watson (Jude Law) look up; a rifle swivels from right to left, and a zoom into an extreme close-up reveals something bullet-like wedged at the end of its barrel. This triggers a flashback, via a masked edit to another close-up of the same object, this time corked in the end of a stick in the clasp of a gloved hand. A series of short shots reveals the bullet to be a lipstick, the gloved hands to be Holmes's clad unconvincingly as those of a woman. After locking himself in the lavatory, Holmes managed – as viewed via another retrospective 'Holmesavision' sequence involving the cistern chain, the tap and a bottle of phosphorus – to swap the lipstick for a bullet in the killer's machine-gun belt. The action then reverts to the present and a short close-up shot travels from the end of the rifle, up its barrel to its cocked trigger moving forward in exaggeratedly slow motion to the moment of impact with the gun. A sequence of almost abstract images of the gun's internal mechanics subsequently shows a bullet travelling down its barrel, towards the lipstick, eventually causing the bullet to backfire and explode in the assassin's face. The sensuality of these images, especially the final tight, fluid shot up, inside and down the gun that culminates in the explosion, parallels – and is, indeed, generated by – the frisson created by Holmes's cerebral, swashbuckling machismo.

The style of Ritchie's *Holmes* is at once freshly exciting and derivative. There are debts, for example, to the comic book action heroes of many contemporary Hollywood action movies (*The Matrix*, *X-Men*, *Iron Man* and animations) as well as to the aesthetics and style of video games, especially when it comes to plot crafting and the switching of point of view and subjectivity. Finally, there is the increased role in all contemporary action adventure movies played by computer graphics. In all, Britain-based Framestore created some 550 shots for *Game of Shadows*, including the entire train and its environments, save for one studio-bound carriage.[14] The interactive visualisations of video games (such as the repetition and reworking of a sequence or the graphic depiction of the internal workings of something), allied with the fantasy-creating possibilities of computer graphics are harnessed specifically in the *Sherlock Holmes* films to construct an aesthetic rooted in the camaraderie between spectator and fictional subject. The masculinity that results from this interaction is compellingly ironic. Though spectators experience empathy for the masculinity on display, they also know perfectly well that Holmes and Watson are not clawing their way along the outside of actual train carriages to Hans Zimmer's familiar-sounding heart-racing, waltz-time score.

All these elements come together particularly effectively for the climactic Reichenbach Falls fight between Holmes and Moriarty. Overall, *Game of Shadows* is more technically complex than its predecessor, one of the results of which is the diffusion and proliferation of 'Holmesavision' to other characters, notably Holmes's nemesis Moriarty who is granted an equivalent 'Moriartyvision' (as Ritchie refers to it in the DVD extras to the film). In addition, Watson becomes, through the film, increasingly active and far more than Holmes's lumpen sidekick. According predictive 'thought-vision' to more than one male character affects conclusively the question of identification, as the de-indivualisation of 'Holmesavision' makes for a more fluid concept of male subjectivity whose transferral from individual character on to the body of the film appears most overtly in the form of the multilayered aesthetic experience.

In an attempt to avert world war, a peace summit is taking place in Reichenbach in a castle on a spectacular cliff edge above a high waterfall. Holmes and Watson have arrived to thwart Moriarty's plans to ignite the conflict by killing one of the ambassadors present. The climax is the final fight between Holmes and Moriarty, intercut with Watson's pursuit of the disguised spy, about to shoot the ambassador, though both strands are effectively

Figure 3.17 *Sherlock Holmes: A Game of Shadows* (Guy Ritchie, 2011). Holmes and Moriarty about to fight.

Figure 3.18 *Sherlock Holmes: A Game of Shadows* (Guy Ritchie, 2011). Holmes and Moriarty fight in 'Holmesavision'.

Figure 3.19 *Sherlock Holmes: A Game of Shadows* (Guy Ritchie, 2011). Holmes and Moriarty continue their fight in 'Holmesavision'.

controlled by Holmes, for, overlaid on to Watson's derring-do sleuthing in the ballroom, is not Watson's but his master's voice accurately predicting the course of events as they unfurl.

In their endgame, Holmes and Moriarty play chess on the castle's freezing balcony as a prelude to their fight to the death. First, as Moriarty lights his pipe, it is Holmes's turn to imagine their imminent duel. In balletic, ultra-slow slow motion interspersed as previously with super-fast interludes, as punches land accompanied by the amplified sounds of arms whistling through the air and the painful crunch of fist on flesh, he runs through the sequence of moves and blows. The fantasy run-through stops abruptly with an edit to a close-up of Moriarty (Jared Harris), a wry smile on his face and saying to himself: 'Come now, you think you're the only one who can play this game?', at which point a second predictive fantasy of how the fight might go ensues. Moriarty's version is visually indistinguishable from Holmes's – the contiguity highly relevant to the dispersal of subjective male point of view – and soon the hypothetical enactment becomes a fusion of Moriarty's and Holmes's as they exchange fantasy words and synchronised fantasy blows. In this climactic macho dance, the slow-motion lurches and the camera encircle the two men until it seems as if Moriarty will prove victorious, getting Holmes (lying in the foreground) on to the balcony ledge, about to swing a fist at him as Holmes's voice predicts 'prognosis increasingly negative'. The images slow even more until Moriarty's voice concludes confidently 'we both know how this ends', as Holmes (having glanced vertically down at the waterfall in what has become a virtually obligatory shot of the embattled action hero up a tall building contemplating the vertiginous fate that logically awaits him) tumbles out of frame, leaving Moriarty triumphant, his arms outstretched like some corrupt formally attired messiah. But there is a cut back to the initial two-shot and Holmes's voice declaring 'conclusion, inevitable . . . unless' at which point he blows hot cigar ash into his adversary's face, locks Moriarty to him and, as Watson comes in from the ballroom, pulls both himself and Moriarty over the ledge to their presumed deaths. In a moment of high 'bromantic' pathos, Watson closes his eyes and imagines, as Holmes has in a sense taught him to do, a sequence of events he does not actually witness, namely the fall. It is now Watson's imagination that conjures up images of the rivals spiralling downwards, frozen in mid-air or dropping and separating as they reach the water. Watson walks over to the ledge and stares down into the abyss and is subsequently shown typing his friend's obituary.

Of course, Holmes is not dead and this is just another premature announcement of a hero's death, much like 007 at the beginning of *Skyfall* who, having been shot off the roof of a moving train, is also presumed dead and also gets an obituary. The hero's non-death in this way after a dramatic and, in *Skyfall*'s case, extended action sequence has odd effects. In both instances, the spectator

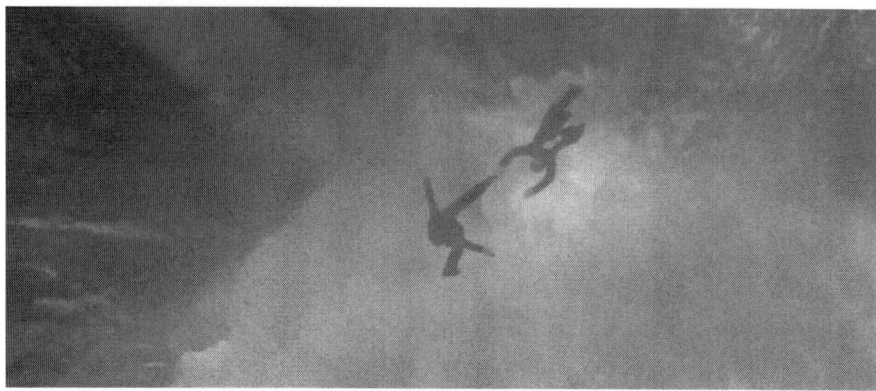

Figure 3.20 *Sherlock Holmes: A Game of Shadows* (Guy Ritchie, 2011). Holmes and Moriarty plunge into the waterfall.

no doubt guesses that the hero has not died but that, by the same token, he has not won the previous spectacular confrontation either, a realisation that works to deflate the fantasy of masculine supremacy and to supplant it with a rather more limply and ironically postmodern play on the differences and mergers between fantasy and reality. But, this duality allows all such contemporary action-adventure films to conform to the contradictory convention that predictability is, indeed, pleasurable while also playing with expectations and traditions of narrative. Thinking back to Dyer's deduction that 'It is no accident that the word climax applies to orgasm and narrative': just as now making out that the hero is dead is no longer such a surprise tactic, there is no longer (at least where narrative is concerned) one 'great single climax' (Dyer, 1985: 40). Instead, in its place there are often repeated computer graphics-assisted *petit-morts* which can be endlessly repeated, refined, bettered and ultimately undermined, a tactic that divests the male body at the sequence's core of its credible physical power, which is perhaps why in the *Sherlock Holmes* films, so much attention is paid to Downey Jr's perfect pectorals and washboard stomach. The end of *Game of Shadows* is especially deflating of the male protagonist as, unlike Daniel Craig who, in *Skyfall*, reappears traumatised and battle-torn after his near death, Holmes comes back from the dead as urban camouflage, disguising himself as the upholstery of an armchair in Watson's study.

SHUTTER ISLAND AND *INCEPTION*: PUZZLES AS ACTION

A significant number of so-called 'puzzle films' have been released recently, not exclusively by Hollywood. Warren Buckland, in the introduction to his edited collection *Puzzle Films: Complex Storytelling in Contemporary Cinema* defines contemporary puzzle films as 'a popular cycle of films from the 1990s that rejects classical storytelling techniques and replaces them with complex storytelling' (2009: 1). After outlining Aristotle's discussions in *The Poetics* of simple and complex plots, Buckland extends his opening definition by suggesting that 'A puzzle plot is intricate in the sense that the arrangement of events is not just complex, but complicated and perplexing: the events are not simply interwoven, but *entangled*' (Buckland, 2009: 3). What has this got to do with men's cinema? With reference to the greater emphasis being placed in contemporary Hollywood on masculine interiority, something that is interesting, from my perspective, is the preponderance of 'puzzle films' that centre on men and which, in turn, use the puzzle element of their plots to explore male psychology and introspection, frequently via a convoluted, layered visual style. There are, of course, feminine puzzle films, such as *Sliding Doors*, *Mulholland Drive*, *The Others* or *Black Swan*; the list of male-focused counterparts is significantly longer, however, and includes: *The Sixth Sense*, *Fight Club*, *Memento*, *The Matrix*, *Donnie Darko*, *The Machinist*, *A Beautiful Mind*, *Source Code*, *Inception* and *Shutter Island*. In Chapter 1 I began by discussing ways in which the ostensibly classical text couches, is disrupted by or is unable to contain 'classical' masculinity; I intend to conclude here with a short analysis of non-classical contemporary masculinity within the non-classical, but nevertheless mainstream, film with reference to *Inception* (Christopher Nolan, 2010) and *Shutter Island* (Martin Scorsese, 2010).

In *The Bourne Identity*, Jason Bourne's interiority, expressed as the traumatic flashbacks, signals a fragility at the core of his action-hero identity; in *Sherlock Holmes* interiority, externalised as Holmes's ability to think through confrontations and problems before they occur, is an indication of his intellectual *and* physical superiority. Interiority in both *Inception* and *Shutter Island* is directly threatening to the protagonists' mental and physical stability. These puzzle movies share an interest in the workings of the (primarily masculine) subconscious and denote those workings via more or less well-defined strata of consciousness; both also have teasing twist endings which might or might not signal their protagonists' successful return to reality. As it is in the majority of puzzle films, the lack of clarity between layers of consciousness is a key narrative element, and the role of visual style within this intended blurring is an important factor in keeping the spectator confused and surprised. Here I shall simply compare two features: the way in which *Shutter Island adds* to our confusion about the identity of its protagonist via its use of style elements – colour and editing especially – and the contrasting manner in which *Inception* uses its 'puzzle' elements – to *clarify* things (that is, until the very end).

Shutter Island, though not so obviously on first viewing, is a journey through the mind of a father sent mad by grief and guilt: grief at the loss of his three children, whom his wife Dolores killed, and guilt at his subsequent murder of Dolores. Andrew Laeddis (Leonardo DiCaprio) then represses all of this, thinks he is still a federal officer under the adopted name 'Edward (Teddy) Daniels', an anagram of his real name, and ends up on Shutter Island, a high-security prison for the criminally insane. The bulk of the film, it emerges at the end, is an elaborate role play orchestrated by the prison's forward-thinking director, Dr Cawley (Ben Kingsley), to bring Laeddis back to reality and help him avoid a lobotomy. In the end, however, Daniels is escorted off to be lobotomised but with the suggestion that he does so willingly and so is, by this point, faking delusional insanity.

For most of the film, therefore, all we are less than explicitly shown is that 'Daniels' suffers from migraines and is traumatised by the case of a disappeared prisoner he has ostensibly come to solve. *Shutter Island* is visually and stylistically ornate, and the interlocutions between the various layers of fantasy, dream, nightmare, flashback and 'reality' become muddied as the lines between Daniels's different levels of consciousness become increasingly porous. Bolstered by Robbie Robertson's perpetually unsettling score (sampled snatches of mainly modern classical music), present-day 'reality' in *Shutter Island* is the most unsettling layer of the lot: a coldly desaturated world of gangrenous blues, greens and greys which contrasts strongly and ironically with the manically overintense vividness of Daniels's hallucinations and flashbacks. These internalised sequences were reputedly inspired by George Stevens's 16 mm colour Kodachrome footage of the liberation of the concentration camp at Dachau which features in the narrative because Daniels/Laeddis was part of the liberation force, and they intentionally adopt a comparably heightened look of 1950s Kodachrome: all luminous reds, richly yolky yellows and summer grass greens. Conversely, the subdued and drained colour palette of the present-day action echoes the decolourised, post-nuclear pallor of *The Road* (John Hillcoat, 2009) or *The Ghost* (Roman Polanski, 2010) and, coupled with the restless camera and editing, has the amorphous effect of agitating and depressing us, without it being exactly clear why this is.

At one point nearing the end of the film, Daniels and his federal officer buddy Chuck (who is, in fact, his psychiatrist performing in the role-play exercise) reach the shore of this perpetually storm-blown island,[15] looking out at the lighthouse, Daniels's final destination in his search for the lost patient. In part, the morose colour tones of the present-day scenes disturb because the boundaries between fantasy and reality have become blurred, as Daniels's wild imaginings start to intrude on them. They, like Daniels, become increasingly unstable. In this scene, Daniels and Chuck run towards the edge of the slate-like rock face as the camera cranes up and away from them, hovering in mid-air above the sea. With an edit to a closer vertiginous shot looking straight down the rock face past the men, the sea seems especially angry. As Daniels despairs of ever being able to get to the lighthouse, there is a notably artificially lit image

Figure 3.21 *Shutter Island* (Martin Scorsese, 2010). Unstable angles for Teddy Daniels.

of the two of them that emphasises the fact that they are actors on a stage set, a recurrent technique that tells us to look beyond the surface by ironically drawing attention to it. Daniels elects to proceed to the lighthouse alone.

After creeping through a wood, he arrives at an alternative rock face but bassy strings start up and Robert Richardson's agitated camera first lurks furtively behind a tree as if spying on Teddy and then pulls up to the right. Cutting mid-movement, and from one moving shot to another as happens here, are always unsettling and make us realise something is not right. The forward-moving shot continues just long enough (before also being edited mid-motion) to indicate that Daniels, who is afraid of water, has reached another shoreline with no dry route to his intended destination. After a couple of mid- or close shots of an anguished DiCaprio, there follows an obtrusively panicked pan up from behind a rock as, clambering back up, he starts to talk to Chuck but realises he is no longer there. Daniels shouts Chuck's name, then catches sight of a smoking cigarette butt. In a close, distorting shot DiCaprio stoops down to pick it up, the extreme foreshortening of his hand forewarning us again of trouble to come, which arrives in the form of a jagged, fast montage of various images of the brooding sky and the angry sea until, returning to Daniels, we realise he has seen something near the water. In a classic way, the jerky montage reflects Teddy's mental instability, while the reverse shot of what he has seen confirms this, as intermittently disappearing under the lapping waves there is Chuck's body. In a predictably uncertain and unsteady series of shots, Daniels clambers down, clinging precariously to the dripping rocks. But, though, in men's cinema, images of active heroes performing such climbing feats with ease are frequently commonplace, this little sequence totally lacks the surety of those. This scene instead resembles a nightmare over which one is losing control, exemplified by the moment when, as a sheet of paper flutters past, the camera undulates after it rather than stay on and with

DiCaprio. The constant, restless shifts in perspective make both the sequence and Daniels hard to 'read'; we are never simply looking at our protagonist, we are always moving, always made to worry about our own footing and – metaphorically – our own stability. As Daniels descends to sea level, we strongly infer he is also descending into madness. At the end of this sequence is one of the moments *Shutter Island* could do without when Daniels sees a cord of rats come tumbling out of a hole in the rock and then discovers the imaginary lost patient Rachel Solando hiding in a cave. The palpable, but figurative, potency of the insanity that invades the 'reality' sequences loses all its eerie edginess the moment it becomes this literal.

Shutter Island's focus is the traumatisation and ensuing mental frailties of one individual, its cryptic conclusion providing a tidy solution to his plight, as we never discover whether or not Daniels/Laeddis consciously elects to be lobotomised in order to escape the debilitating invasions from his subconscious. Conversely, *Inception* uses a similar puzzle format (in this instance focused on layers of controlled dreaming with the addition of a deeper stratum of unstructured subconscious or 'limbo') to construct a more ambitious metaphor for masculine subjectivity. Though they are largely male centred, the dream layers in *Inception* are not gender specific. A key member of the group of dream 'extractors' (who can extract thoughts from the subconscious of others), for example, is a woman, Ariadne. *Inception* is roughly comparable to *Shutter Island* in that it renders literally the consciously uncontrollable, that is: the subjective and imaginary phenomenon of dreams. *Inception*, however, via its protagonist Cobb (Leonardo DiCaprio again) and the addition of the deep layer of 'limbo' (access to which is centred on and controlled by him), ultimately also constructs a metaphor for the unknowableness or masculine subjectivity and the mysteries related to its visualisation.

The subconscious strata in *Inception*, though elaborately constructed, are relatively clearly demarcated. In the protracted, climactic sequence as the group of extractors takes its two business clients down through three dream levels, the *mise en scène* and narrative environment of each remains distinct: a rainy, urban downtown; a plush, futuristic hotel; a snowy mountain fortress. Linking them on the level of style, all three exhibit some of the recognisable traits and motifs of men's cinema, such as extreme slow motion juxtaposed with frenetic activity, fast-cut chase sequences, rough hand-held camera at points of high action and dizzy camera angles. These shared stylistic elements, therefore, render the different tiers parts of a shared consciousness, as do the edits between them which usually occur mid-movement, leaving them incomplete, hanging in the balance until the extreme synchronisation of all the characters' exits from the various levels, including 'limbo'.

Inception's long and interlayered final section can, in many ways, be argued to offer a reflexive dissection of these subgeneric features, but with a twist.

A narratively important example of this is the minibus, in which the extractors are travelling during the first and most conventional dream layer, which crashes over the edge of a bridge well before the dreams need to end. In extreme slow motion, the van plunges towards the water, an action that takes approximately twenty-five minutes of screen time to complete and is intercut with action from the other dream layers. The intermittent image of the white van cascading gently down or suspended in time is the logical, if extreme, extension of other uses of slow motion to heighten the tension and impact of an otherwise furious sequence. The falling van provides both the extended sequence's moments of hiatus and its crucial punctuation marks. It also allows us all to catch our collective breath for, when it hits the water, all the characters will be kicked out of the respective dream worlds. As the van inches closer to the water, so the deeper levels move at normal, action-sequence speed and therefore still use the 'action' cinematic conventions that the upper level – which had hitherto contained the most conventional visual elements, such as ragged hand-held camera, short shots and hurried pans – has now left behind.

Once Cobb and Ariadne have descended into limbo, there comes a more complex interweaving of signification, *mise en scène* and style, exemplified by the eclectic, incoherent mix of architectural styles within limbo itself, a city created by Cobb's subconscious that puts side by side crumbling post-apocalyptic edifices, post-atomic shells of buildings, homogenised, featureless skyscraper towers and domestic houses marooned in water. There is a literalness to this configuration of the unkempt and abstract subconscious but how could it be otherwise? Salvador Dali's dream sequence for Hitchcock's *Spellbound* is childishly literal and goes little way towards approximating the character's unconscious inner core. Just as there remains doubt over *Inception*'s teasing ending, however, so there remains a dislocation at the heart of why limbo is so problematic for, although it is Cobb's wife Mal who is the character who can no longer tell reality and dreaming apart, it is to Cobb that this dangerous blurring matters most. The hyper-constructedness of the layers of dreams in *Inception* and their relationship to the mishmash world of limbo can be taken two ways. It could suggest that human identity, and masculinity in particular, are merely a series of Butlerian performative exercises, staging and refining previously observed and learnt generic gestures, which ultimately prove the emptiness at masculinity's core. Alternatively, we can look more precisely at limbo and proffer a far simpler understanding of that core as a metaphor for Hollywood masculinity, as all that Cobb really wants to do is to return to reality to be a good father. This is one of Hollywood's favoured myths about masculinity but here it is given a further cruel twist in that the only way, the end of *Inception* implies, that Cobb can reach this idealised state (and after all, the 'real' at the end of *Inception* is bathed in the unreal golden light of the perfect sunset) is to renounce and destroy all the other potentially more exciting aspects of masculinity along the way, its performative outer layers, its dream states. That at the end his spinning totem wobbles but does not fall could also mean that what awaits Cobb is the even harsher realisation that even that relatively bland domesticity is illusory, and so masculinity is nothing but instability.

The corroborating evidence for this restorative narrative reading is, of course, that at the heart of the deepest tier in this final section of *Inception* is Robert Fischer's (Cillian Murphy) quest for his dying father's love and recognition through the frigid alpine landscape to the inner sanctum of the fort. What Fischer discovers there is that his father was not disappointed in him after all and had, until his death, kept in his safe alongside his last will and testament a memento of his son's childhood: a paper wind spiral. As Fischer reaches his point of tearful rapprochement with his now dead father, one of the dream extractors nods, a gesture that triggers the final 'kick' back to reality: over a range of different shots the fort explodes; the lift from the second-level dream hurtles towards the surface; the vertical white van finally dips into the water. Then, on returning to the third level, before another huge explosion, there is the cheesiest reminder of all of this narrative's centrality: a shot of Fischer senior's bedside photo of him with his son as a child. (Distractingly inappropriate though this is, this image recalls the end of *Fatal Attraction*). There follows the inevitable rapid montage of the fort disintegrating, the lift travelling in slow motion, the extractors and clients beginning to wake and Ariadne hurling herself backwards out of one of limbo's towers in order to propel herself back to reality. In the uppermost dream level, the extractors and clients in the minibus awake, scramble in slow motion (inevitably) out of it and then, in normal time, swim ashore. Finally everyone really wakes up and Cobb goes home via the grim mundaneness of the 'Welcome to the United States' sign at the airport and the warm domestic beauty of his Frank Lloyd Wright house.

CONCLUSION

I set out to discuss something that seemed to be lacking within film studies, namely an extended examination of masculinity that prioritised the analysis of *mise en scène* and film style over narrative or character. I have argued, via a series of wide-ranging representative illustrations, for a liberating and flexible way of thinking about this relationship. Whereas I began, in Chapter 1, by focusing on instances in which aspects of masculinity are particularly strongly evoked and articulated through *mise en scène*, Chapters 2 and 3 have sought to delineate more concretely the category 'men's cinema', not as a cinema for and by men, but as a by now conventionalised way of making films about men and masculinity that adopts certain recognisable tropes, motifs and styles. These motifs and styles form the basis, I have argued, for a 'masculine aesthetic' – one that encapsulates masculinity but also, by virtue of not being slavishly shackled to representation, occupies the 'third term', the meeting place between the binaries of on-screen images of masculinity on the one hand and the films' spectators on the other. The reason for having consistently stressed the importance of *feeling* and the attendant sensualities of watching men's cinema is that I have sought ways of articulating two things: how films about masculinity effect their audiences and why or how films *about* masculinity are not necessarily, or even primarily, *for* male audiences. At the start of her book *Extra-Ordinary Men: White Heterosexual Masculinity in Contemporary Popular Cinema* Nicola Rehling explores hegemonic masculinity or what 'has historically been considered the most "ordinary" . . . identity' against the backdrop of the recent challenges mounted to hegemonic masculinity's neutrality by 'the politics of identity' (Rehling, 2009: 1). Rehling continues by considering the issue of how hegemonic masculinity's 'very ordinariness means that it is also haunted by the anxiety that it is a vacuous identity' (1), that it is sterile and empty. These fears emerge, I would argue, at the end of a film such as *Inception* or in Hollywood's frequent problematisation of 'normal' masculinity and sexuality. To escape being, or being found, boring, redundant or marginal, 'ordinary' masculinity reinvents itself as 'extra-ordinary'.

Another way in which 'ordinary' masculinity can be reinvented, though, is by its destabilisation, and concomitantly through the questioning of its hegemonic status by that destabilisation. The decoupling of 'hegemonic' and 'masculinity' is the essential first step towards this, after which the potentially universal appeal of masculinity becomes the appeal, not of the dominant and reactionary identity position, but of a more fluid and flexible one that encompasses, for example, masculinity as more akin to Robin Wood's conceptualisation of Mozart's music as the perfect embodiment of the 'ideal human being' (Wood, 2003: xvii–xix). Similarly, there is Kosofsky Sedgwick's first 'Axiom' in *Epistemology of the Closet*: 'People are different from each other', a 'self-evident fact' she goes on, for which we have only a 'tiny number of inconceivably coarse axes of categorization', such as gender, race, class, nationality and sexual orientation (Sedgwick, 1994: 22). Difference, Sedgwick proposes, is the new normality, so it need not be the case, by extension, that, in enjoying its masculine aesthetic, the diverse audiences for men's cinema are accepting the 'universality' and dominance of (hegemonic) masculinity. Placed alongside Judith Butler's contemporaneous questioning in *Gender Trouble* of the stability and performativity of identity or the coherence of gender categories, then heterosexual masculinity appears less monolithic and the pleasures of men's cinema appreciably more diverse.

This book's focus on style and *mise en scène* has wanted to open up the possibility of identification with a more abstract, symbolic and comparably non-fixed notion of masculinity which, by virtue of having been distanced from the straightforward representation of that masculinity, is more receptive to these ideas and less problematically tied to conventionally established hierarchies of identity and gender. With her belief that gender resides not in the body but in 'the understanding of identification as an enacted fantasy of incorporation' whose 'words, acts, gestures, and desire produce the effect of an internal core or substance, but produced [this] *on the surface* of the body' (Butler, J., 1990: 136), Judith Butler was already indirectly propounding a prototype for the performative potential of film spectatorship: that, for instance, the figure on the screen is less important to our absorption or excitement than a film's non-corporeal stylistic elements. The 'normality' of heterosexual masculinity, like other genders and sexualities, is consistently undermined by films' non-narrative or stylistic elements, remaining perpetually out of reach, unobtainable or unidentifiable. As I argued in the introduction, this 'normal' heterosexual masculinity becomes the ultimate perversion through its performative superficiality (that it is a series of imitations) and relative rarity. Masculinity, then, is defined not just in contrast *to* what it is not but *as* what it is not.

This is where the complex jouissance of men's cinema comes in: the defined, though not necessarily prescriptive, pleasures of spectatorship; the viscerally instinctual and physical enjoyment of its actions, tensions and so on. The act of watching is not inevitably gendered nor, as I have argued repeatedly, is identity fixed, which means, therefore, that the jouissance remains abstract though allied to a literal, actual presence of masculinity on the screen. Another crucial component of this jouissance is the familiarity of the tropes, motifs and styles identified in this chapter; motifs and the like that, though certainly not exclusive to 'men's cinema', have been repeatedly deployed, refined and modified in conjunction with masculinity. I described my introduction as being 'cobweb-like' as opposed to linear, and the cobweb remains as apposite a simile for men's cinema, too, as its styles, motifs or tropes most frequently woven into it become significant only in this context through association.

The starting point for my thinking about men's cinema was the crane shot used in *Once upon a Time in the West* to mark Claudia Cardinale's arrival at Flagstone station. It is definitely not the case that the crane shot acquires resonant signification only within the context of men's cinema; in certain contexts, however – especially during the scaling of high natural or man-made structures – it has become an indispensible and recognisable term within its lexicon. Thinking of men's cinema's many climbing sequences, however, the vertical high-angle shot down the side of the building, rock or the like *is* now specifically affiliated to men's cinema. Conversely, the many uses of the Steadicam, either crane or harness mounted, have featured a lot in my textual analyses but without Steadicam being *innately* masculine. What has happened to the use of Steadicam is that, through its repeated adoption in 'men's cinema' contexts, it has become an *inherent* feature of, for example, the action sequence. The things that matter more than anything are context and conjunction, hence the conglomeration of specific style elements, motifs and tropes around masculinity. In several instances (*The Wild Bunch, Once upon a Time in the West, Goodfellas, Reservoir Dogs, The American President*) the act of men walking has been discussed, sometimes but by no means exclusively in relation to the use of Steadicam. The Steadicam/walking link is only one factor in this 'chain'; arguably the more important conjunction is between walking and slowness, whether this be walking slowly as in the Leone, or walking in *slow motion* as in the Peckinpah. The effects achieved through men moving either slowly or in slow motion are arguably very similar.

Slow motion, however, has become an especially interesting entry in the men's cinema roster. In no coherent or legible way is a technique, such as slow motion, gendered but the prominence accorded it within the framework of men's cinema is noticeable. Most conspicuously, slow motion is juxtaposed with action, the contrast often proving most potent in subsidiary alignment with close-ups of the hero at the epicentre of a fast sequence, a combination of elements used to powerful effect in *Gladiator*, for instance. Following on from this, the close-up is of fundamental importance to men's cinema but, once again, contextualisation and alignment are key. For example, the close-up into Henry Fonda's face after the fluid track in *Once upon a Time in the West* as he is about to shoot the McBain son is very different from the close-ups of Tom Cruise as he grafts his way up the skyscraper in *Ghost Protocol* which, in turn, have a very different effect to the tight shots of Robert Downey Jr in *Sherlock Holmes* that act as preludes to the rapid thought-process montages.

I have referred consistently to the abstract or more nebulous ways in which men's cinema entices and beckons us, as viewers, to identify with it; just as ambiguously defined, are the multiple ways in which men's cinema uses movement. Speed at both ends of the spectrum (slow or fast) has featured in many of the film analyses above, whether with reference to editing, or movement of men through space, or the movement of the camera, and self-evidently, speed itself can serve an important function in men's cinema, as in Maverick and Goose's mantra 'I feel the need . . . the need for speed'. Similarly, the style of the movement is telling. Elegant, sweeping moves frequently figure in relationship with crane shots (for example, plunging out of the window after Tom Cruise) whereas scruffier, jerkier moves are often favoured for more realistic, earth-bound settings, from the chase sequences in *Dirty Harry* to the action sections in each dream tier in *Inception*.

As in these instances, the relatively specific union of stylistic elements is significant, but again in context. The synchronisation of music, editing and movement, though a recurrent combination in men's cinema, is far from exclusive to it or to men (think of the music video editing of Julia Roberts's successful shopping expedition in *Pretty Woman*) but it is symptomatic of men's cinema's tendency towards establishing synchronicity between various stylistic elements. I have examined diverse forms of synchrony, an obvious one being the use of a song in relation to movement; but, whereas the relationship between what is going on during the title sequence of *Blue Collar* and what is being narrativised in the lyrics of Jack Nitzsche's 'Hard Workin' Man' is close, it is not the lyrics of 'Little Green Bag' but its cool 1970s languidness that enriches the images of the 'reservoir dogs' walking in slow motion. *Top Gun*'s adoption of the same pop-promo editing style as *Pretty Woman* is striking; in the volleyball sequence, however, the standard music/editing synchronisation is augmented by the addition of other more men's cinema-specific elements, such as the repeated close-ups of Tom Cruise. A recent example of men's cinema synchrony is between physicality and thinking in films as diverse as *The Bourne Identity*, *Sherlock Holmes* and *Inception*. Interesting in itself, this emphasis on interiority has been even more intriguing for its adoption of many of the same features and techniques as I am describing here, fusing, as opposed to differentiating, sharply between thinking and action. Hollywood's treatment of masculinity has been both varied and consistent and its masculine aesthetic both established and perpetually evolving.

NOTES

1. The only sequence in colour in *Raging Bull* is the home-movie montage showing, for example, Jake and Vicky's marriage, that of his brother Joe and footage of their kids playing in the garden.
2. The apostrophe is missing in Pennebaker's original title.
3. Gordon Cooper poses the rhetorical question 'Who's the best pilot you ever saw?' to his wife several times, before supplying the answer, 'You're looking at him'.
4. For an extended discussion of these musical themes cf. http://www. filmtracks.com/titles/gladiator.html.
5. Boccherini instructed his string players to put their cellos – and presumably also their violins, as Russell Crowe does in *Master and Commander* – on their knees to play them as they might guitars.
6. Originally, the piece was written for a string quintet.
7. Tarantino is referring to Melville's remark that Jef Costello in *Le Samourai* wears 'a suit of armour' in Dargis 1994: 17.
8. As shown in *Apollo 13*, the capsule window played a vital part in the pilots' safe return to Earth.
9. For Fassbinder, Ballhaus was cinematographer on several key films

including *The Bitter Tears of Petra von Kant*, *The Marriage of Maria Braun* and *Lili Marleen*.

10. Recalling President Lyndon Johnson's set of domestic programmes through the 1960s, the central policies of which aimed to eliminate poverty and racism.

11. See above (p. 126) for a brief discussion of Hans Zimmer's music for *Gladiator*.

12. It is also problematic to only equate 'spectacle' with the over-the-top 'spectacular', as King does.

13. Conan Doyle's Sherlock Holmes was versed in the art of Bartitsu, a Japanese form of wrestling which blended ju-jitsu, boxing and cane fencing.

14. Cf. http://www.cgw.com/Press-Center/Online-Exclusives/2011/VFX-Sherlock-Holmes.aspx#.UO18DKXeM5Q

15. *Shutter Island* is based on the islands in Boston Harbour.

Bibliography

Aaron, Michele (2007) *Spectatorship: The Power of Looking*, London: Wallflower Press.

Arroyo, José (2002) 'Mission: Sublime', in José Arroyo (ed.) *Action/Spectacle Cinema: A Sight and Sound Reader*, London: British Film Institute, pp. 21–5.

Barr, Charles (1963) 'CinemaScope: before and after', *Film Quarterly*, 16: 4, summer, pp. 4–24.

Bazin, André (1967) *What is cinema?*, trans. and ed. Hugh Gray, Berkeley: University of California Press.

Berliner, Todd (2005) 'Visual Absurdity in *Raging Bull*', in Kevin L. Hayes (ed.) *Martin Scorsese's Raging Bull*, Cambridge: Cambridge University Press, pp. 41–68.

Beugnet, Martine (2007) *Cinema and Sensation: French Film and the Art of Transgression*, Edinburgh: Edinburgh University Press.

Bordwell, David (2002) 'Film Futures' *SubStance*, Issue 97 (31: 1), pp. 88–104.

— (2006) *The Way Hollywood Tells It: Story and Style in Modern Movies*, Berkeley and Los Angeles: University of California Press.

Bordwell, David, Staiger, Janet and Thompson, Kristen [1988 (1985)] *Classical Hollywood Cinema: Film Style and Mode of Production to 1960*, London: Routledge.

Bovenschen, Silvia (1976) 'Is There a Feminine Aesthetic?', in Gisela Ecker (ed.) *Feminist Aesthetics*, London: The Women's Press, pp. 23–50.

Brunsdon, Charlotte (1986) *Films for Women*, London: British Film Institute.

Bruzzi, Stella (2005) *Bringing up Daddy: Fatherhood and Masculinity in Post-war Hollywood*, London: British Film Institute.

Buckland, Warren (2009) *Puzzle Films: Complex Storytelling in Contemporary Cinema*, Oxford: Blackwell.

Butler, Alison (2002) *Women's Cinema: The Contested Screen*, London: Wallflower Press.

Butler, Judith (1990) *Gender Trouble: Feminism and the Subversion of Identity*, London and New York: Routledge.

— (2004) *Undoing Gender*, London and New York: Routledge.

Charity, Tom (1997) *The Right Stuff*, London: British Film Institute.

Christie, Ian and Thompson, David (eds) (2003) *Scorsese on Scorsese*, London: Faber and Faber, revised edition.

Cixous, Hélène [1997 (1975)] 'The Laugh of the Medusa', in Robyn R. Warhol and Diane Price Herndl (eds) *Feminism: An Anthology of Literary Theory and Criticism*, revised edition, Basingstoke: Macmillan Press, pp. 347–62.

Cohan, Steven (1997) *Masked Men: Masculinity and the Movies in the Fifties*, Bloomington and Indianapolis: Indiana University Press.

Cohan, Steven and Hark, Ina Rae (eds) (1993) *Screening the Male: Exploring Masculinities in Hollywood Cinema*, London and New York: Routledge.

Connell, R. W. [2003 (1995)] *Masculinities*, Cambridge: Polity Press.

— (2009) Connell, Raewyn *Gender*, 2nd edition, London: Polity.

Cook, Pam (1982) 'Masculinity in Crisis?', *Screen*, 23, 3: 4, September–October, pp. 39–46.

Cowie, Elizabeth (1998) 'Storytelling: classical Hollywood cinema and classical narrative' in Steve Neale and Murray Smith (eds) *Contemporary Hollywood Cinema*, Routledge, pp. 178–90.

Dargis, Manohla (1994) 'Quentin Tarantino on *Pulp Fiction*', *Sight and Sound*, 4: 11, November, pp. 16–20.

Dawson, Jeff (1997) *Quentin Tarantino: The Cinema of Cool*, London: Applause Books.

Doty, Alexander (2000) *Flaming Classics: Queering the Film Canon*, London and New York: Routledge.

Dyer, Richard (1985) 'Male Sexuality and Media', in Andy Metcalf and Martin Humphries (eds) *The Sexuality of Men*, London: Pluto Press, pp. 28–43.

— [1992 (1982)] 'Don't look now: the male pin-up', (eds) *Screen, The Sexual Subject: A Screen Reader*, London and New York: Routledge.

— (1993a) 'Homosexuality and Film Noir', in *The Matter of Images: Essays on Representation*, London and New York: Routledge.

— (1993) 'White', in *The Matter of Images: Essays on Representation*, London and New York: Routledge.

— (1997) *White*, London and New York: Routledge.

— [2000 (1994)] 'Action!', in José Arroyo (ed.) *Action/Spectacle Cinema: A Sight and Sound Reader*, London: British Film Institute, pp. 17–21.

— (2007) *Pastiche*, London and New York: Routledge.

— (2012) *In the Space of a Song: The Uses of Song in Film*, London and New York: Routledge.

Elsaesser, Thomas [1985 (1972)] 'Tales of Sound and Fury: Observations of the Family Melodrama', in Bill Nichols (1985), *Movies and Methods II*, Berkeley and Los Angeles: University of California Press, pp. 164–89.

— [2012 (1973)] 'Narrative Cinema and Audience Aesthetics: The *Mise-en-scène* of the Spectator', in Thomas Elsaesser, *The Persistence of Hollywood*, London and New York: Routledge, pp. 95–104.

Elsaesser, Thomas and Hagener, Malte (2010) *Film Theory: An Introduction through the Senses*, London and New York: Routledge.

Foucault, Michel (1976) *The History of Sexuality:* Volume 1, *An Introduction*, Harmondsworth: Penguin.

Fraiman, Susan (2003) *Cool Men and the Second Sex*, New York: Columbia University Press.

Frayling, Christopher (2000) *Sergio Leone: Something to Do with Death*, London: Faber and Faber.

— (2006) *Spaghetti Westerns: Cowboys and Europeans from Karl May to Sergio Leone*, London: I. B. Tauris.

Freud, Sigmund [1991 (1905)] 'The Sexual Aberrations', in *On Sexuality* (Penguin Freud Library, Vol. 7), London: Penguin, pp. 45–87.

Gaines, Jane (1990) 'Costume and narrative: how dress tells the woman's story', in Jane Gaines and Charlotte Herzog (eds) *Fabrications: Costume and the Female Body*, New York and London: Routledge.

Garber, Marjorie (1992) *Vested Interests: Cross-Dressing and Cultural Anxiety*, London: Penguin.

Garwood, Ian (2003) 'Must You Remember This? Orchestrating the "Standard" Pop Song in *Sleepless in Seattle*', in Kay Dickinson (ed.) *Movie Music, The Film Reader*, London and New York: Routledge, pp. 109–18.

Gledhill, Christine (1995) 'Women Reading Men', in Pat Kirkham and Janet Thumim, Janet (eds) *You Tarzan: Masculinity, Movies and Men*, London: Lawrence and Wishart, pp. 73–93.

Grant, Barry Keith (2011) *Shadows of Doubt: Negotiations of Masculinity in American Genre Films*, Detroit: Wayne State University Press.

Grønstad, Asbjørn (2008) *Transfigurations: Violence, Death, and Masculinity in American Cinema*, Amsterdam: Amsterdam University Press.

Halberstam, Judith (1998) *Female Masculinity*, Durham and London: Duke University Press.

Jeffords, Susan (1993) *Hard Bodies: Hollywood Masculinity in the Reagan Era*, New Brunswick: Rutgers University Press.

Johnston, Claire [1976 (1974)] 'Women's Cinema as Counter-Cinema', in Bill Nichols, (ed.) (1976) *Movies and Methods*, Berkeley and Los Angeles: University of California Press, pp. 208–17.

Kael, Pauline (1986) 'The Current Cinema: Brutes', *Village Voice*, 31, 26 May, pp. 114–17.

Kaplan, E. Ann (1983) *Women and Film: Both Sides of the Camera*, London and New York: Methuen.

Kinder, Marsha (2001) 'Violence American Style: The Narration Orchestration of Violent Attractions', in J. David Slocum (ed.) *Violence and the American Cinema*, London and New York: Routledge, pp. 63–100.

King, Geoff (2000) *Spectacular Narratives: Hollywood in the Age of the Blockbuster*, London: I. B. Tauris.

— (2002) *New Hollywood Cinema: An Introduction*, London: I. B. Tauris.

Kinsey, Alfred (with Wardell Pomeroy and Clyde Martin) (1948) *Sexual Behavior in the Human Male*, London: W. B. Saunders Company Ltd.

Kirkham, Pat and Thumim, Janet (eds) (1993) *You Tarzan: Masculinity, Movies and Men*, London: Lawrence and Wishart.

— (1995) *Me Jane: Masculinity, Movies and Women*, London: Lawrence and Wishart.

Kitses, Jim (2004) *Horizons West: Directing the Western from John Ford to Clint Eastwood* (new edition), London: British Film Institute.

Klevan, Andrew (2005) *Film Performance: From Achievement to Appreciation*, London: Wallflower Press.

Krutnik, Frank (1991) *In A Lonely Street: Film Noir, Genre, Masculinity*, London: Routledge.

Lacan, Jacques [1993 (1958)] 'The Signification of the Phallus', in *Écrits: A Selection*, trans. Alan Sheridan, London and New York: Routledge, pp. 280–91.

Langford, Barry (2010) *Post-Classical Hollywood: Film Industry, Style and Ideology Since 1945*, Edinburgh: Edinburgh University Press.

Lawrence, Amy (1991) *Echo and Narcissus: Women's Voices in Classical Hollywood Cinema*, Berkeley and Los Angeles: University of California Press.

Lehman, Peter (2001) *Masculinity: Bodies, Movies, Culture*, London and New York: Routledge.

Lynes, Russell (1953) *A Surfeit of Honey*, New York: Harper.

Mellen, Joan (1977) *Big Bad Wolves: Masculinity in the American Film*, London: Elm Tree Books/Hamish Hamilton.

Merck, Mandy (2007) 'Mulvey's Manifesto', *Camera Obscura*, 66, 22: 3, pp. 1–23.

Mulvey, Laura [1985 (1975)] 'Visual Pleasure and Narrative Cinema', in Bill Nichols (ed.) (1985) *Movies and Methods II*, Berkeley and Los Angeles: University of California Press.

— [1987 (1977)] 'Notes on Sirk and melodrama', in Christine Gledhill (ed.) *Home is Where the Heart Is: Studies in Melodrama and the Woman's Film*, London: British Film Institute.

Neale, Steve [1993 (1983)] 'Masculinity as Spectacle', in Cohan and Hark, pp. 9–22.

Nichols, Bill (ed.) (1976) *Movies and Methods*, Berkeley and Los Angeles: University of California Press.

— (ed.) (1985) *Movies and Methods II*, Berkeley and Los Angeles: University of California Press.

— (1994) *Blurred Boundaries: Questions of Meaning in Contemporary Culture*, Bloomington: Indiana University Press.

Nicol, Bran (2013) 'Sherlock Holmes: Version 2.0: Adapting Doyle in the Twenty-First Century', in Sabine Vanacker and Catherine Wynne (eds) *Sherlock Holmes and Conan Doyle: Multi-Media Alternatives*, Basingstoke: Palgrave Macmillan, pp. 125–31.

Nowell-Smith, Geoffrey [1985 (1977)] 'Minnelli and Melodrama', in Bill Nichols (1985), pp. 190–4.

Perkins, V. F. (1972) *Film as Film*, Harmondsworth: Penguin.

Porter, Lynnette (ed.) (2012) *Sherlock Holmes for the 21st Century: Essays on New Adaptations*, Jefferson and London: McFarland and Company Inc.

Powrie, Phil, Davies, Ann and Babington, Bruce (eds) (2004) *The Trouble with Men: Masculinities in European and Hollywood Cinema*, London: Wallflower Press.

Prince, Stephen (1998) *Savage Cinema: Sam Peckinpah and the Rise of Ultraviolent Movies*, Austin: University of Texas Press.

Pye, Douglas (1992) 'Film noir and suppressive narrative: *Beyond a Reasonable Doubt*', in Ian Cameron (ed.) *The Movie Book of Film Noir*, London: Studio Vista, pp. 98–109.

Ray, Robert B. (1985) *A Certain Tendency in the Hollywood Cinema, 1930–1980*, Princeton: Princeton University Press.

Rehling, Nicola (2009) *Extra-Ordinary Men: White Heterosexual Masculinity in Contemporary Popular Cinema*, Plymouth: Lexington Books.

Rivette, Jacques *Texts and Interviews* (1977), trans. Tom Milne, London: British Film Institute (out of print but the majority still available at: http://www.dvdbeaver.com/rivette/ok/about.html).

Rodley, Chris (ed.) (1992) *Cronenberg on Cronenberg*, London: Faber and Faber.

Rothman, William (1982) *Hitchcock – The Murderous Gaze*, Cambridge, MA: Harvard University Press.

Rowbotham, Sheila (1973) *Women's Consciousness, Man's World*, Harmondsworth: Penguin.

Ryan, Michael and Kellner, Douglas (1990) *Camera Politica: The Politics and Ideology of Contemporary Hollywood Film*, Indianapolis and Bloomington: Indiana University Press.

Schrader, Paul [1990 (1972)] 'Notes on Film Noir', in Paul Schrader and

Kevin Jackson (eds) *Schrader on Schrader and Other Writings*, London: Faber and Faber, pp. 80–93.

Sedgwick, Eve Kosofsky (1985) *Between Men: English Literature and Male Homosocial Desire*, New York: Columbia University Press.

— [1994 (1990)] *Epistemology of the Closet*, London: Penguin.

Shaviro, Steven (1993) *The Cinematic Body (Theory Out of Bounds)*, Minneapolis and London: University of Minnesota Press.

Slocum, John David (2005) *Rebel Without a Cause: Approaches to a Maverick Masterwork*, New York: SUNY Press.

Smith, Paul (1996) (ed.) *Boys: Masculinities in Contemporary Culture*, Boulder Colorado: Westview Press.

Sobchack, Vivian (2004) *Carnal Thoughts: Embodiment and Moving Image Culture*, Berkeley and Los Angeles: University of California Press.

Spender, Dale (1982) *Man Made Language*, London: Routledge and Kegan Paul.

Stacey, Jackie (1987) 'Desperately Seeking Difference', *Screen*, 28: 1, winter, pp. 48–61.

Tasker, Yvonne (1993) *Spectacular Bodies: Gender, Genre and the Action Cinema*, London and New York: Routledge.

Thomas, Deborah (1992) 'How Hollywood Deals with the Deviant Male', in Ian Cameron (ed.) *The Movie Book of Film Noir*, London: Studio Vista, pp. 59–70.

Wollen, Peter (1999) '*Rope*: Three Hypotheses', in Richard Allen and S. Ishii-Gonzalès (eds) *Alfred Hitchcock: Centenary Essays*, London: British Film Institute, pp. 75–86.

Wood, Robin (2003) *Hollywood From Vietnam to Reagan . . . and Beyond*, New York: Columbia University Press.

Index